W. W. Loring

Florida's Forgotten General

W. W. Loring

Florida's Forgotten General

by

James W. Raab

Sunflower University Press®

P. O. Box 1009 • 1531 Yuma • Manhattan, Kansas 66505-1009 USA

ISBN 0-89745-205-4

Cover: W. W. Loring sketch by Jean Light, St. Augustine, Florida.

Artist Jean Light, of St. Augustine, Florida, is known for her pen and ink drawings and pallette knife paintings. A native of Roanoke, Virginia, she has a Bachelor of Fine Arts degree from Richmond Professional Institute and taught art in the public schools for over 30 years. Her award-winning work is in many collections in the South.

Edited by Julie Bush

Layout by Lori L. Daniel

City Gates of St. Augustine, by Jean Light.

To my wife Doris

Contents

General
W. W. Loring

Few officers resigned from the United States Army to enter the Confederate service with a richer experience than Loring. In May, 1861, he was six months past his forty-second birthday and had been soldiering since he was fourteen. He had been in Seminole wars in Florida at a time when most of his later associates were learning parade-ground tactics on the fields of West Point. Later he studied law, and when Florida became a state Loring sat in the state legislature. Then, when the Mexican War called for valorous men, the twenty-seven-year old Loring abandoned law and politics forever. He became a captain, a major, a lieutenant colonel. He won brevet promotions for gallant and meritorious conduct. At Mexico City he led an assault on Belen Gate and lost an arm. Thereafter his empty sleeve bore its eloquent testimony to his courage and gallantry. When the war ended, Loring stayed on in the army.

For a dozen years young Loring proved that the army made no mistake in keeping him in the service. No product of West Point looked more like a soldier than he. He was five feet nine inches tall, sturdy — even stout — in build. His carriage was erect, commanding. His hair and imperial-cut beard were coal black, matching his jet-black eyes. His nose was large, his complexion swarthy. His head — his whole bearing, in fact — struck men as Napoleonic. And his deeds confirmed the impression his appearance gave. He led his regiment, with six hundred mule teams, for twenty-five hundred miles across the mountains to Oregon without losing a man. A generation later it was called "the greatest military feat on record." He commanded the Department of Oregon. He fought Indians on the Rio Grande and on the Gila in Arizona. He fought Mormons in Utah. He went to Europe to study the military systems of the continent. He came back to command the Department of New Mexico. At thirty-eight he was the youngest line colonel of the American army. When he entered the Confederate service, even his enemies bore him tribute: a man of "unflinching honor and integrity," said the Federal officer who replaced him in his western command.

From *The Blue and Gray on the Nile*, by William B. Hesseltine and Hazel C. Wolf (The University of Chicago Press and The University of Toronto Press, 1961). © 1961 by The University of Chicago. Used by permission.

Preface

*W*ILLIAM WING LORING, a career soldier, left few personal letters to rely on for information about his life. He did not keep a diary, and he died before he could write his memoirs. Studying him from a perspective of over 100 years, I had to become a literary detective, finding documentation of the events in which he participated, chasing down clues, and ferreting out enough details to clothe him with sufficient flesh to make a story and convince the reader that my subject was, after all, worthy of attention.

The historical significance of W. W. Loring was elusive at times. Viewed from different angles, at different times, for different purposes, by different people, the well-established facts sometimes took on different meanings, compelling me to dig deeper.

My investigation's purpose was to elicit the truth. I began separating myth from reality, reexamining Loring's 50-year military career and eliminating incorrect statements that deliberately manipulated his Civil War record. I became determined to set the record straight and publish the story of "Old Blizzards."

After six years of research, I can now tell Loring's life story, which, when revealed, places him equally alongside the many famous historical personalities that make up the 425-year history of St. Augustine.

James W. Raab
St. Augustine, Florida

Chapter 1

Early Years in Florida and the Seminole Indian War

R*EUBEN AND Hannah Kenan Loring, married in Wilmington, North Carolina, on 18 May 1812, gave birth to their second son, William Wing — whose name came from a famous family of the original Plymouth Colony — on 14 December 1818.*

On 10 July 1821, the red and gold ensign of Spain that had fluttered over the Florida Territory was replaced by the 23-star American flag. The Americanization of the Terri-

tory would begin, and during this time, in 1823, Reuben Loring brought his family to St. Augustine.

St. Augustine was an old, walled city, essentially an 18th-century town with a central plaza and Catholic church. Two-hundred-year-old sandy streets were surrounded by earthen and wooden walls, moats, drawbridges, redoubts, and an aging fort called St. Mark, later named Fort Marion.

As the ancient city began to change and assimilate Northern neighbors, it became rough and disorderly, where luxury and debauchery reigned amid scarcity and poverty. Its heterogeneous population — transient soldiers, sailors on shore leave, Indians, freed blacks, and others — provided a multicultural community for young Loring to observe.

In 1827, Reuben Loring purchased a coquina house one block south of Fort Marion. At age nine, within the shadow of the fort, Loring and his sidekicks — including such later notables as E. Kirby Smith and Stephen Vincent Benét — would emulate what they saw daily and played soldier and Indian. The real war would come later.

Young Loring was a handsome child with earnest eyes, black, wavy hair, and a fearless high spirit, with more than a touch of the passionate determination that characterized him in later years. He was described as impulsive, warmhearted, and always a leader of other boys in the games they played.

W. W. Loring was born to be a soldier, and it did not take many years for him to prove it. At the age of 14, he volunteered for service with the Florida Militia. He accompanied the 11th Regiment, 2nd Brigade, on its marches and earned himself the title of the "Boy Soldier." At 17, he was promoted to sergeant.

In the same year, W. W. Loring participated in the most memorable of Florida's Indian wars, the Great Seminole War of 1835-1842. Two-thirds of the entire American Army would be involved and would pass through St. Augustine for Loring to observe. Thousands of citizen volunteers from Florida and states as far away as Missouri came to seek revenge on the Seminole and his depredations. It was during this conflict that Loring, from a hazardous boyhood spent on the Florida frontier, would evolve into a skilled and resourceful fighter.

The Seminole, numbering no more than 4,000 across the Florida Territory, were being driven from their land by white settlers, who were frequently brutal in killing them. In retaliation, the Seminole and their Negro allies, starving and freezing because of the extremely cold winter of 1835-1836, began to attack, plunder, and destroy one plantation after another. The Dade Massacre of 28 December 1835, where 105 of 108 of Brevet Major Francis L. Dade's troops were shot and killed at point-blank range in an Indian ambush, ignited the wrath of the American nation. When General Joseph M. Hernandez heard of the event, he sent a detachment of militia to central Florida under the leadership of Major Leigh Read. Young Loring went along with these mounted volunteers and was under the command of Captain J. J. Finley. On 29 February 1836, as part of the advancing west wing, Loring took part in the battle of the blockhouse at Withlacoochee. He was now a part of the fighting militia.

As a steady stream of troops began arriving in Florida, Loring was given his first glimpse of the U.S. Army in action. Indeed, the cast of military personalities involved in the Great Seminole War reads like a playbill for the future Mexican War and Civil War: Winfield Scott, Joseph E. Johnston, Zachary Taylor, William Tecumseh Sherman, William J. Hardee, John C. Pemberton, Braxton Bragg, and many others offered their service in Florida.

Loring was inspired by the military life that unfolded. He distinguished himself at the Battle of Wahoo Swamp in November 1836 and was appointed second lieutenant of his company in the 11th Regiment, 2nd Brigade, from 11 June to 16 August 1837.

The Seminole War seemed to slow down with the removal of several of the chiefs from Florida to South Carolina in 1838. The war did not come to an abrupt end; it simply dragged itself out. With less demand on militia activity, Loring turned to another interest: education.

He had received at home the rudiments of early schooling, and when he was 20 it was decided that he should attend Georgetown College in Virginia. Making the 800-mile trip by steamboat and railroad, Loring arrived at Georgetown on 15 November 1839, but stayed in school only until 3 April 1840. Contrary to several historical profiles on Loring, he did not attend Georgetown Law School, which in fact did not exist until 1870, some 30 years after Loring's enrollment.

Young Loring returned to St. Augustine in the spring of 1840 and entered into a "clerkship" in Judge Robert R. Reid's office. Without a law school in the Territory, it was a common practice, if one qualified, to apprentice in a law office, "reading law" as it was called, and then becoming licensed to practice law. Being a lawyer was prestigious, and certainly Loring's father must have approved.

Loring's next five years in the Florida Territory became the most formative years in his life, partially as a result of his association with Judge Reid and a young attorney named David Levy. In January 1841, Judge Reid was appointed governor of the Territory by President Martin Van Buren and took office at the capitol in Tallahassee. However, Reid's governorship was short-lived, for he was stricken with yellow fever on 28 June 1841 and in three days was dead at the age of 52.

Loring was a smart and eager young man and saw the advantage of politics. In April 1843, he decided to run on the Democratic ticket of St. John's County for a seat on the Territorial Legislature in Tallahassee to fill the vacated seat of David Levy, who had been elected in 1841 to the U.S. Congress by the Whig Party. The *Florida Herald Southern Democrat* on 13 November 1843 announced the triumph of the whole Democratic ticket of St. John's County for legislative representatives; Colonel Joseph S. Sanchez and W. W. Loring were elected. Shortly after the election, an advertisement began to appear weekly:

William W. Loring
Attorney & Counselor at Law
St. Augustine, East Florida
December 23, 1843

There was no street address listed, and 23 December was when the court issued him a license to practice law. This date appeared in all of his ads in 1844 and 1845.

Loring went to Tallahassee, probably in January 1844, when the legislature convened, and became associated with all of the leading men of the Territory at that time. His local friends were Colonel Sanchez and Douglas Dummett from Mosquito County. For a man of 25 years, these political lessons and connections were invaluable stepping stones to bigger things.

The St. Augustine *East Florida* newspaper reported on 2 April 1844 that "William W. Loring, Esq. one of the Representatives to the legislative Council from St. Augustine returned home on Thursday." It was a long horseback ride from Tallahassee.

Florida entered the Union as a state on 3 March 1845, and with statehood came new elections for state and national seats. The *Florida Herald Southern Democrat* on 6 May 1845 published the results: David Levy was elected to Congress, and W. W. Loring went to Tallahassee for the first General Assembly as the elected representative from St. John's County. He was thus in the first House of the State of Florida.

In July 1845, Loring nominated Levy as a candidate for the U.S. Senate, and Levy indeed took his seat in the Senate on 1 December 1845. Levy became known as the Florida "fire-eater" because of his passionate pro-slavery oratory. Loring heard every word of it over again, and he believed it.

Chapter 2

The Mexican War, 1847

OR THREE YEARS, Loring traveled between his law office in St. Augustine and the new state capital of Tallahassee. Although Florida had everything to offer him at his young age, he apparently was not satisfied as a politician. He always seemed to keep his eyes open for an opportunity to return to the military life.

From Washington he wrote in late February 1846 that he had heard a Senate debate

Early photo of W. W. Loring as a young man. (Courtesy, Library of Congress)

on "the Oregon question," which dealt with an end to the Anglo-American joint occupation of that Territory. It was a "day of thrilling interest," he reported, when "I heard the thundering Webster, a beautiful speech from

Crittenden, a cross fire between Colquit and Breese and Allen — also speeches from Calhoun and Johnson." Many thought the tensions would lead to war with England, Loring added, and while he had no opinion of that, he wished "they would hurry and raise the Rifle Corps in which my friends think I stand A-no. 1" (Waterbury 87-88).

In May 1846, the 29th U.S. Congress passed an act to provide for raising a regiment of Mounted Rifles. Whether through the assistance of David Levy, renamed David Levy Yulee, or the U.S. proclamation of war with Mexico on 13 May, President James K. Polk offered Loring the sword that he had tried so hard to win in his teens. This offer came as an appointment as the senior-ranked captain — on the threshold of field grade rank and regimental staff command — of the newly authorized Regular regiment of Mounted Riflemen, with the date of rank to be set from 27 May 1846. At the end of his third term in Tallahassee, 27-year-old Loring accepted the appointment.

To belong to the pre-Civil War U.S. Army Officers' Corps was to belong to a unique brotherhood of traditions and customs that would give Loring rank and privilege, which he desired. Even though the pay was low, promotions very slow, and retirement pensions almost nil, W. W. Loring could certainly fit into this group, which included the likes of Ulysses S. Grant, Jefferson Davis, Robert E. Lee, and William J. Hardee.

The Riflemen's exact purpose was to establish military posts along the Oregon Trail for the protection of the emigrants on their way to the Pacific Coast. Also, as Manifest Destiny led settlers Westward, the U.S. government wanted the troops to back the American claim to the Oregon country and to challenge the Hudson's Bay Company trading posts north of the Columbia River. However, the regiment's commander, Colonel Persifor F. Smith, was in Mexico commanding the 2nd Brigade of Regulars involved in the Mexican War, and it was decided that the Riflemen would join Smith there and that the Oregon Trail would wait. Captain Loring, after being assigned to Bowling Green, Kentucky; Jefferson Barracks, Missouri; and the mouth of the Rio Grande in New Orleans, became the regimental major on 12 February 1847 before embarking on the siege of Vera Cruz.

On 22 February, the Mounted Riflemen set out for Lobos Island, the staging area for the coming invasion of Mexico. Here, the Riflemen were joined by their commander, Colonel Smith, and were assigned to the 1st Brigade of General David E. Twiggs's division.

The goal of Major General Winfield Scott, the senior general of the U.S. Army, was to end the war by capturing the enemy's capital, Mexico City. To accomplish this, the Army first struck a decisive blow at the key seaport of Vera Cruz, the most heavily armed city in the Western Hemisphere, and then headed toward Jalapa, Mexico, one of two principal way stations on the 270-mile road that led from Vera Cruz to Mexico City. On 8 April, General Twiggs and the Mounted Riflemen began moving up the national highway; 74 miles away lay Jalapa.

On 17 April, the Riflemen of Loring's company and part of Twiggs's division were following along a makeshift trail, intending to bypass Santa Anna's 4,000 troops that were dug in in the hills overlooking the national highway near Cerro Gordo, a mere 12 miles from Jalapa. Suddenly, a rifle company on a reconnoitering mission clashed unexpectedly with some Mexican troops on the trail. Colonel William S. Harney's brigade was sent to rescue the rifle company; they drove the Mexicans up and down the mountainside, but the Mexicans made counterattacks. Harney was outnumbered 50 to 1, and his men were tired, shattered, and bleeding from the melee. Major E. V. Sumner of the 2nd Dragoons, who was in overall command of the Dragoons and Riflemen, was severely wounded, leaving Loring in complete charge of the action.

It was here that Loring heard the cry, "Send up the Rifles!" During the long, hot night of 17 April, the Riflemen helped drag the heavy guns of the 1st Artillery into position on the side of the mountain for the purpose of attacking Santa Anna and his troops. By 3:00 a.m., the task was complete and the men fell exhausted, only to have to fight in a few hours.

Loring's Riflemen — without horses or mules, for the terrain was too difficult — were ordered to pass to the left of the column to attract the attention of the enemy and to keep them in check until the storming of the heights commenced. During this diversion, the Rifles were exposed to destructive rounds of fire from the enemy, but the mission was successful: a large force of the enemy was held in check, a force that would have been able to resist and turn the assaulting column.

Cerro Gordo was the first major battle of the campaign and was a huge American success. General Scott was elated and wrote to Secretary of War William L. Marcy: "Sir, the plan of attack was finely executed by this gallant army. We are quite embarrassed with the result of victory. . . . It is a most pleasing duty to say that the highest praise is due Harney, Plympton, Loring, and Alexander, their gallant officers and men for their brilliant service" (Wessels 15). In his first time in command of a regiment, W. W. Loring was praised by the senior general of the U.S. Army — what higher honor could be asked for?

The American Army advance on Mexico City began on 7 August, but the passes on the direct road to the city had been well fortified and garrisoned by the Mexicans, and between the roads were great tracts of marshland that artillery and supply wagons could not cross. General Scott was thus faced with a direct assault on the little village of Churubusco, which lay in his path and had been strongly fortified by the Mexicans, and the well-defended camp of Contreras, with a garrison of about 6,000 men. In the rear, between the camp and Mexico City, was a reserve force of 12,000 men.

But General Scott lost no time in moving against the enemy's works. On 20 August 1847, the Americans attacked Contreras at dawn, completely surprising the Mexicans and forcing a surrender in 17 minutes. A longer battle was waged at Churubusco. For four hours, the Mexican guns behind the massive walls of the San Mateo convent thundered, cutting down the Americans. By 3:00 p.m., Colonel Smith and Major Loring and their Riflemen joined and began to push back the Mexican skirmishers. Soon after, General William Worth's battered men began to make their presence felt. American artillerymen blew the Mexican defenders back with rounds delivered as rapidly as musket fire. As U.S. infantrymen flowed over the convent walls into the fortress, many defenders went over the opposite walls.

As a result of the victories at Contreras and Churubusco, both on the same day, Scott's forces had reduced Santa Anna's army by about a fourth, with over 4,000 killed or wounded and 3,000 taken prisoner. American losses were fewer but sobering: 133 killed, 865 wounded, and 40 missing in action. Scott halted the advance.

Also on the same day, 20 August, Major Loring was promoted to lieutenant colonel by brevet for gallant and meritorious conduct in the battles of Contreras and Churubusco.

General Scott moved his headquarters to Tacubaya, a village two and a half miles southwest of Mexico City, and with the U.S. Army at the gates of the capital, Scott decided to try to negotiate a peace with Santa Anna and the Mexican government. On 24 August, a truce went into effect but lasted only two weeks, as the Mexican commissioners, after delays designed to gain time, declined the American conditions of the armistice. Indignant at such treachery, General Scott at once resumed his advance upon Mexico City.

To take the city, the Americans first had to take the Castle of Chapultepec, which had served as Mexico's military academy since 1833. It stood on a hill 200 feet above the surrounding plain and was supported by a huge retaining wall four feet thick. Beyond that were two routes to the city: one causeway ran from the castle to the *Garita* (or gate) *de Belen*; another headed north about two miles and connected with the causeway to the *Garita de San Cosme*.

Early on the morning of 12 September, the bombardment and cannonade of the castle commenced under the direction of Captain Benjamin Huger; batteries reopened fire on the 13th. Colonel Smith and Lieutenant Colonel Loring with their Riflemen, part of Twiggs's division, arrived on the 13th with a brigade to support Major General John Quitman's division at the southern gates.

Raising storming ladders against the castle wall, a number of men climbed up against the increasing Mexican fire. The first wave was mowed down, but so many ladders rose that 50 Americans could climb abreast at one time. The castle wall was finally mounted, and within minutes the American flag floated over Chapultepec.

The two routes to Mexico City were then open, *Garita de Belen* to the south and *Garita de San Cosme* to the north. Each of these routes was an elevated causeway, resting upon arches and massive pillars. Generals Worth and Quitman were prompt in pursuing the retreating Mexicans from the castle. Quitman's column, taking the *Belen* Gate causeway, was led by Loring and his Riflemen. General Smith reports:

> The Rifle Regiment under Lt. Col. Loring led then the South Carolina and Pennsylvania Volunteers and the 1st Artillery and 3rd Infantry, and a portion of the 6th Infantry, which had missed its own brigade and joined mine. . . . After taking a large building which the Mexicans had occupied, the Division carried a

Battery to the length of the aqueduct. The Riflemen, long the leading Regiment, entered it first. . . . They surged forward and took the strongpoint, while the Mexicans fell back to the Garita de Belen. Slowly creeping from arch to arch, we lost many men by the batteries in front, while the fire from flanking batteries coming through the arches killed many who were safe from that in front. (Nevin 216)

It was early afternoon when Loring and the U.S. troops breached the *Garita de Belen*, and here Loring was joined by General Quitman. After a short advance, a shot from the *garita* shattered Loring's left arm. Grabbing the rifle from the wounded Loring, Quitman fired its last cartridge, tied his red silk handkerchief to the weapon's muzzle, and waved it in signal for the Riflemen and the volunteer troops from South Carolina to follow him over the breastwork. With loud cheers they charged the garita, taking it by storm. John Quitman witnessed his soldiers enter the city and plant their various standards.

Lieutenant Colonel Loring was immediately removed from the battle. In the Mexican War, medical care for the wounded was simple and direct, and the medical instruments were often merely knives and saws. Dr. H. H. Steiner of Augusta, Georgia, reported: "Loring laid aside a cigar, sat quietly in a chair without opiates to relieve the pain, and allowed the arm to be cut off without a murmur or a groan. The arm was buried on the heights by his men, with the hand pointing toward the City of Mexico" (Wessels 18).

Thirty-one years later, Loring remembered:

When I was wounded they carried me up to the castle of Chapultepec, which we had captured, and there, with the battle gates and citadel going on before my eyes, my arm was amputated.

The excitement of the spectacle drove away all sense of pain, and like Poreau, I smoked a cigar while they were sawing into my poor bones. . . . None but an army of heroes could have accomplished the conquest of Mexico. (Wessels 18)

While the severely wounded Loring observed the battle from Castle Chapultepec, Quitman entered Mexico City, adding several new defenses

Brevet Colonel William W. Loring, on his return from the Mexican War, at age 29.

to the position he had won. Finally, all ammunition was exhausted, and the American pieces were silent.

Both *garitas* had fallen, and during the night Santa Anna, with the remains of his defeated army, retreated from the city, leaving the authorities to make the best terms they could for its surrender. At 4:00 a.m., a white flag was flown, and Mexico City was in General Scott's power.

W. W. Loring was removed to the Church of the Franciscans, which was used as a general hospital in Mexico City, and on the same day, 13 September 1847, he was made colonel by brevet. In fact, for gallant and meritorious conduct, he was breveted three times — for bravery at Cerro Gordo, Churubusco, and Belen Gate.

With the fall of Mexico City, the Mounted Riflemen did provost and police duty for the remainder of the war. Their commander, Persifor F. Smith, recently made general, was appointed commander of the military department of Vera Cruz. The Riflemen were then sent back to the States via New Orleans and arrived at Jefferson Barracks on 24 July 1848 under the direction of Major Winslow F. Sanderson.

The one-armed Loring was ordered home to St. Augustine for rest and recuperation on 26 October 1847. The *Florida Herald Southern Democrat* carried on that day: "Our fellow citizen Maj. Loring has again distinguished himself in his Country's cause. He has been severely wounded. We are hoping to learn that he is not considered in a dangerous condition. We confidently hope he may soon recover and reap further laurels. Florida has been well represented by him in the service and bloody contests of this war." The same newspaper announced on 16 November that "his mother reports he is coming home via New Orleans on the 15th . . . completely healed."

In December, the Florida House and Senate passed a resolution of appreciation for the military services of Loring.

Chapter 3

The Mounted Riflemen and the West

*T*HE ORIGINAL MISSION of the Mounted Riflemen in 1846 had been part of a series of moves made by the U.S. government against the British government and the Hudson's Bay Company as a result of the deterioration of the Oregon Joint Occupancy Accord. As early as 1815, the two nations with equal claims to this section of the territory could not agree on which would have exclusive ownership of that Territory. Possession

and occupancy of the land, and not merely discovery, represented ownership.

As part of the Manifest Destiny that America was pursuing, the War
Department in 1846 established the 10th Military Department, which
would take in the Oregon Territory as well as upper and lower parts of California. The strategy was to form a mounted rifle unit to march to Oregon
to back up President Polk's U.S. claim to Oregon; show the world that the
U.S. was prepared to fight for those claims; convince the British that an
American army could arrive in Oregon much faster than they could; and
give the American frontiersmen in the Willamette Valley professional
leadership against the Hudson's Bay Company. On the move to Oregon,
the Riflemen were also to establish posts to protect the emigrants from the
Indians and to open up a mail route. However, participation in the Mexican War postponed the Mounted Riflemen's mission to Oregon for three
years.

With peace in Mexico and the Treaty of Guadalupe Hidalgo in February 1848, the boundary between Upper and Lower California was defined.
The discovery of gold in that same year caused such an unsettled state of
affairs that the War Department decided to strengthen the military command on the Pacific Coast.

The old established 10th Military Department was split into the 10th
and 11th Departments. These two would be designated as the Third or
Pacific Division, and joint military operations could be conducted if necessary. General Persifor Smith, serving as military commander at Vera
Cruz, Mexico, was appointed to head the 10th Military Department. Smith
set out for his new post on 24 November 1848 by way of New Orleans and
the Isthmus of Panama and arrived at Monterey, California, on 23 February 1849. He brought with him Lieutenant William Tecumseh Sherman as
his adjutant.

The leadership of the 11th Military Department went to W. W. Loring,
who was in St. Augustine. Quickly, President Polk appointed Loring as a
full lieutenant colonel. Loring, at the age of 30, was placed in command
of the Mounted Riflemen and would be their "march commander" for the
upcoming move to Oregon. He was selected to put the government's
power politics into motion.

By 1 August 1848, Loring left St. Augustine and returned to Jefferson
Barracks, Missouri, to take over his new command. Upon his arrival, however, he found that the whole regiment, in effect, had disbanded: Congress

had passed an act that gave permission to the enlisted men of the regiment who had served in Mexico to receive an honorable discharge, as if they had served out the full period of their enlistment. This would entitle them to three months' extra pay plus some bounty land.

Loring would have to organize a new recruiting campaign. He sent recruiting officers to Ohio, Illinois, Pennsylvania, and Indiana, but they met with poor results. With the popular Mexican War over, who wanted to go into the Army? Out of necessity, Loring resorted to obtaining his raw recruits mainly from the new immigrants stepping off the boats from the old country. Germans, Dutch, and Irish made up the bulk, but they were mostly farmers, not military men. The balance recruited were those who wanted a free ride to the goldfields in California. From the start they were a disorderly and troublesome lot to command.

If the newly recruited enlisted men presented one kind of problem, the officers who would be commanding them created another type for Loring. With the onset of the Mexican War, many junior officers were deliberately appointed, a number from top political circles, and they represented the high-spirited, adventure-loving, independent-thinking, short-tempered cavaliers. Joining Loring at Jefferson Barracks were many of these returning junior officers and noncommissioned men. The combination of questionable recruits plus the returning "cavalier" officers led the rest of the Regular Army military units to refer to them as the "Kangaroo Regiment" — a 19th-century term indicating that this was one "fouled-up" outfit. Fortunately, Loring did have a cadre of key Regular officers and noncoms who were career soldiers and who did their work, kept to themselves, and followed the day-to-day military routine with little or no comment.

Normally, the crew of any army train of this period — the wagon masters and teamsters — were civilians hired from a general contractor. However, regular channels for such contracts dried up with the swarming of the gold rushers to California in early 1849. Many of the contractors, as well as the experienced drivers, had already left for the goldfields. Loring then had to recruit individual civilians for the crews, a dangerous alternative. The regiment would be at the mercy of these men who might desert at the first opportunity or turn off to the gold claims in California.

Lieutenant Colonel Loring was consumed not only with the immense responsibility of making the regiment ready for the 2,000-mile march to Oregon but also with the hundreds of civilians who wanted to go West. As the weeks in early 1849 saw the regiment filling up with recruits, the civilians looking for safe passage to California assembled and began to resemble a flotilla of prairie schooners. What better way to go West than with the U.S. Army?

By 10 May 1849, everything was ready to move out. Could Colonel Loring and his high-spirited officers and dedicated noncoms combat the agonizing march to Oregon City? This would be Loring's supreme test of resourcefulness and courage and prove him an able man and military expert.

Brevet Major General David E. Twiggs and Colonel Aeneas Mackay, deputy quartermaster general, came from St. Louis to Camp Sumner, the rendezvous point for the beginning of the march, about five miles west of Fort Leavenworth, to see the Rifles off. Five companies were reviewed, and General Twiggs himself gave the order that pointed them toward Oregon. For the first time in American history, a full U.S. Army regiment complete with wives, children, relatives, baggage, household goods, small arms, equipment, supplies, and even a cattle column would cross the "Great American Desert" to the sand hills of the Nebraska Territory and then on to Oregon.

Judge William H. Packwood gives an eyewitness account of the departure:

> On the . . . bright, sunshiny morning, Colonel W. W. Loring broke camp and the panorama then viewed was never to be forgotten. The companies, mounted, filed out in columns of two, their arms shining in the sun; horses gay and prancing; sabers dangling by their sides; officers riding here and there giving commands. As soon as the regiment was well under way the quartermaster and commissary trains began to string out, and in a short time — between 9 and 10 o'clock — the rifle regiment was on the long journey for Oregon. . . .

Army life on the Oregon Trail was difficult. Being absent from civilization for five months pressed the military as well as the emigrants far more than anyone had dreamed. The Army offered little to attract enterprising men or to elevate them once enlisted. A recruit signed up for a five-year hitch. He received $7 a month in the infantry and artillery, $8 in the cavalry, and $13 a month if he made sergeant. In remote garrisons and while on extended service in the field, they often went six months or more without pay.

The daily ration, repeated with deadly monotony, consisted of fresh or salt beef or pork, bread, coffee, and beans, peas, or rice. In the West, the soldiers sought to vary the fare whenever the opportunity offered hunting or fishing, and buffalo, elk, deer, wild turkey, grouse, and other game often appeared on the mess table. Fresh vegetables were priceless rarities. In a garrison, a soldier might be lucky to have a mud hut or a permanent rack to sleep in, but in the field and on the march, he slept in a tent, or in or under a wagon.

The officer corps was not much better off. Low pay and slow promotions coupled with a dearth of other forms of reward prompted the resignation of the more promising men. A second lieutenant received $25 a month; Colonel Loring received $75 a month. Allowances for rations, fuel, forage, servants, quarters, and other necessities helped triple the base pay, but the total was still far below salaries in comparable civilian occupations. Even the General in Chief had a base pay of only $2,400 a year. Most frontier officers were hard drinkers, and all too many slipped into the grip of alcoholism.

When most of the recruits signed up for the trip with Colonel Loring, they had only a notion of the hardships they would face. Driven by their lust for gold, they thought they could sacrifice five months of their lives to go West on the cheapest vehicle available, the U.S. Army, and then desert. They survived basic training, but when the time came to get on the trail and move daily, they began to realize that there was a lot more to "this here army" than five months in the saddle.

One thing they did not bargain for was the threat of Asiatic cholera, which was sweeping Missouri. The emigrants accompanying the troops fared the worst. If one member of a family caught the disease, that family's wagon would likely be cut out of the line of march. Major Osborne Cross of the Quartermaster Corps reported, "They were to be pitied, as no aid in any way could be afforded them" (Clark, n.p.). It is estimated that in 1849, between 4,000 and 5,000 emigrants lost their life to cholera on the trail, never to see California or Oregon.

Paramount among the hazards of the trail, and usually not known by the rookie recruit who had signed on, was the harsh and unremitting discipline of the U.S. Army. The Articles of War catalogued every offense imaginable, and the 99th — "to the prejudice of good order and military disci-

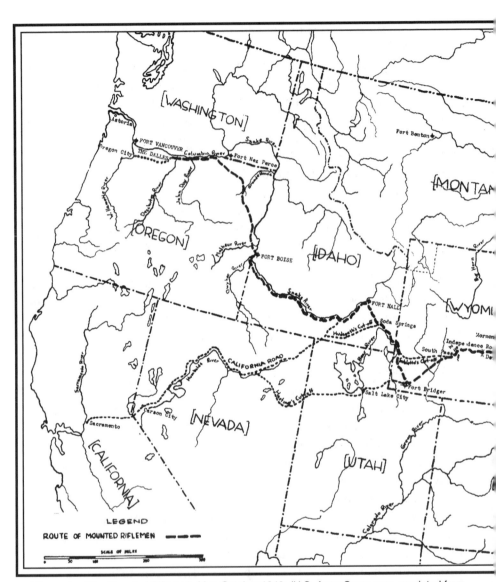

The route of the Mounted Riflemen, May-October 1849. (U.S. Army Corps map, reprinted from *The March of the Mounted Rifleman: From Fort Leavenworth to Fort Vancouver, May to October 1849*, ed. by Raymond W. Settle (University of Nebraska, Lincoln © 1940; renewed 1968, Arthur H. Clark Company)

pline" — covered everything that had been missed in the first 98. Solitary confinement on bread and water or forfeiture of pay and allowances were normal sentences handed down by garrison court-martial for minor trans-

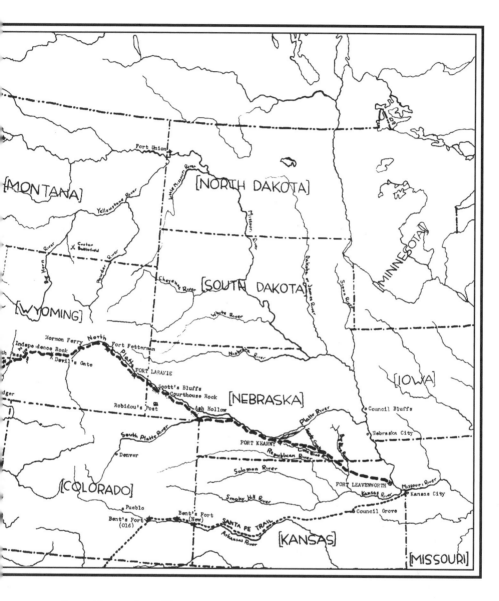

gressions. For major offenses, the punishment was generally left to the discretion of the officer in charge of the court-martial. The man could be whipped, hung by the thumbs, marched around the parade ground for days with a pack full of bricks, or subjected to almost any other torture an officer might think up.

The sentence for desertion was the worst, short of being sentenced to death. Stripped to the waist, the deserter was tied to a pole and his back was flogged with up to 50 lashes by a rawhide whip. Later, branded with a large "D" and his head shaved, he was drummed out of the post to the strains of the "Rogue's March."

On the march, the source for all this punishment was young W. W. Loring. He was an unknown quantity to the officers accompanying him; they did not know what to expect. The enlisted men and the noncoms thought that the garrison rules of punishment would be put behind them on such a march, but these ideas were shattered quickly by Loring. He was fair but firm, and his legislative background plus two years in the Mexican War as an officer prepared him to lead. Loring was not going to give any quarter in maintaining discipline. Shape up or be punished.

Loring was a roaring officer who spat out commands and orders, and when they were not followed, he chewed up individuals with forcible language that would make a first sergeant blush. Without West Point training and not a member of the wealthy Eastern elite, his uncouth behavior at times offended some. But for the next dozen years in the West, he would train hundreds of officers from the Point, forming them into tough, fighting officers. He was the extension arm of West Point for training in the field, even though he never attended West Point himself.

Reveille was sounded at 3:00 a.m. each day, and the signal to advance was given at 6:00 a.m. By 29 May, the caravan had reached Fort Kearny, Nebraska. On 2 June, Colonel Loring separated the command into three divisions of two companies each in order to have better control of the men and wagons; it was impossible to move everything at the same time. Five miles were to separate the first and third divisions. The column then moved out and wound itself toward the Northwest and Fort Laramie in the Wyoming Territory, reaching it by 22 June. The travelers had advanced one-third of the way to the Pacific; they were 639 miles from Fort Leavenworth.

On 5 August, the column arrived at Fort Hall in the Idaho Territory, the regiment's last place to stop for supplies. The condition of the trains, which were to carry the regiment another 700 miles, was not encouraging.

It was now important to reorganize the whole train by leaving unfit animals and wagons behind.

Fort Hall was owned by the Hudson's Bay Company, which would advise emigrants that the Oregon Road was impassable by wagon. In this manner they could control the number of Americans going to Oregon, which at this time still belonged to the British. The road to California was recommended. Many emigrants, including some of the civilians with Loring's column, followed the Hudson's Bay Company's advice, but equally as many were unwilling to make last-minute changes in their plans. Disposing of their wagons, some emigrants walked overland to the Pacific Northwest.

Colonel Loring, under orders from General Persifor Smith, was supposed to establish military posts to protect the emigrants on their Westward movement. Accordingly, he ordered two companies to set up Cantonment Loring, three miles up the Snake River from Fort Hall. The British were then on notice of the American intentions in the West.

At Fort Hall, the command, which had been reunited, was again split into two divisions. On 7 August, the first division resumed the march; the second division commenced on 8 August.

According to Major Cross's journal: "We had traveled three months and had only accomplished 1400 miles, two thirds of the journey, over the most uninteresting route. Stout hearts and willing dispositions to brace difficulties will be needed for the next leg of the trip, 700 miles to Oregon City" (Settle 175).

On 29 August, the Rifles straggled into Fort Boise, Idaho, another trading post established by the Hudson's Bay Company in the same manner as Fort Hall. The 177-mile trip from Fort Hall through a country of waste had been very difficult for Loring and his men. The mules became weakened for want of food, and many horses, entirely unfit for service, had died upon the road.

Because the train had become so weak, Loring sent an express to Fort Vancouver on the Columbia River for transportation to meet him at The Dalles in Oregon, as it would be impossible to get the stores and troops over the Cascade Mountains with the present means of transportation. Loring then ordered the principal portion of the train to be left behind, with all the broken-down horses and mules, to be escorted by one company left for that purpose. This meant the command was dismounted, and the horses were driven for the remainder of the march. Five companies with their baggage and provisions were placed in advance; the remainder of the train, the weakest horses, and one company followed. Major Cross recorded in his journal:

> September 1 — The stores were weighed and arranged in proportion to the strength of the teams. The commissary stores were daily decreasing, which would greatly relieve the teams. . . .
>
> The men on foot were placed under the command of Lt. Lindsay. This day's march of twenty miles was performed in shorter time and with much less difficulty because the number of wagons broken up had given us an additional number of good mules. This gave the Rifles an opportunity to travel more rapidly. (Settle 24, 213-214)

The first large division of the regiment arrived at The Dalles on 22 September, and some of the men by then were "barefooted and unable to walk" (Van Arsdol 92). On 26 September, the second division arrived "so completely broken down," the quartermaster reported, that it "could not possibly have gone farther." This division had 30 wagons left, and the 190 mules were so exhausted that they could not travel until rested. En route, the command had abandoned 45 freight wagons and one ambulance, and 35 horses and 295 mules had died from overwork and lack of forage. To compound their problems, Loring found that the transportation he had sent for was not enough for the whole command.

He thus directed Major Stephen S. Tucker with 100 men to proceed by the trail on the north side of the Columbia River to Fort Vancouver, from where they were to proceed to Oregon City. Loring and the remainder of the command, with the baggage, were transported by way of the Columbia and Willamette Rivers on mackinaw boats, canoes, a yawl, and a whale boat. They arrived in Oregon City on 8 and 9 October 1849.

Loring reported:

> It is gratifying to state that the expedition has reached its destination safely after one of the longest marches that has ever been made, a distance of over two thousand miles across a country — a large portion of which approaches a waste and much of it

mountainous — by a regiment just recruited, an outfit that was certainly inadequate to such an undertaking — besieged with temptation to desert to California and the gold fever — to the officers and non-coms — my warmest thanks for your energy and ability to perform your duties. (Loring report)

The accomplishments of this historic march were exactly what General Scott and the War Department had hoped for. Fort Laramie and Fort Hall with Cantonment Loring had been established as trail stations for the emigrants. Several companies from the Mounted Riflemen remained on active duty at these stations for the next year.

But while Loring's fame grew in the Eastern newspapers — "Loring's march was considered the greatest military feat of the kind on record" (*National Cyclopedia* 364) — he could use little of it in the tough West.

No group coming across the Oregon Trail in 1849 had commanded more anticipation and attention from the American citizens on the Pacific Coast than the Mounted Rifles under Colonel Loring. Newspapers in California and Oregon had given descriptions of the troop's movements from official government dispatches.

The arrival of the regiment was a satisfactory end to an era of pleading for forts and protection of American emigrants and for forces to occupy Oregon. The settlers would now have protection from the Indians and the manipulations of the Hudson's Bay Company.

But the Territory was a glaring example of the problems faced by the Army. A third of the continental land mass of the United States was suddenly dropped in its lap, and when the new scale of distances was imposed upon the existing problems of supply, finance, and recruitment, the burden was staggering. The new country to be protected seemed full of displaced and misplaced people: wandering families looking for Eden, Indians expelled from their land for reasons they could not appreciate, irresponsible spoilers of all kinds, especially miners and land speculators, forever restless.

Secretary of War Charles M. Conrad had ordered a skeleton force to police the Pacific Northwest. Loring, with limited manpower, did his best. But at Cantonment Loring he had stationed two companies with 122 rank and file; at Fort Steilacoom, 1st Artillery, 75 rank and file; at Astoria, a small detachment of 10 men; and at Fort Vancouver, 1st Artillery, 70 rank and file, leaving Loring with 297 men at Oregon City, a small force to patrol the vast new Oregon Territory.

Loring's mission had been to establish military reservations along the Oregon Trail and then in the Territory of Oregon. General Smith indicated that he favored military posts at Fort Vancouver and The Dalles. On 27 April 1850, Colonel Loring established headquarters at Fort Vancouver; in May, two companies of Rifles established Camp Drum (later Fort Dalles) at The Dalles. Loring also posted two batteries at Astoria.

But the settlers who had taken up claims near Fort Vancouver and the other military reservations contested such an appropriation of property. The complainants held that they preferred fighting their own Indian wars to submitting to military usurpation and urged the government to withdraw the rifle regiment at its earliest convenience. Petitions soon bombarded the office of Secretary of War Conrad.

By the next year, Conrad had examined the situation in the Pacific Division and decided to move the Mounted Riflemen to a frontier post where they were more needed: Texas. In a letter to Oregon Governor Jon P. Gaines, Conrad explained that "Texas and New Mexico are surrounded by tribes of Indians far more formidable, both from their numbers and their character, than those of the Pacific. . . . The presence of [the Mounted Riflemen] . . . is indispensably necessary in Texas" (Utley 104).

When word got out in April 1851 that the troops were leaving the Territory, attitudes changed. The governor issued a long letter to the Indian Commission on their virtues: "The news of the withdrawal of the Rifle Regiment from Oregon has been so sudden and unexpected, that I had no time to address a remonstrance to the Department of War upon the subject" (Utley 104). But the breakup was swift. Military Departments 10 and 11 were dissolved and merged into the Pacific Division. Aging General Persifor Smith was reassigned to command the 8th Military Department at San Antonio, Texas. The regiment of Mounted Riflemen under Brevet Colonel Loring was broken up, to be re-formed in Texas, but first they returned to Jefferson Barracks, Missouri.

After arriving at Jefferson Barracks, Loring went on detached service at

Baltimore, Maryland, where General Winfield Scott and the U.S. Army were located. Undoubtedly there were debriefings of Loring's activities in Oregon.

Colonel Loring returned to St. Augustine in late October 1851 and stayed until February 1852, when he rejoined the regiment at Indianola, Texas, the beginning of his service on the Great Plains, where Sioux, Cheyenne, and Arapaho were to make their last stand over the next 15 years against the white man. Loring was now commander of the Department of Rio Grande.

It is interesting to note that at this time, the military hierarchy seemed to prefer a formal military education, like that gained at West Point, in order to lead troops in battle, rather than having field service suffice. But the fact was that an appointee learned his "frontiersmanship" by serving with veterans like Colonel W. W. Loring. The need for an academic background tended to fade. Loring was the grand master in the field for educating and training these men. Serving with him in Oregon in 1849 and 1850 with the Mounted Riflemen were no less than ten future generals who would serve in the American Civil War: Daniel Marsh Frost, George Bibb Crittenden, and William Edmonson Jones (Confederate States of America), and Osborne Cross, Charles Frederick Ruff, John Porter Hatch, Rufus Engalls, A. Porter, Gordon Granger, and J. B. Fry (Union army). These were the cavaliers of the early West. There were not many of them.

From Indianola, Loring's troops were sent to Fort Merrill, Texas, and on 22 June, the regiment was again moved to Fort Ewell, 40 miles southeast of Cotulla, located on an old Indian thoroughfare between Texas and Mexico. When Loring arrived at this post on 26 June, there was no real framework or strategy to follow, and few policy guidelines emanated from the War Department to give direction and coherence to frontier defense measures. Frontier officers, such as Loring, pursued their missions and met each crisis largely with policies and courses of action developed from previous experience. They erected their defenses and employed their troops as they saw fit.

Loring's Texas mission was easily defined on paper, but the implementing of the actions against the Indians was complex. The Mounted

Riflemen spent much time and frustration in tracking and trying to find the Comanche, Kiowa, and the confederated Kiowa-Apache, tribes the army considered "bad" — barbarous, cruel, dishonest.

Field service consisted of scouting for the Indians trying to move in either direction, in or out of the new state of Texas; guard duty; mapping the area; and fighting the bugs, sunburn, heatstroke, desert, cactus, mesquite, and rattlesnakes. By the end of 1852, Loring had seen little success with the Indians. However, his troops had suffered a high death rate on the frontier; monthly reports always showed several deaths from sunstroke or disease. It was lonely duty, to say the least.

In 1854, the War Department stepped up the scouting and reconnaissance programs with a design to control the Comanche and Kiowa. To do this meant constant work for Loring on the barren frontier. Excessive Texas heat again took its toll on men and beast, as the monthly regiment report showed: eight to ten desertions a month; four or five deaths; a few transfers but seldom new recruits. But by the end of 1854, Loring had the companies spread all over the 2,000-mile-long frontier, intercepting and menacing the Indians of the vast area to a point where the safety of the inhabitants and new emigrants was far more guaranteed than it had been four years previous. The cantankerous regiment of Riflemen did their job well.

In 1855, when Loring was on the Rio Grande frontier, President Franklin Pierce signed on 4 March a bill authorizing four new regiments in the U.S. Army, two cavalry and two infantry, orchestrated by Secretary of War Jefferson Davis. At the time, three mounted regiments existed: the 1st and 2nd Dragoons, authorized in 1833 and 1836, and the Mounted Rifles, authorized in 1846. Now there would be more of them on the frontier. With Pierce's plan for additional cavalry, Colonel Loring, after four and a half years on the Texas frontier, would be going to the New Mexico Territory.

On 4 July 1856, Loring returned from a leave of absence in Baltimore to Fort Clark, Texas, from where he left with part of the regiment, en route to New Mexico, on 10 July. On 3 August, they arrived at Fort Bliss, Texas. This movement of 400 miles in the dead Texas heat took 24 days on horseback. From here they proceeded to Camp Holmes, Texas, where they met up with the rest of Loring's troops. On 1 September, Loring moved his headquarters and nine companies of the regiment to a point on the Rio Grande, ten miles below Fort Fillmore, and established Camp Crawford.

On 4 September, the command set out for Fort Union, New Mexico, arriving on 27 September. This move covered 375 miles and took 23 days. All total, in 79 days Loring moved 800 miles out of Texas and into New Mexico. Loring was becoming famous for his long treks.

The administration of a regiment that was to control over 250,000 square miles was not an easy task. Within the boundaries of New Mexico resided an Indian population of about 40,000; Loring would have to deal with the three tribes that were considered a menace: the Ute, Navajo, and Apache. Supplies from the Atlantic states for the men stationed so far West was an expensive transportation problem, with a 12-month time lag in shipping. Contracts for local flour, salt, and beans could be supplied only on a limited basis.

After spending some time in the field pursuing Indians, Loring returned to Fort Union on 22 December and found out eight days later that he had been promoted to full colonel in the Regular army — no more brevet. At the age of 38, W. W. Loring became the youngest colonel in the history of the army at that time.

On 11 February 1857, the Department of New Mexico ordered the Mounted Riflemen to participate in the spring expedition of the U.S. Army in a sweep of the Gila Apache Indians, a murderous band who had stolen thousands of sheep on the Rio Grande during the summer and fall of 1856. Colonel Loring was to command the northern column of the army. His detachment of 300 included three companies of his own regiment, and added to the Rifles were two companies of the 3rd Infantry and a detachment of Mexican and Indian Pueblo trailers and scouts, led by Captain Manuel Chavez. The total number of troops moving southward out of Fort Union to Santa Fe involved around 800.

By 1 May, the troops had arrived at the Gila supply depot. Loring wrote that "the country passed over, mostly waste of mountains, rough and destitute of grass and water, severe in weather, will never be forgotten by those who participated" (Loring to Army Headquarters). The campaign got off to an inauspicious start. From the depot, the troops of Loring's northern column beat the brush throughout much of the surrounding country, and as they approached their rendezvous with the southern column on the Gila, they found the entire country fired by the Indians. So complete was the destruction that the troops had difficulty in finding enough grass in protected spots to maintain their horses and mules. Screened by the smoke and flames, the Indians quickly migrated to the safety of the mountains of Arizona and Chihuahua, Mexico.

Signs were soon discovered, however, of the passing of another large party of Indians — and sheep. The Indian scouts of Loring's column picked up the broad trail of Mimbres chieftain Cuchillo Negros, who for three years had been a pillar of the government's agricultural experiment and who now had entered, at a most unpropitious moment, the zone of operations of the U.S. Army with a herd of more than a thousand stolen sheep.

The pursuit began and continued day and night. On 25 May, the troops found the fugitives in a rocky mountain valley some 70 miles northeast of the Gila supply depot. The bugle sounded and the attack began at dawn. Loring and Captain Chavez, with a small band of their Indians, guides, and spies, slid down the crater's wall and defeated the whole party of the infamous sheep thieves. Cuchillo Negros was killed along with six of his warriors; two were wounded and nine captured. The rest scattered up the narrow valley, abandoning the sheep and all other property to the Mounted Rifles. The Rifles pursued the Indians to a neighboring canyon where they discovered another band of thieving Indians; these escaped, leaving behind 500 sheep.

After a 200-mile march in six days, Loring and his troops arrived back at the Gila depot, bringing in about 1,500 sheep and nine prisoners and a large quantity of packed meat, skins, and tents.

Loring and his regiment remained in camp until 14 June 1857, when they marched from the Gila depot for the invasion of the country of the Coyotero Indians. On the 29th, Loring finally found the farms of the Coyotero, in Arizona Territory. He had been instructed to destroy all corn, and on 2 and 3 July, he proceeded to lay waste to extensive cornfields in the valley of the Tularosa belonging to the Indians.

The Riflemen were determined to inflict a deadly blow at the strength of the Coyotero Nation, but the Coyotero fled with their herds of horses, and Loring was unable to catch them. After 4 July, Loring began the 188-mile trek back to the Gila depot, arriving on 15 July.

The *Santa Fe Weekly Gazette* characterized the Gila expedition as the most arduous, trying, and dangerous military operation undertaken since

New Mexico had become a possession of the United States. Unfortunately, the expedition had not solved the Indian problem in the Territory.

On 15 July, Loring received orders relieving the column from further duty in the Gila expedition and ordering him to Fort Defiance, Arizona, because of disturbances created by the Navajo Indians. Loring and the Rifles left on 20 August and reached Fort Defiance, the command post for all the troops serving in the Navajo Indian country, 400 miles away, by the end of the month.

The fort lived up to its name as the Indians reacted against it in like fashion. The garrison was one that Colonel E. V. Sumner had established in 1852 with the idea that it would keep the Navajo quiet after several treaty attempts had been miserable failures.

Late in August 1857, the cry went up: "The camels are coming, the camels are coming!" Jefferson Davis's camel experiment was on its way to California in hopes that these animals would be the answer to the military logistics problem — moving supplies over great distances in hot weather with animals that needed little water or food — in the Southwest.

Edward F. Beale was assigned the task of moving the 25 camels. "Aboard his swaying white ship on the desert, Beale, the ex-sailor, rode into Fort Defiance in order to make an impression on the post commander, Colonel Loring" (Hart 60). Beale taught Loring how to ride, but Loring had no opportunity to use the camels on the trail of Indian raiders. After the short stopover, Beale continued Westward, over the Colorado River at Fort Mojave and across the Mojave Desert, following the U.S. surveyor's trail to Los Angeles.

After making a short treaty regarding grazing land with the recognized head of the Navajo, Loring and his troops ended their short tour at Fort Defiance. The troopers rode 360 miles back to Fort Union. Since April, the mounted riflemen had traveled over 1,500 miles on worn-out, broken-down cavalry horses and mules.

During Loring's ten-year movement over the Southwest, he dealt with many of the various Indian tribes on behalf of the U.S. Army, lending to his creditability as an important, patriotic frontier officer dealing with a very complicated social problem — the movement and settlement of the Indians. Few others could claim such an Indian-fighting and peace-making status for such a long period of time in the early days of settling the West.

The year 1857 was not a good one for the nation. A financial panic helped fan the flames of secession of the Southern cotton states from the industrial states of the North. The South wanted out of the Union.

During the time that Loring was preparing for the Gila Apache expedition, James Buchanan was inaugurated as President. One of the first things Buchanan did was to relieve Brigham Young of his authority in Utah and instead appoint Alfred Cummings as territorial governor. The Mormons, who constituted virtually the entire population of the Utah Territory, were embittered over the removal of Young, who retorted that he would remain as governor. He described the federal government as "a stink in our nostrils" and challenged the armies to come against them, believing God would smite them with pestilence and storms. But open rebellion by a Territory would not be permitted by Washington; it would be met by force.

This action by the new President sent a clear message to all states: don't consider dissolving the Union. President Buchanan directed that a force be assembled at Fort Leavenworth, Kansas, sufficient to quell Brigham Young's Mormon legions and rebellion and to escort the new governor and other federal officials to the Utah Territory immediately.

General Persifor Smith was selected to take command of the force, but within a week of his arrival at the post, he became fatally ill. Loring, next in line for the command, was in the field in New Mexico and Arizona, so it was offered to Colonel Albert Sidney Johnston, who was delayed and did not arrive at Fort Leavenworth until 11 September 1857, two months after the first contingent of troopers had left for Utah.

Colonel Johnston, Governor Cummings and other federal officials, and six companies of the 2nd Dragoons moved out on 17 September. Bad weather plagued them the whole trip. Over 1,200 miles and two months later, the army of 2,500 men and thousands of animals made it to Utah Territory.

However, the Mormons, anticipating the military, had burned Fort Bridger, Colonel Johnston's destination. They also had ambushed and destroyed his supply trains, which contained clothing, medicine, and rations, and the grasses, so essential to grazing, had been burned.

Johnston constructed a new fort at the old location, naming it Camp Scott, but was forced to send Captain B. Marcy with a small detail back to Fort Massachusetts in New Mexico to acquire horses and mules for the Army. After learning that the Mormons had destroyed the Army's supplies, Congress immediately voted an appropriation for 4,000 reinforcements to be sent to Utah, including the Mounted Riflemen.

In March, three and a half months after leaving Camp Scott, Marcy purchased the necessary horses and mules in New Mexico; he then received word from Colonel Loring to wait for him and the Riflemen for the return trip to Utah. On 29 April a severe snowstorm struck the party and scattered the horse herd. Extreme cold, which accompanied the storm, and the swollen streams added to the hardship of both men and beast. Loring and Marcy arrived in Johnston's camp on 4 June, having traveled an estimated 702 miles.

In the meantime, negotiations between Brigham Young and the new governor had settled the differences. A compromise was reached: the new governor of the Territory would be received, and the Mormons would pledge acceptance of federal authorities and permit the Army to enter Salt Lake City as long as no troops were quartered in or occupied the city.

The U.S. troops moved out from Camp Scott to Salt Lake City on 13 June. One-armed veteran Colonel W. W. Loring led his battalion of Mounted Riflemen as the Army of Utah, with the American flag flying proudly, guidons flapping in the warm breeze, and bands playing loudly, began its march down Main Street. With over 3,000 officers and enlisted men and the quartermasters' trains, the Army, marching straight through the city, took eight hours to pass a single point, showing off its power and might but playing to an empty house: the 30,000 residents had fled the city and were streaming south some 40 miles to Provo, where they lived in temporary shanties and tents for several months. Had they remained, they would have seen a number of future generals of the coming Civil War, including Joseph E. Johnston, Samuel W. Ferguson, John Pegram, John C. McCown, John H. Forney, and Philip S. Cooke. Within a few years, they would be scattered by the fury of the War Between the States, facing one another in valleys of death and destruction. This was the first military maneuver by a great part of the U.S. Army since the Mexican War, ten years earlier.

Loring was ordered back to Fort Union, New Mexico, on 19 July 1858 and was instructed to lead a military detachment comprised of 50 wagons with teamsters, 300 men: those of Company K and detachments of Companies H and G, the Mounted Riflemen, and Companies A, E, and F, 3rd Infantry. They took the central route across Utah and Colorado and saved 200 miles; the route became known as the Loring Trail.

On 23 April 1859, Loring left the regiment for a leave of absence. In June, the leave was extended 11 months. An article in the 7 July 1859 *West Arizonian* stated: "No less than thirteen officers of the U.S. Army have obtained leave of absence for the purpose of visiting Europe in general and the seat of war in particular. Among the number . . . Col. Loring of the Rifles."

Loring's itinerary during this long leave is not easy to document. Various unofficial sources stated that in mid-1859, Loring was sent by the War Department to Europe to observe the armies and training procedures of a number of European nations, including France, Great Britain, Prussia, and a number of smaller German states. He made a tour of Europe, devoting much time to a study of the military tactics and systems.

On returning home from his European tour in 1860, Loring discovered that the nation was on fire. In this year, many occurrences were leading up to the beginning of the American Civil War, and by summer, it was clear that a Lincoln presidential triumph in the fall elections would mean possible secession by several Southern states.

Colonel Loring reported to Secretary of War John B. Floyd, still in office under the Buchanan administration. The instructions given to the colonel, who would return to New Mexico and take command of 25 percent of the active field U.S. Army, are unknown.

The election of Abraham Lincoln, the Declaration of Secession in December 1860, and the firing of the first shots at Fort Sumter, South Carolina, in April 1861, saw the collapse of the U.S. Army for a brief period.

In states such as Virginia, South Carolina, Florida, Alabama, Georgia, Mississippi, and Louisiana, the governors ordered the seizure of all Federal property — forts, posts, barracks, arsenals, ships, naval yards, hospitals, and mints. This was done with no opposition. The big bang came in February 1861 when Loring's mentor, General David E. Twiggs in Texas, surrendered the whole U.S. Army that was stationed in Texas to the state of Texas without firing a shot.

Loring was aware of the dissension and turmoil in Texas and the secessionist movement in the South. From New York on 14 February 1861, he wrote to Governor M. S. Perry of Florida, "I shall always hold myself

ready to serve my State and the South, should the time come when my services will be usefull to them" (Joseph F. Siano private collection).

Since the Army was dominated by Southern officers and noncoms,
these men had little trouble in making their decisions known: they would
resign and support their home states and the new Confederacy. Loring, like
all other Southern officers, was faced with the same decision in February,
and yet he returned to his command in New Mexico.

In the next few months, the isolated Army detachments scattered in
New Mexico found themselves with their pay half a year in arrears, without animals, lacking the proper ordnance stores and artillery necessary to
deal with the Apache menace, and dispersed in half a dozen different
posts. They were being deserted by their officers and were being enticed
by such men as Simeon Hart in Texas to desert and join the new Confederacy. As a consequence, discipline and morale fell apart.

It became the considered opinion of many that the Army had been
unnecessarily scattered by Secretary of War Floyd, who himself had been
forced to resign in December 1860 after being accused of stacking the
Federal armories in the South with arms and munitions. Did he likewise
stack the Western commands with soldiers of the South — Albert S. Johnston in California, Twiggs in Texas, and Loring in New Mexico?

Although no longer stationed in Texas, Loring's long duty and service
in the state permitted him to brush elbows and dine with some of the leading secessionists. Maybe it was on military business and maybe at time
social, but Loring was privy to their thinking and plans. As the events of
secession unfolded in Texas, his past association with men such as Judge
Simeon Hart, James (Santiago) Wiley Magoffin, District Judge J. F. Cros-
by, and even General David E. Twiggs, who was in charge of the Department of Texas, would have profound implications and innuendoes on his
part of the coming seceding actions.

Abe Lincoln's election in November of 1860 accelerated Texas's exit
from the Union. On 28 January 1861, the Texas Convention met at Austin
and adopted an ordinance of secession. Governor Sam Houston, although
objecting to secession, asked General Twiggs if he would turn Federal
property over to the State of Texas. It is reported that Twiggs informed
Washington he did not want to start a civil war, and thus he would comply
with Houston's demand!

Thus Twiggs, with one stroke of his pen, without firing a shot, surrendered Texas to the secessionists. Under the agreement, all U.S. troops

would collect their weapons, clothing, and camp equipment and march out of Texas unharmed, leaving behind 44 cannons and howitzers; 1,900 muskets, rifles, and carbines; 400 Colt pistols; two magazines full of ammunition; 500 wagons; 950 horses; and a large amount of commissary stores. It was the biggest giveaway in the Civil War.

Twiggs became the scapegoat and was immediately branded a traitor throughout the North. On 5 March 1861, the new government in Montgomery exercised military jurisdiction of the new Confederate state, and sent Colonel Earl Van Dorn on 26 March to assume command.

During the spring of 1861, the New Mexico Department began to unravel, and the doctrine of the "Rights of Secession" — the belief that any state could withdraw from the Union of states at its pleasure, that the states were sovereign, and that the government was but their agent that any one of them could repudiate at will — would prevail. This doctrine led the Southern officers right out of the Federal army with mass resignations.

Arriving at his decision, Colonel Loring held a conference with the officers of the various posts around Santa Fe. "For my part," he told them, "the South is my home, and I am going to throw up my commission and shall join the Southern Army, and each of you can do as you think best" (Wessels 52). Colonel W. W. Loring resigned on 13 May, as did Colonel Thomas T. Fauntleroy and Major Henry H. Sibley. Such resignations were body blows to the weakening U.S. Army and at the same time were a source of great encouragement to the Confederate leadership.

For 31 days, Loring retained control of the Department of New Mexico. Was he waiting for a column of secessionists from Texas to come and secure New Mexico for the Confederacy? The newly formed Confederacy expected the population of New Mexico to espouse the Southern cause and California to secede from the Union. New Mexico was the gateway to California and the outlet to the Pacific Ocean. It would control the immense gold and silver treasury flowing from the mines of the West into Union coffers to finance the war. South of New Mexico was Mexico with its 600 miles of frontier, the only neutral country from which the Confederates could gain supplies from abroad. Loring was clearly marking time and waiting. On 11 June, he placed Major E. R. S. Canby in charge of Santa Fe, while he moved to Fort Fillmore, still waiting for a move by the Texas Confederates.

Canby was reluctant to believe that there was any truth in rumors that Loring had gone over to the Confederacy. But on 24 June 1861, Canby expressed doubt about Loring's loyalty in a letter to Major Isaac Lynde, commanding officer at Fort Fillmore: "When Col. Loring left this place, every officer here had implicit confidence in his integrity, but I am sorry to say that some information received since he left has shaken that confidence. It is a long step from confidence to absolute distrust, but it is necessary that you should be on your guard against any betrayal of the honor or interests of the United States" (Keleher 193, 194).

One might construe that Loring's move to Fort Fillmore was a strategic retreat since the fort was only 38 miles from El Paso, Texas. Most of the deserting officers passed through the fort on their way to Texas. Loring could wait no longer; his loyalty to the U.S. Army was thus severed.

Safely back in Texas, Loring hurried along to San Antonio where on 1 July he sent a short letter to Confederate Secretary of War Leroy Pope Walker in Richmond, Virginia: "I am now hastening to the scene of war, fearing that my application both through officers who have resigned and also by letter, may not have reached you. I again offer my services and shall leave here tomorrow via New Orleans for Richmond" (National Archives).

Why didn't Loring return to Florida as he stated in his letter to Governor Perry of 14 February? The Confederate leaders in Richmond expected little action in Florida since it was 900 miles away. They needed experienced officers immediately in Virginia. Consequently, Loring went to Richmond. Loring never commanded any Florida troops during the war.

Eventually, 286 West Pointers, including 19 of Northern birth, chose to serve the Confederacy during the Civil War. Secretary of War Simon Cameron declared that the South's rebellion could never have reached formidable proportions without the help it was receiving from West Pointers. When Jefferson Davis became President of the Confederate states, he did not hesitate to appoint other West Point graduates to important commands, often to the exclusion of other officers. Davis held to this elitist doctrine to the end, and it undoubtedly was one of the mistakes he made in running the Confederacy.

For 14 years, the Brave Rifles under Loring's command had produced an enviable record. When the Mounted Riflemen left Oregon in 1850 Lor-

 ing had under him future Confederate and Union generals, as he had in 1855, when he left the Department of Texas for New Mexico: Dabney H. Maury, John S. Bowen, Laurence S. Baker, John G. Walker, and Henry Hopkins Sibley would join the Confederacy; John S. Simpson, Washington L. Elliott, Benjamin Stone Roberts, Thomas Duncan, and Alfred Gibbs would be part of the Union. All of these men were ranked by Loring, who at 42 was the youngest full colonel in the U.S. Army. As the Civil War progressed, squabbles arose time and time again about rank in the "old" U.S. Army and the "new" Confederate army. In the U.S. Army, Loring was a legend, but his days in the sun were numbered.

On 3 August 1861, after Colonel Loring had resigned, Congress called for all mounted regiments to be designated as cavalry and for renumbering them as such by seniority of authorizations.

The 1st Dragoons thus became the 1st Cavalry; the 2nd Dragoons became the 2nd Cavalry; the 1st Cavalry regiments became the 4th Cavalry; and the 2nd Cavalry regiments became the 5th Cavalry.

The Mounted Riflemen became the 3rd Cavalry (which later became the world-famous 3rd Armored Cavalry Regiment). Colonel Loring commanded the 3rd Cavalry longer than any other officer, because Persifor F. Smith, the first commander, was on detached service in California and never did command the regiment. Loring was in command for 14 years.

Chapter 4

Loring and Lee
at Cheat Mountain,
Western Virginia

Being punished, he resisted. Resisting, he died.
— Carlton McCarthy, a Confederate soldier,
Eisenschiml and Newman, *The American Iliad*

*T*HE STARTLING DEFECTION of *Southern officers permitted the rebellion to assume formidable proportions in a short time. Needless to say, the Federal authorities were furious over the number of officers, trained at the taxpayers' expense, who were "going South." The scattered U.S. Army at the end*

of 1860 numbered 16,367 men and officers, and 313 of the officers, nearly 25 percent, joined the Confederacy.

The bulk of Southern officers waited until after the South's attack on
Fort Sumter and Lincoln's call for troops in April 1861 to quit the service
and start for home. But Colonel Loring did not report to his home state of
Florida for rank and position; instead, he journeyed directly to Richmond
for his appointment. On his long trek from New Mexico to Virginia, he
certainly had time to reflect on his career and accomplishments. He surely had to be concerned about his forfeiting the pension and all future rela-
tionships with the U.S. Army. And it would take more than a service
record to advance in the Confederate army.

A handful of the chosen and elite were picked to command the Southern resources and military, and while Richmond welcomed the influx of
able, energetic, and brainy men from other states, her acceptance of "out-
siders" was based upon their recognition that in accomplishments, Vir-
ginians were "first among equals."

Colonel Loring reached Richmond in July; it had taken him six long
weeks to come from New Mexico. The shooting war had been going
on since late April and the army had been formed; consequently, he
wondered, what could be left in the way of good commands for a late-
comer?

Loring had received his appointment as a brigadier general in the Regular Confederate army (formed when the Confederacy was created) and in
the provisional Confederate army (formed when it became apparent that
thousands of troops would be needed from all states). Upon reaching
Richmond on 20 July, Robert E. Lee assigned him to the command of the
Northwestern Army (*OR*, p. 986, ser. I, vol. 2) and to proceed without
delay to stop Union General George B. McClellan's movement from Ohio
into Virginia, which had begun in the spring of 1861. In addition, Loring
was instructed to bring some semblance of military order and peace
between the feuding Confederate Generals Henry A. Wise and none other
than former Secretary of War John B. Floyd.

General Loring arrived in Monterey, Virginia, 25 July and assumed
command of the forces on both the Monterey and the Huntersville lines,
which had a common objective in containing the invading Federal force on
Cheat Mountain and near Huttonsville. Loring found it a difficult task to
instill confidence and morale into a discouraged, disgruntled, and disappointed Confederate army. Many men were sick, necessary supplies were

lacking, and guns and ammunition were inadequate. The transition from civil life was too sudden: the men were still raw recruits, and the officers were scarcely better trained in the business of war. There was bumbling incompetence, and mistakes were many.

On the same day, Loring sent a dispatch to Colonel George Deas in Richmond:

> Yesterday I received the letter of General Lee of the 16th, in which he refers to the importance of defending the mountain passes to prevent the advance of the enemy on the Virginia Central Railroad. I have been exceedingly anxious that the general should be apprised by *personal inspection* of the indescribable condition into which this branch of the army has fallen.
>
> The condition of Colonel Ramsey's command is in truth pitiable. Officers and men are absolutely stripped of everything — tents, clothing, cooking utensils, shoes — and I am sorry to believe that many may have thrown away their arms.

Loring then questions, "Is the whole country thus to be surrendered?" (*OR*, vol. 2, p. 95).

On 31 July, Loring sent a dispatch to General Floyd:

> The enemy are on Cheat Mountain, with a considerable force at its base and along the road to Beverly. If the enemy is not pressing in the direction of Wise, and the different commands can join me, I think we can give the enemy a decided blow in the vicinity of Cheat Mountain and also strike the column sent in the direction of Wise. I beg that you will give me the earliest information of the movements of both General Wise and yourself. (*OR*, vol. 51, pt. 2, p. 206)

On 1 August, General Loring rode to the front, accompanied by his staff, and crossed the Allegheny Mountains, reconnoitered the enemy's position on Cheat Mountain, and concluded that a direct attack by way of the Parkersburg Road was impractical.

He then decided to take immediate command of the force that had been ordered to rendezvous at Huntersville and attempted to turn Cheat Mountain by way of the Valley Mountain pass. He directed General Henry R.

Jackson to advance his whole force of some 6,000 men to the Greenbrier River and hold himself in readiness to cooperate when the advance should be made from Huntersville toward Beverly, 50 miles away.

General Loring then rode down the valley of the Greenbrier to Huntersville, where he established his headquarters and his army's supply depot, and began to make arrangements for the proposed forward movements on the Federal forces at Huttonsville and on Cheat Mountain.

On 3 August, General Robert E. Lee and his companions rode into Huntersville and went immediately to Loring's headquarters. Although General Lee had been placed in command of all Confederate troops in Virginia in May, there is no evidence that he ever usurped General Loring's command other than by cooperation.

After conferring with Loring for several days, Lee rode forward 28 miles to Valley Mountain and established his headquarters. Loring joined Lee there around 12 August, and they addressed the immediate task of how to dislodge the capable Federal commander General J. J. Reynolds from his strongholds at Elkwater and on Cheat Mountain. Loring was in immediate command of the Army of the Northwest. His right wing was made up of troops on the Monterey line and the Huntersville line; his left wing was under General Floyd.

But the crucial factor in Lee and Loring's campaign would not be Reynolds's Federal forces, which were being added to daily, or the lack of adequate supplies, which weakened the Confederates' fighting effectiveness; rather, it was the weather. The months of July and August had seen a steady downpour of rain, which saturated the whole country. The mountain roads, cut up by the constant passing of heavy army trains, became axle-deep mud traps, and the many unbridged streams, swollen by the steady rain, added to the difficulties of transportation. For weeks the army was short of rations.

This continuous damp and chilly weather resulted in sickness of every kind among the thousands of unseasoned troops. By the middle of September, nearly half of Loring's men were laid up in poorly provided hospitals, and the mortality rate from illness among the young recruits, so far away from home, became very great.

In early September, Lee and Loring decided that a show of resistance by an attack on the Federal position at Cheat Mountain and Elkwater was demanded. The weather changed for the better, improving the roads. Orders were issued for a simultaneous movement by the

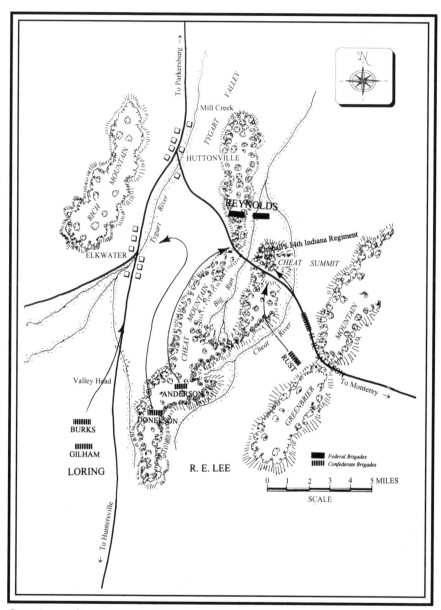

Operations at Cheat Mountain, September 10-15, 1861. (Courtesy, William R. Scaife)

Huntersville line on the enemy camp at Elkwater and by the Monterey line on that of Cheat Mountain.

But the best of plans can go awry. The simple attack plan — the Confederate left wing under Lee and Loring would unite with General Jackson's right wing to attack the enemy's position at Elkwater, breaking the rear of the enemy's column, cutting his line in two, and ensuring the capture of the position at the top of Cheat Mountain — was changed at the last minute due to new information from Colonel Albert Rust, who had just returned from a reconnaissance of the enemy's station on the summit. General Jackson, using Rust's information, then urged that *three* concerted attacks be made: one by Loring from the valley, one by Jackson from the east, and one by Rust from the rear, using the route he had just surveyed.

One of the difficulties of waging war in the mountains of western Virginia was that the tree foliage hid the troops. Frequently, Lee and Loring didn't know where the blueclads were located and in fact didn't know where their own troops were. Consequently, communication was very difficult to maintain in executing a combined attack.

Before the dawn of 12 September, each of the commands had reached its appointed position undetected, and all waited for the opening fire of Rust's assault as the signal to attack. However, no fire came: Rust had faltered at a crucial moment, believing he was plunging into a Union trap. The element of surprise had been lost — and so the battle of Cheat Mountain was never fought (Andrews 293-295). The conduct of the attack was kept so well in hand by the Confederates that they were without serious loss of numbers.

General Lee then turned his attention to the New River area where Generals Floyd and Wise were positioned, Floyd at Meadow Bluff and Wise at Camp Defiance. On 22 September, Lee rode forward to inspect Camp Defiance, then made a reconnaissance of Sewell Mountain on the following day. The enemy had occupied the western top of Sewell Mountain with infantry, cavalry, and artillery, all plainly visible from the camp, about one mile distant. Skirmishing around Camp Defiance was rapidly beginning to appear more like a general engagement. Lee decided to reinforce Wise at the camp, and on 24 September, he wrote to Loring, encamped at Marlings Bottom, Pocahontas County, some 80 miles away, ordering reinforcement from him.

As Loring and his troops made their way to Camp Defiance, serious skirmishing continued, raising fear and anxiety on both sides of Sewell's summit. On 26 September, Union General William S. Rosecrans arrived at the camp of General Jacob D. Cox and decided to personally conduct a reconnaissance of Lee's encampment, taking with him General Cox and Colonel Robert L. McCook, along with Major Rutherford B. Hayes. He wanted to view for himself the position held by Wise on the eastern crest of Sewell. But near the enemy's works, light rain suddenly became a torrential downpour. The cold rains and strong winds that had set in would prove to be a deluge of three days' duration. The inundation was complete and disastrous: the turnpike seemed to disappear, the telegraph lines were washed out, bridges were carried away, the streams overflowed their banks, and flooding began. The temperature dropped sharply, and just after dark the rain turned into sleet. Disease and supply problems, which were already at near intolerable levels in both camps, became many times worse before the storm ended. It stopped, most likely, one of the major battles of the war.

Writing after the war, General Lee's aide, Colonel Walter H. Taylor, described the situation:

> The season was a most unfavorable one. For weeks it rained daily and in torrents, the conditions of the roads most frightful. Wagons were hub-deep in mud, measles and a malignant type of fever prostrated hundreds. In the subsequent campaigns of the Army of Northern Virginia the troops were subjected to great privations but never did they experience the same heart-sinking emotions as when contemplating the wan faces and the emaciated forms of those hungry, sickly, shivering men of the army at Valley Mountain. (McKinney, *Robert E. Lee and the 35th Star*, 44)

Loring arrived at General Floyd's camp at Meadow Bluff, bringing the 42nd and 48th Regiments of the Virginia Infantry and a battery of artillery. Following behind Loring by about a half a day's march was General Samuel Read Anderson, with the 1st, 7th, and 14th Regiments of the Tennessee Infantry.

Lee and Loring then began formulating a plan to attack the Federals. But in a country that presented formidable natural barriers, it was far better to meet an attack than to deliver one. Cox and Rosecrans, of course, had similar ideas. So both sides marked time.

An order was finally issued by Lee to be ready for action by 4 October. Wagons were loaded and sent to the rear, and the men were told to prepare for a march. The day was spent waiting. Would the Union soldiers attack, or would the Confederates move out? Nothing happened. More sickness broke out: the men suffered from diarrhea, fever, headaches, and body aches, and many died in their tents and were buried on the roadside.

The 5th of October was a calm, sunny day for a change, and it was spent the same as the preceding day, in hourly expectation of a fight. Lee and Loring climbed to a prominent point on the mountain from which they could view the Yankee camp. What the two generals did not know was that General Rosecrans, after several days of badgering by his officers, had decided to retreat and had made preparations to slip away that very night.

Confederate pickets heard and reported noise from Rosecrans's retreat during the night, but it was dismissed as nothing unusual. The Confederate camp was astonished the next morning when daylight showed the opposite hill on Sewell Mountain, which had been filled with tents and moving men for the past 11 days, was perfectly bare.

General Lee ordered an immediate pursuit of the enemy, which was conducted by a detachment of cavalry and four infantry companies. Unfortunately, the poor condition of their horses and lack of fodder prevented the Confederates from making a vigorous chase.

A new plan of advance was developed by the Confederates: move Floyd to the south side of the Kanawha River and have him advance to a point where he could cut the communications of the enemy at the Gauley River. Lee would then attack the enemy with Loring's and Floyd's help and drive them out of the Kanawha Valley. The plan was implemented on 12 October but proceeded very slowly. Lee found it nearly impossible to supply his remaining troops at Sewell Mountain, and he realized that to advance another 32 miles over the sodden turnpike would ruin his precarious system of supply. The situation in which Lee found himself thus dictated his decision. With no food or forage, the hospitals in the rear full to overflowing, morale very low, and winter approaching, he had no choice but to call it quits. On 20 October, Lee wrote to Floyd: "General Loring has received dispatches tonight from Generals [Henry R.] Jackson and [Daniel S.] Donelson confirming several previous reports indicating attacks on both their lines, and calling earnestly for aid. . . . I do not think it proper to retain General Loring any longer" (McKinney, *Robert E. Lee at Sewell Mountain,* 110). On the following day, Lee and Loring departed Sewell Mountain, never to return.

Lee would be much abused by the press for his lack of a decisive victory in western Virginia. In fact, both commanding generals, Lee and Rosecrans, were defamed by the disappointed traveling press covering this early phase of the Civil War. On 5 November, Lee was assigned to the new Department of South Carolina, Georgia, and East Florida. In actuality, Lee's accusers certainly missed the mark in citing Lee and Loring as fighting a losing battle in the mountains. This six-week-long battle, admittedly with few shooting casualties, was surely one of the most trying fights of the Civil War. With thousands lying ill on the mountainside in cold, rainy weather and little or no food for man or beast, these two leaders kept the army together and restrained and discouraged the movement of the Federal forces any farther into Virginia.

Chapter 5

The Romney Expedition
and the Jackson Affair

*ENERAL LORING RETURNED to
his headquarters to prepare for the
coming winter months and the
defense of the backdoor to the Confederacy. It was at this same time that
the newly appointed major general of the
Valley District, Thomas J. Jackson, deemed
it of great importance that northwest Virginia be occupied by Confederate troops that
winter. He requested of Secretary of War
Judah Benjamin that all the troops under
General Loring be ordered to Winchester.*

Four days later, Benjamin wrote to Loring, agreeing to Jackson's proposal of a combined movement. But he made it perfectly clear that he and President Davis did "not desire to direct the movement without leaving you a discretion, and the President wishes you to exercise that discretion. If upon full consideration, you think the proposed movement objectionable and too hazardous, you will decline to make it. If, on the contrary, you approve it, then proceed to execute it as promptly and secretly as possible" (*OR*, vol. 5, p. 969). Thus, Loring was free either to accept or reject Jackson's proposal.

Loring was never one to stay too long in a single location during his army career. The thoughts of spending a lengthy winter on the mountains of western Virginia were even less appealing. Accordingly, he decided that, "agreeable to instructions from the War Department, the Army of Northwest will be withdrawn from its present line of operations for immediate service elsewhere" (*OR*, vol. 5, p. 975) — he chose to be available for service with Jackson.

However, a letter to Secretary of War Benjamin on 29 November laid out Loring's conditions, reflecting his wisdom and experience in such maneuvers. He made clear that moving his troops and equipment out of the mountains could not be done quickly, considering it would soon be December and the turnpikes were mostly washed away.

But more Federal troops were moving into Romney, Virginia, a key position located near the Baltimore & Ohio Railroad, and General Samuel Cooper, the Adjutant and Inspector General of the Confederate army, wired Loring at Staunton on 5 December: "The exigency requires the arrival of your entire command as rapidly as possible at Winchester" (*OR*, vol. 5, p. 978), where Jackson was already situated, 43 miles east of Romney.

The 23rd of December found Loring still at Staunton. Secretary of War Benjamin had sent word that "the measure you have taken in disposing and moving your forces meets the entire approval of the Department" (*OR*, vol. 5, p. 1003), but an impatient General Jackson had written to Benjamin: "I would recommend that General Loring be directed not to postpone the marching of his troops in consequences of a desire to save a large supply of subsistence stores. . . . If General Loring is not here speedily, my command may be a retreating instead of a victorious one" (*OR*, vol. 5, p. 988).

As it got closer to Christmas, Jackson's designs seemed even bolder. On

23 December, he wrote to General Cooper: "I respectfully request that
such of Brig. Gen. W. W. Loring's forces as are on and near the Allegheny
Mountains be ordered to march forthwith to Moorefield County, with a
view of forming a junction with the troops now at and near this point. . . .
If it is the design of the Government to commence offensive operations
against Romney soon, the troops asked for should move to *my aid* at once"
(*OR*, vol. 5, p. 1005).

Jackson proposed to take over Loring's Army of the Northwest and
place Loring as a commander of a division. Jackson quickly reversed
himself after Loring arrived in Winchester on Christmas Eve of 1861,
writing to Major Thomas G. Rhett, the Assistant Adjutant General:
"Brig. Gen. W. W. Loring informs me that, in his opinion, the Secretary
of War designs his command to continue to be known as the Army of
the Northwest and that he should continue to be its immediate commander. This meets with my approbation, and I respectfully request that no
action be taken upon my former application for him to command as a division such part of his forces as might be in this district" (*OR*, vol. 5, p.
1006).

In spite of Loring's initial willingness to join and cooperate with
Jackson, the two generals from the beginning did not and would not
work well together for the coming campaign to Romney. Jackson apparently did not care much for Loring or for two of his three brigade commanders, Colonel William B. Taliaferro, heading up the 1st Georgia,
3rd Arkansas, and 23rd and 37th Virginia Regiments, and Brigadier
General Samuel Read Anderson, who led the all-Tennessee 1st, 7th, and
14th Regiments. Colonel William Gilham, who knew Jackson very well,
commanded the third brigade, leading the 21st, 42nd, and 48th Virginia
Regiments.

Jackson disliked free-thinking subordinates and insisted on blind obedience. His most effective tool for relieving friction was transfer and reas-
signment. Anyone who disobeyed him was subject to arrest and court-
martial, and the redoubtable Stonewall Jackson instituted more court-mar-
tials than anyone else in the Confederate army.

After rushing Loring's movements through the month of December,
Jackson did absolutely nothing between Christmas and New Year's. Then,
having secured all the troops that the Confederate authorities would
entrust him with, he was determined to move on the Federals, despite the
lateness of the season and the difficulties that would be encountered in a

winter trek through the mountainous region of Maryland and western Virginia.

The army's goal — kept a secret from Loring, six years Jackson's senior, and the other officers, thanks to Jackson's eccentric unwillingness to reveal his strategy or destination — was to push northward toward Bath and wipe out the bridgehead, then move six miles farther, cross over the Potomac River, and destroy the supply depots at Hancock, Maryland. On the other side of the Potomac they could interrupt and destroy the telegraph communications between Union Generals Benjamin F. Kelly and Nathaniel P. Banks. Returning over the Potomac, the army would then push westward on the road from Unger's Store through Bloomery Gap to Romney and then secure control of the Baltimore & Ohio Railroad.

Jackson decided to move out on New Year's Day, much to the chagrin of the enlisted men who thought Winchester would make good winter quarters. The unseasonably warm morning prompted the men to stuff their greatcoats into the company wagons, but by the afternoon, the skies darkened, the wind began to whip down from the northwest, and snow and hail fell. With this came a protracted period of intense cold and extremely inclement weather.

Loring's brigades led the move toward Bath, followed by Jackson and his men. The supply train following the caravan began to lag, and the freezing rain and snow never permitted it to get into position where the men could retrieve their overcoats or get their evening rations. By nightfall the van had trudged only eight miles northwest of Winchester to Pughtown; the supply train was strung out for six miles.

The storm continued the next day. The army halted a scant eight miles beyond Pughtown, at Unger's Store. The men were exhausted and, without rations, began to scavenge. Many were compelled by sickness to return to Winchester or to drop out of the march and seek shelter.

Jackson's plan was to strike Bath's Federal garrison of 1,400 men with a surprise attack late on 3 January. He directed the Virginia militia to cross over Warm Spring Mountain some miles south of Bath and push along its western fringe. Simultaneously, Loring was to storm directly into Bath on the main road east of Warm Spring Mountain and herd the enemy northward toward the Potomac or westward into the path of the militia.

But the militia column moving west of Warm Spring Mountain gave up its advance when it found the road obstructed with a few trees felled by the Federals. Later in the day, more snow and sleet set in, making the road

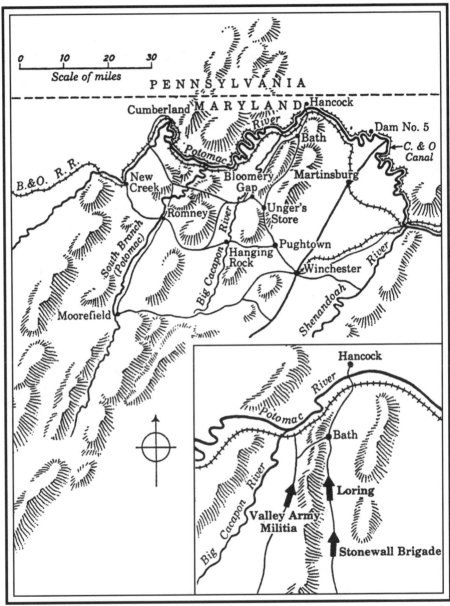

Area of operations against Romney, January 1862. Inset: Action of January 4. From *Stonewall in the Valley*, by Robert G. Tanner (Doubleday & Co., New York, 1976), © Robert G. Tanner, used by permission.

so slippery that the wagons were again unable to keep up. With night and the snow storm approaching, orders were given to bivouac about four miles southwest of Bath.

With a surprise attack vanishing at dusk, Jackson ordered Loring and his brigades to keep moving. When handed the dispatch from Jackson, Loring reportedly exploded, "By God, sir, this is the damnedest outrage ever perpetrated in the annals of history, keeping my men here in the cold without food," or words to that effect. Jackson, in turn, was frustrated by what he perceived as the inert spirit of Loring's command.

When near Bath, the Confederates came upon the enemy's pickets, and there was a halt. During this delay, Jackson and Loring met, and unpleasant words passed between them. Loring complained that if Jackson should be killed, he would find himself in command of an army about whose movements he knew nothing.

The next morning, Jackson ordered his forces to surround Bath. Exhausted by the cold and suffering of the three preceding days, the troops moved slowly, greatly hindered by the ice and sleet that covered the ground.

All the while, the Federal spies knew the frozen Confederates were coming their way. The 39th Illinois Regiment, a squadron of cavalry, and a section of artillery stationed in Bath were reinforced on the morning of the 4th by the 84th Pennsylvania from Hancock, Maryland, and at midday by the 13th Indiana. These Federal troops skirmished for some hours with Loring's advance, led by Colonel Gilham.

But the bluecoats decided not to await an attack on Bath, which was basically a crossroad town that had nothing worth defending. They retreated precipitately to Hancock, six miles distant, leaving their stores and camp at Bath to be captured. Pursuing the retreating enemy sounded good, but the weather, road conditions, and morale of the army prevented a successful overtaking.

Snow fell again on 5 January. Loring ordered the destruction of the railway bridge over the Cacapon River west of Bath, and Jackson sent a message to Hancock's commandant: evacuate within one hour or the town would be shelled. When the enemy refused, Southern artillery opened and bombarded the town most of the day with a large cannon. This of course was a ruse — why would the Federals surrender? Jackson was trying to gain their attention with a bold move so that his engineers could construct a bridge several miles above Hancock to allow the entire force to cross and make a direct assault.

But Jackson and Loring soon saw Northern reinforcements massed around the town. By the following day, the Federals were reinforced to such an extent that Jackson reached the conclusion, again without consulting Loring or any of the other officers, that nothing more of value could be achieved by his forces at Hancock. It would take several days to construct the bridge across the river, and the enemy would have time to reinforce in front of him. The decision was to abandon the siege of Hancock and move on to Romney.

The march back to Unger's Store was slow and difficult. The mountain roads were under a sheet of ice, and the temperature plunged below zero. It was too bitter to even cut firewood. Many were severely frostbitten, and the flesh on their hands and feet peeled off like onion skin. And to boot, Loring's horse fell and rolled over on him, which did not improve the uninjured Loring's attitude toward Jackson and his campaign.

Jackson had no choice but to halt at Unger's Store. One of Loring's brigades carried 300 men on its sick list, another more than 500. While Jackson tried to regroup, he received the startling news: the Yankees had evacuated Romney. They had fled suddenly, leaving tents standing and precious medical supplies. Scouts were already in the abandoned city. To Jackson it seemed a miracle, a blessing from the Almighty. Less devout men correctly surmised the Romney garrison had not been as strong as Jackson had reported to Richmond. The enemy had given Jackson the prize.

When the Confederates left Unger's Store on 13 January, the sun was shining, creating slush on the road, but that night it snowed two inches. The next day it alternated rain and sleet, and the 15th was among the most miserable days ever known in the Alleghenies; sleet fell for hours, covering everyone with ice. Loring's command floundered beneath this inclement pounding. One regiment inched 500 yards and counted it a triumph. Dr. Charles Todd Quintard wrote:

> I cannot begin to tell all that our troops suffered through the stupidity and want of forethought of Major-General Jackson. It is enough to say that we were subjected to the severest trials that human nature could endure. We left Winchester with 2,700 men in General Anderson's Brigade of Tennesseans. That number

was reduced to 1,100. When we reached the position opposite the town of Hancock, Maryland, the First Regiment numbered 680. In Romney, it mustered only 230 men fit for duty. I felt that General Loring ought to demand that he might be allowed to withdraw his forces from the command of Major-General Jackson. . . . (Noll 39)

The Valley Army entered Romney on the 15th. "Of all the miserable holes in creation, Romney takes the lead . . . a hog pen," protested Private Ted Barclay of the Headquarters Guard (Ambler 81). Every street was an open sewer thanks to the indiscriminate dumping by the Yankees, who had also left the courthouse building stacked high with rotten meat. The streets decayed into slimy pools so deep even the horses could hardly move.

Possession of Romney had aroused Jackson's ambition, and he drew up a plan to strike the gigantic New Creek railroad bridge west of Cumberland, 30 miles distant, in order to sharply cut the flow of supplies to the Federals in that town. Stonewall alerted General Richard B. Garnett's and Colonel William Taliaferro's brigades to prepare for another march.

Cumberland was girded with 12,000 Federal troops, yet Jackson planned to march into their vicinity with two shrunken, sick brigades, which were by then, in effect, a reinforced regiment. No more than one-third of Jackson's men appeared fit for action. Taliaferro's 23rd Virginia Regiment was smaller than a company; its Company C had 15 able to walk.

Worst of all, Loring's men seethed on the edge of open rebellion. They were unaccustomed to Jackson's demands and could not believe the terrible weather had not convinced Jackson to return to Winchester days ago. They equated his tenacity with insanity. They talked mutiny and swore to follow Jackson no longer. Included in the dissenters were men of Jackson's own brigade.

As rain and thaw set in and changed the frozen roads to slush and mire, Jackson reluctantly submitted to the discontent of his troops and the unfavorable conditions, relinquishing his aggressive intentions and preparing to defend what he had won by going into winter quarters. On 16 January, Jackson wrote to headquarters: "Unless otherwise directed, I will proceed to construct winter quarters, and will station General Loring's troops and General Boggs' militia brigade in the South Branch Valley" (*OR*, vol. 5, p.

1034) — he intended to leave Loring's Army of the Northwest stranded in Romney while he returned to Winchester with his men on 24 January.

As Jackson and his army departed from Romney, a surly group of Loring's command watched and screamed out, "Jackson's lambs," believing that Jackson had showed favoritism to his own command with a comfortable winter assignment in Winchester. "There go your F.F.V.'s [First Families of Virginia]" (Noll 44). They left a garrison of smoldering resentment. The invited guests, Loring's Army of the Northwest, were being left out in the cold.

More trouble than ever broke out in Loring's command. The prospect of finishing the winter at Romney whipped the men into an insubordinate frenzy. Officers of one regiment refused to leave their quarters during foul weather. They complained bitterly of the campaign that had been conducted at the expense of so much suffering. They were now left to be exposed to the enemy in an inhospitable mountain region, out of the reach of adequate supplies. Soldiers of all ranks utilized a new grant of furloughs to hasten out of the county, telling tales of Jackson's madness. Loring did little to quiet the discontent.

On 25 January, 11 brigade and regimental officers signed and handed a petition to Loring condemning the occupation of Romney.

> The undersigned officers of your command beg leave to present their condition to your consideration as it exists at Romney.
>
> It is unnecessary to detail to you, who participated in it all, the service performed by the Army of the Northwest during the last eight months. The unwritten (it will never truly be written) history of that remarkable campaign would show, if truly portrayed, a degree of severity, of hardship, of toil, of exposure and suffering that finds no parallel in the prosecution of the present war, if indeed it is equaled in any war. And the alacrity and good-will with which the men of your command bore all this hardship, exposure, and deprivation would have done honor to our sires in the most trying times of the Revolution.
>
> After being worn down with unremitting toil and wasted by death and disease, the remainder were about preparing quarters to shield them from the storms of winter in a rigorous climate. Many had prepared comparatively comfortable quarters, when they were called upon to march to Winchester and join the force

under General Jackson. This they did about the 1st of December, with the same alacrity which had characterized their former conduct, making a march of some 150 miles at that inclement season of the year.

After reaching Winchester, as expected, was ordered in the direction of the enemy, when all cheerfully obeyed the order, with the confident expectation that so soon as the object of the expedition was attained they would be marched to some comfortable position, where they could enjoy a short respite and recruit their wasted energies for the spring campaign.

The terrible exposure and suffering on this expedition can never be known to those who did not participate in it. When men pass night after night in the coldest period of a cold climate without tents, blankets, or even an ax to cut wood with, and without food for twenty-four hours, and with some of the men nearly two days at a time, and attended by toilsome marches, it is not to be thought strange that some regiments which left Winchester with nearly 600 men should now, short as the time has been, report less than 200 men for duty.

Instead of finding, as expected, a little repose during midwinter, we are ordered to remain at this place. Our position at and near Romney is one of the most disagreeable and unfavorable that could well be imagined. We can only get an encampment upon the worst of wet, spouty land, much of which when it rains is naught but one sheet of water and a consequent corresponding depth of mud, and this, too, without the advantage of sufficient wood, the men having to drag that indispensable article down from high up on the mountain side.

We are within a few miles of the enemy and of the Baltimore and Ohio Railroad, which imposes upon our men the continued hardship of very heavy picket duty, which will in a short time tell terribly upon their health and strength. We regard Romney as a place difficult to hold, and of no strategical importance after it is held. Besides, the country around it for some distance has already been by the enemy exhausted of its supplies. Your army could be maintained much more comfortably, and at much less expense, and with every military advantage, at almost any other place.

Another consideration we would endeavor to impress upon your mind: All must be profoundly impressed with the paramount importance of raising an army for the next summer's campaign. When we left Winchester, a very large proportion of your army, with the benefit of a short furlough, would have enlisted for the war, but now, with the present prospect before them, we doubt if one single man would reenlist. But if they are yet removed to a position where their spirits could be revived, many, we think, will go for the war.

In view of all these considerations and many others that might be presented, we ask that you present the condition of your command to the War Department, and earnestly ask that it may be ordered to some more favorable position.

Respectfully,

Wm. B. Taliaferro,
    Colonel, Commanding Fourth Brigade Northwestern Army.
Saml. V. Fulkerson,
    Colonel Thirty-seventh Virginia Volunteers.
Van H. Manning,
    Major, Commanding Third Arkansas Volunteers.
J. W. Anderson,
    Major, Commanding First Georgia Regiment.
A. V. Scott,
    Captain, Commanding Twenty-third Virginia Volunteers.
Jesse S. Burks,
    Colonel, Commanding Third Brigade Northwestern Army.
D. A. Langhorne,
    Lieutenant-Colonel, Commanding Forty-second Virginia Volunteers.
P. B. Adams,
    Major, Forty-second Virginia Volunteers.
J. Y. Jones,
    Captain, Commanding First Battalion P.A.C.S.
R. H. Cunningham, Jr.,
    Captain, Commanding Twenty-first Virginia Volunteers.
John A. Campbell,
    Colonel, Commanding Forty-eighth Virginia Volunteers.

(*OR*, vol. 5, pp. 1048-1049)

Loring immediately dispatched the petition to Secretary of War Benjamin, but by the way of Jackson in Winchester, as this was the proper chain of command and he did not want to appear to be working behind Jackson's back. Jackson, after reading the petition, sent it on to Benjamin, instead of to General Joseph Johnston, his immediate superior and commanding officer. Jackson's four-word comment: "Respectfully forwarded, but disapproved." Now the fat was in the fire.

Rumors of an enemy stab into the lower Shenandoah indicated Jackson's Valley Army might be in trouble if the Federals were moving on Harper's Ferry or Winchester. An alarmed President Davis suggested that Benjamin have General Johnston review the valley defenses. Johnston sent his chief engineer, S. M. Barton, whose bottom line was, "For a small force this point [Romney] is indefensible" (*OR*, vol. 5, p. 1056).

But without waiting for Johnston's evaluation, President Davis had already instructed Benjamin to write to Jackson: "Our news indicates that a movement is being made to cut off General Loring's command. Order him back to Winchester immediately" (*OR*, vol. 5, p. 1053). General Jackson promptly issued the necessary orders for Loring's withdrawal to Winchester. And with compliance of this order from Benjamin, Jackson submitted his resignation on 31 January 1862:

> Your order requiring me to direct General Loring to return with his command to Winchester immediately has been received and promptly complied with.
>
> With such interference in my command I cannot expect to be of much service in the field, and, accordingly, respectfully request to be ordered to report for duty to the Superintendent of the Virginia Military Institute. . . . Should this application not be granted, I respectfully request that the President will accept my resignation from the Army. (*OR*, vol. 5, p. 1053)

Jackson found many friends throughout the Shenandoah and across the state who implored him not to resign. And within a week, Jackson had changed his mind and decided to remain in the army. Not satisfied with resigning, Jackson readied a court-martial charge against Loring, accusing him of neglect of duty and conduct subversive of good order and military discipline. He specified that on 3 January, near Bath, Loring had failed to attack the enemy and "press forward with requisite promptness," that on 4 January, he "did permit the head of his column, without sufficient cause, repeatedly to halt and lose . . . much time," that on 18 January, he "permitted part of his command to become so demoralized as not to be in a condition for active service at Romney," and that he "did permit officers of his command, in violation of Army Regulations, to unite in a petition against their commands being required to pass the winter in the vicinity of Romney," among other complaints (*OR*, vol. 5, pp. 1065-1066). Jackson then submitted them to General Johnston for approval. Johnston concurred and asked Adjutant and Inspector General Cooper to assemble a tribunal of high-ranking officers.

President Davis was apprised of the situation and became very upset. He read the charges of the court-martial, and after Loring was allowed to respond to them ("This allegation is . . . without foundation," "The evidence of the promptness of the movement [near Bath on 3 January] is found in the fact that they killed 4 . . . and took 8 prisoners," "This order [to proceed at double-quick time] was countermanded by General Jackson to await re-enforcements, and the delay [near Bath on 4 January] was occasioned by him and not by me," "I obeyed the instructions of my superior," "An intimate acquaintance with the Army Regulations . . . has failed to inform me of the fact that a respectful and truthful statement by commanders of the condition of their commands was other than a duty") (*OR*, vol. 5, p. 1070), Davis made the decision that the charges would not be prosecuted. "The good of the service does not, it is believed, require a court-martial" (*OR*, vol. 51, pt. 2, p. 469). The President saw the folly of the whole event. Loring had followed Jackson's orders at all times.

Chapter 6

Service at Suffolk

ORING HAD QUICKLY returned to Winchester after Jackson's telegram on 31 January instructed him to abandon Romney. On 9 February, Secretary of War Benjamin wrote to General Johnston indicating that President Davis "thinks the good of the service requires that no part of General Loring's command be left with General Jackson. You are also requested to order General Loring to report to the Adjutant-General at Richmond for orders. He is assigned to duty with General [Robert E.] Lee, in Georgia" (*OR*, vol. 5, pp. 1066-1067).

General Loring was thus cut free from Jackson, but he also lost his command of the Army of the Northwest: because Jackson's Valley Army as well as other Confederate departments needed immediate replacements, Loring's army was broken up and dispersed to meet the need.

As Loring traveled to Richmond, the military situation at the time appeared bleak; disasters had swept the Confederacy. After early victories, Fort Henry on the Tennessee River had been taken as had nearby Fort Donelson, with 14,000 Confederate soldiers being surrendered. Nashville was expected to fall at any hour. All western Tennessee was overrun. Albert Sidney Johnston was in retreat to Murfreesboro, Tennessee. And closer to Richmond, on the east coast of North Carolina, Union General A. E. Burnside occupied Roanoke Island after capturing more than 2,500 men. Secretary of War Benjamin was being charged with the responsibility for the defeat at Roanoke Island and was being assailed for incompetency.

On 19 February 1862, Loring was promoted to major general, a suitable compensation to "right the wrong" of his losing the Army of the Northwest. Two days later, Loring and his staff boarded the train to Norfolk. Loring had been assigned second in command to an old army veteran, 56-year-old Major General Benjamin Huger, who was in charge of the Department of Norfolk. Loring would not be joining Lee in Georgia as Davis had originally indicated, as Lee had been put in charge of all the Confederate armies and would thus be headquartered in Richmond.

Sick with pneumonia on his arrival in Norfolk, Virginia, on 22 February, General Loring was confined to a sick bed at the Norfolk Naval Hospital for most of March 1862, under the care of his friend Dr. Charles Todd Quintard, who had accompanied him from western Virginia. Once Loring was on his feet again, it was decided that General Huger would be in command of Norfolk and that Loring would go to Suffolk and lead the 1st Division at Fort Huger, an open fortification named for the general and constructed in 1861 by the Confederates to protect Suffolk. It stood near the confluence of the western branch of the Nansemond River and the main stream.

General Lee decided to hold Norfolk because of its strategic value, its dry dock, and the machinery at the navy yard. Twenty-two miles to the southwest, the important Norfolk & Petersburg Railroad crossed the

Nansemond River at Suffolk. To that point, the Nansemond was navigable for light craft that could enter its mouth at will from Hampton Roads, an eight-mile-long water corridor running into Chesapeake Bay and then the Atlantic Ocean. Lee foresaw the ease with which the Union gunboats could ascend the river, take Suffolk, put a landing force ashore, cut the railroad, and take Norfolk in reverse.

Such an operation would also cut the Seaboard & Roanoke Railroad, which ran through Suffolk from Norfolk to Weldon, North Carolina. With both roads cut, not only would Norfolk be isolated, but North Carolina would lie wide open to invasion along the line of the Seaboard & Roanoke. To guard against such possibilities, Loring was sent to protect the railroad at Suffolk until batteries could be planted on the banks of the Nansemond. Opposite Norfolk was Huger's old post, Fort Monroe, which was still occupied by Federal troops.

On 1 April, the huge Northern army began moving from near Alexandria, Virginia, to Fort Monroe via the Potomac and Chesapeake Bay in preparation of the assault on Yorktown, 17 miles to the north. On 3 April, General Huger sent a telegraph dispatch to Loring, informing him that the enemy was landing a large force at Newport News and above it and that he should keep a bright lookout at Barrett's Point. This was the beginning of the siege of Yorktown.

Six days later, Loring reported that the enemy in their gunboats had landed at Elizabeth City, North Carolina, and captured the Pasquotank Militia. General Joseph Johnston, in a hastily called meeting with the President, proposed that one large army be formed for the defense of Richmond, sitting only 78 miles from the action at Yorktown, by uniting all forces of the Confederacy in North Carolina, South Carolina, and Georgia with those at Norfolk and on the Peninsula and bringing them close to Richmond. Through the spring of 1862, the Confederate withdrawals were not so much retreats as concentrations of Southern power.

Secretary of War George Randolph (who had on 22 March replaced Judah Benjamin, the new Secretary of State) did not want to give up the naval base or Norfolk, and General Lee opposed it because he believed it endangered South Carolina and Georgia. Compromise reigned with Generals Gustavus W. Smith's and James (Pete) Longstreet's divisions joining the Army of the Peninsula and the Department of Norfolk being added to that of Northern Virginia. Now Huger and Loring would take orders from General Joe Johnston.

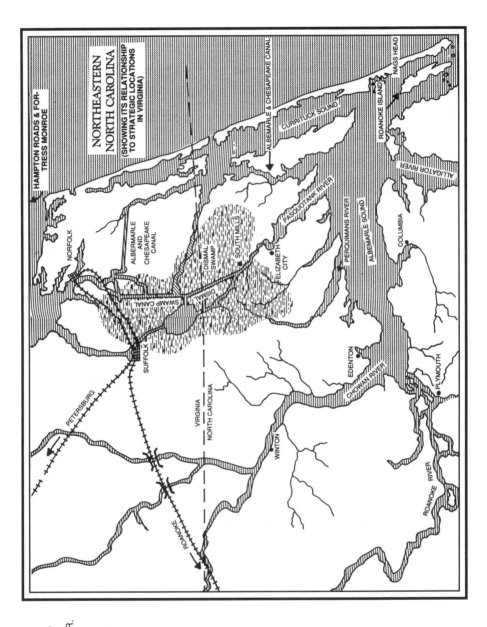

From *Ironclads and Columbiads*, by William R. Trotter (William R. Blair Publisher, Winston-Salem, NC, 1989), used by permission.

As the Federal advance quickened, Generals Huger and Loring countered as best as possible with limited forces. Loring, covering such a large area from Suffolk into North Carolina, was especially pressed for manpower.

The loss of New Bern, North Carolina, on 14 March had made the Confederate command reevaluate the state scene. They quickly realized that a sweep of General A. E. Burnside's army across North Carolina would divide the upper Confederacy. On 26 April, Burnside captured Beaufort. He then had 17,000 troops available to move northward toward Suffolk and Norfolk.

Suffolk would now become the hub of the defense force south of the James River. Loring could move by ship, railway, or turnpike toward any point — Norfolk, Portsmouth, Yorktown, Richmond, Petersburg, or down into the Great Dismal Swamp of North Carolina, which was a natural barricade and fortification for the defense of Suffolk and Norfolk.

On 21 April, Loring received word that the Federals were moving through the Dismal Swamp toward South Mills. Loring immediately ordered two regiments and two batteries in the direction of South Mills where on 19 April Colonel A. R. Wright of the 3rd Georgia Regiment defeated Union General J. L. Reno and sent his fatigued troops back to their transports at Elizabeth City.

In the same time frame, Union General McClellan had transported his massive army of approximately 105,000 men from the vicinity of Washington to Fort Monroe, opposite Norfolk and Suffolk. Cautious McClellan spent the month of April laying siege to the Yorktown line, then on 4 May began his grand assault on the Southern defenses and Yorktown and found them unoccupied. Joe Johnston had withdrawn his army up the peninsula.

General Huger was instructed to prepare to evacuate Norfolk, and Loring at Suffolk headquarters would begin to handle the skillful retreat of the Confederate forces toward Petersburg, Virginia.

President Lincoln ordered a landing of Union troops at Willoughby's Point, some seven miles north of Norfolk. In the early morning of 10 May, General John E. Wool landed 5,000 men and began marching toward Norfolk. Huger received notice of the landing, and since he did not have a force sufficient to defend the city, he called for an evacuation immediately to Suffolk.

At Suffolk, Huger found Loring issuing a bevy of orders to all points of his department with instructions to retreat toward Zuni, Virginia, which would become the collection point for all troops, supplies, and the sick on their move to Petersburg. As Loring retired toward Petersburg, the troops tore up the tracks of the Norfolk & Petersburg and the Seaboard & Roanoke Railroads east of Suffolk and destroyed railroad bridges to hinder any pursuit by the Federals. On 11 May, Norfolk fell to the bluecoats.

General Huger and his brigades moved forward quickly to Richmond and were assigned to active duty with Lee's army. W. W. Loring, his job as second-in-command completed, would not be joining Huger. His experience and steady hand were needed in another department. He was being assigned back to western Virginia to guard the back door of Richmond, which was still ajar from the winter campaigns of 1861. The Federals were at the front door of Richmond with 100,000 bluecoats. Lee would handle them.

Chapter 7

The Department of Southwestern Virginia and the Kanawha Valley Campaign, 1862

Richmond, May 8, 1862

Maj. Gen. William W. Loring is relieved from duty with Major-General Huger, and is assigned to the command of the Department of Southwestern Virginia, embracing the commands of Brigadier-Generals Heth and H. Marshall.

By command of the Secretary of War.

(*OR*, vol. 10, pt. 2, p. 504)

ENERAL LORING and his staff hurried toward the mountains of Virginia, arriving at Giles Court House in Giles County, deep in the Appala-

chians, on 19 May. This became the headquarters for the Army of Southwestern Virginia. In the immediate area was General Humphrey Marshall of Kentucky, commanding the Abingdon District with about 2,000 troops. Near Lewisburg, General Henry Heth had gathered his small force of fighters, called the Army of the New River, which numbered 1,400 men.

The Federals called this the Mountain Department, and it was headed by the famed "pathfinder," General John C. Fremont with headquarters at Wheeling in western Virginia. General Jacob D. Cox commanded the brigade of the Kanawha.

The newly formed Department of Southwestern Virginia was in immediate need of a competent, seasoned commander who could, with a minimum number of troops, contain the enemy and restrain the instability of the southwestern region of the state. What the President needed for the campaign that lay ahead for General Lee in defending Richmond was a mature general, such as Loring, to carry into effect a steadfastness of law and order that had been elusive in the region since the opening days of the war.

This was a tall order to be placed on Loring as the area to be covered was west to the eastern boundary of Kentucky, and then as far west of that boundary as circumstances required. This meant his command would extend to the Cumberland Gap and even farther if necessary. It linked the theoretical thin line of defense that extended some 400 miles from the Mississippi River to the Cumberland Gap, with the middle anchored at Bowling Green, Kentucky.

This vast area would not be easy to defend. The Confederate commanders and forces were required to look in all directions and at the same time rush troops from one extremity to the other to meet any Federal threats. It was an extremely fluid situation and almost impossible to defend.

Between the two great Confederate armies in Virginia and Tennessee lay a long stretch of country, principally covered by the Allegheny and Cumberland Mountains. From the beginning of the war, east Tennessee had been a prize much desired by both sides. Strong Union sentiment in that area had resulted in the addition of several regiments to the Union armies, and many who remained behind constantly begged for protection against what they claimed was unbearable Confederate oppression.

Of still greater importance to the Confederates was the railroad through east Tennessee connecting Virginia with the Deep South and New Orleans. This was the only means of direct communication and transportation between these two Confederate armies. The railroad moved the vital supplies of lead, salt, and food. It also was used to transport troops to meet Union attacks from Chattanooga to Richmond. Richmond's instructions were that the Virginia-Tennessee Railroad must be protected against both local enemies and the organized Federal forces.

The first three weeks in the new department kept General Loring very busy. His capable management of the four brigades at his disposal held the Union men in check from the Cumberland Gap all the way to Fincastle, Virginia.

However, 700 miles to the south, at St. Augustine, Florida, now occupied by Federal troops, things were not going well at all for the general. On 7 June 1862, an act was approved by the U.S. government permitting taxes to be levied in Insurrectionist Districts on secessionist-abandoned property, and such property was to be sold for the unpaid taxes. With the Loring family gone from 138 St. George Street, the Federals confiscated the old homestead. Consequently, unlike most Confederate commanders, he was now unable to return to his home.

The quick move to the Department of Southwest Virginia did not annoy Loring, as he was always seeking combat. To others, it was a bittersweet promotion. West Point graduate Humphrey Marshall, a politically appointed general from Kentucky, reluctantly accepted Loring as his commander, but he refused to cooperate with Loring. This prompted a letter to Marshall from no less than the President, dated 29 May 1862: "Have you received a copy of the instructions given to General Loring? If so, note reference to yourself. You can not doubt my goodwill towards you, and I do not doubt your willingness to make any proper sacrifice for our cause" (*OR*, vol. 10, pt. 2, p. 561).

On 9 June, Loring wrote the Assistant Adjutant General and tactfully suggested certain changes: "Cannot General Marshall be given a command somewhere else? He is undoubtedly an officer of great mind and experience, and could no doubt render great service in some field where his talents could have a fair opportunity. In this mountain service you want active and vigorous young men" (Wessels 63).

The 50-year-old, 300-pound Marshall resented his assignment to the western Virginia mountains. Accordingly, he resigned his commission on 16 June. However, Confederate plans to drive the Federals from Kentucky and arouse Confederate loyalties required the presence of Kentuckians in responsible command. So Marshall was cajoled by President Davis into accepting reappointment as brigadier general again on 19 June.

If any factor was the single greatest cause of unrest in the mountains, it was the Confederate government's imposition of the draft on the "mountain boys." All 18- to 35-year-old men were subject to the draft, but conscription agents appearing in the hills were often met with shotguns. Desertions increased as the conscription agents filled their quotas. The opportunities for desertion on the front lines were numerous and the path back home not hard to find at all. Loring was to prevent this as much as possible.

Two other Confederate policies Loring would have to enforce were the tax-in-kind act and the policy of impressment. The tax-in-kind act was essentially a "tithe tax." Farmers were required to contribute one-tenth of everything they produced to the Richmond government. For the gentlemen farmers on the coast and in the Piedmont, this was not necessarily a burden, but for the farmers of the mountains, it was an agonizing turn of the screws. Already stricken by a shortage of manpower, horses, and usable farming implements, most rural families were barely able to feed themselves. There was no surplus.

The policy of impressment allowed the government to seize provisions, animals, slaves, wagons, or whatever else was needed for the cause. The compensation was invariably pegged much lower than the inflated market value of the commodities taken.

In addition to these hated policies, the farmer in southwestern Virginia was subject to the terror of the bushwhackers — deserters and outlaws who hid in the mountains and made predatory raids on those sympathetic to the Southern cause, including women, children, and the elderly. As western Virginia had broken away from Virginia and remained loyal to the Union, the unpopular war had led those with Union sympathies to prey upon those who supported the South, and vice versa.

The Federals soon learned about the bushwhackers and recruited them as guerrilla troops in the Federal service. The Union provided them with food, rifles, and ammunition. Some were mounted on horses and moved from farm to farm, destroying property, burning houses, and killing the inhabitants.

In addition to the Confederates, Yankees, and bushwhackers, there was a fourth force in the mountains of Virginia: partisan rangers. In April 1862, the Confederate Congress had passed an act authorizing "partisan bands" for the purpose of making inroads against the enemy, even though there had been irregular Southern partisans, loosely organized and wholly irresponsible, acting since the beginning of the war. The Partisan Ranger Act gave the authority to military department commanders to authorize and to commission officers to form these bands. The ranger service was very useful in the mountains, especially when the men knew the country.

General Loring was responsible for the formation of a number of partisan ranger groups while he served in command of the department. However, without adequate reinforcements, Loring was forced to continue recruiting to build his own army. He met very little success — the mountains had been stripped of those faithful to the cause — plus, the Confederate draft motivated many to volunteer for Governor John Letcher's Virginia State Line troops.

On 9 June, General Heth circulated a proclamation stating that if conscripts would not report for duty, he would shoot them. This created quite a stir among the conscripts of all classes, and on 16 June Loring wrote Heth:

> With hesitancy, for I have respect for your judgment, I differ with you in the policy of shooting conscripts ordered out under the law. . . . There is a very good feeling shown us by the best people of S.W. Va in aiding the military to bring into service the people. It is well to cultivate this feeling. . . . Let a single man be shot as stated, unless in the act of resistance, and the whole matter would present another phase. It is my judgment we would not get another conscript — and our time would be employed in hunting them down. . . . I do not wish to sway my authority against yours, but I beg you will suppress the proclamation and urge upon the conscripts the necessity of joining your command . . . without the extreme course of taking life. . . . I am sure that after a further reflection you will agree with me. (Letter book)

Loring's wisdom and maturity are obvious.

In August, General Loring began setting the stage for his own movement against the Federals in the Kanawha Valley, some 20 miles away. He sent two of his men to Richmond with his plan, which was approved by Secretary of War Randolph. He then entreated Randolph to get General Marshall to work with him: "The enemy has precipitately withdrawn from Meadow Bluff & the Flat Top Mountain & probably has gone to Gauley Bridge. If you promptly [get] Gen Marshall to cooperate with me, I am ready to take the offensive" (*OR*, vol. 12, pt. 3, p. 922).

But Marshall wanted to make an expedition into Kentucky, believing his presence in his home state would help General Braxton Bragg there. Loring pointed out to Randolph that such a movement would leave the enemy free access to the fruitful valley between the Cumberland and Clinch Mountains, and Randolph at first sided with Loring: "A small expedition of infantry [Marshall's] will effect nothing and will run great risk of being captured. If General Marshall co-operates with Loring I understand that Loring will take the offensive" (*OR*, vol. 12, pt. 3, p. 922). But after ten days, Randolph unexpectedly reversed himself and said General Marshall was a part of an extensive plan of cooperation with Generals Bragg and E. Kirby Smith in Kentucky. Randolph was apparently caught between the strategies of General Robert E. Lee and President Davis.

On 5 August, Lee remarked, "General Marshall and General Loring have better opportunities. It may now be better for the two officers to unite, if they can sweep the enemy out of the valley and then enter Kentucky together. It may be necessary to re-enforce General Loring, but it is a bad time to diminish this army" (*OR*, vol. 12, pt. 3, p. 922). It was apparent to Loring that he was not to receive any help from Marshall and no reinforcements from Lee's army. Loring, more resolved than ever, moved rapidly to put his Kanawha Valley plan of operation into effect.

In his letter of 12 August to Dr. Quintard, Loring mentions, "I have just had made a new General of my cavalry in the person of Colonel [Albert Gallatin] Jenkins; he is a bold and dashing man and will do a good service" (William R. Perkins Library). At this same time, Union General Jacob D. Cox began to remove some of his troops from the Kanawha Valley to the fighting in Virginia. With this, Loring saw a splendid opportunity to strike. He quickly ordered newly appointed General Jenkins to compose a fast-moving strike force cavalry and move out.

On 24 August, General Jenkins, with 600 fresh cavalry and a mountain howitzer, headed toward the northwest. After sweeping around the Baltimore & Ohio Railroad near Cheat, Jenkins then exhibited his force in the enemy's rear, in the Kanawha Valley, and by diversion permitted General Loring to begin moving out toward the valley with his infantry. Jenkins and his men reclaimed 40,000 square miles of territory for the Confederates and were the first to invade the North via Ohio. Loring heaped praise upon the 32-year-old general.

Incidentally, in the same 12 August letter to Dr. Quintard, Loring reveals a much different side of himself — a man in love:

> What little time I have to devote to my lady love I make good use of in the form of letters, now and then by the kind offices of my friends. I get at long intervals a very short note, she is determined not to be so easily won — "War and love do not seem to thrive together" — at least I believe it to be the case. Though only a few miles distant I have only been able to make this one visit. . . . I am however I believe on the best of terms with the whole family including the father.

On 18 August, Loring wrote to Randolph: "News has just reached me that the enemy have fallen back from Meadow Bluff. They had previously fallen back from the Flat Top, in Mercer County. . . . I am pushing my reconnaissance on both sides of the New River" (*OR*, vol. 12, pt. 3, pp. 935-936). Then on 22 August, 175 miles to the northeast, the big break came: "While there was skirmishing between Lee's and [Union General John] Pope's armies along the Rappahannock, Jeb Stuart made a daring raid on Catlett's Station, to the rear of the Federal Army, and captured General Pope's baggage train. Included in this prize was Pope's current Letter-book" (*OR*, vol. 12, pt. 3, p. 942).

After examining the information in the letter-book, General Lee wrote to Randolph on 25 August:

> I have the honor to transmit to you herewith some of the correspondence of the enemy captured by our cavalry. . . . I call your attention particularly to a letter in the book of August 10th from General Cox to General Pope, and the reply of the latter on the 11th, directing General Cox to remain in Western Virginia with

5,000 men, and send the rest to General Pope by river and rail.
I deem it important that General Loring should be informed of
the force opposed to him and directed to clear the valley of the
Kanawha and then operate northwardly, so as to *join me*
[emphasis added] in the valley of Virginia. (*OR*, vol. 12, pt. 3,
p. 943)

General Lee was preparing to move into Maryland.

On 29 August, Randolph notified Loring at Dublin Depot: "Pope's letter-book has been captured. . . . Clear the valley of the Kanawha, and operate northwardly to a junction with our army in the valley. Keep us advised
of your movements" (*OR*, vol. 12, pt. 3, p. 946). Loring's reply may have
been crossed in the mail, for he wrote to Randolph on the same day, "I am
deferring my advance a few days, fearing that a premature demonstration
would only detain the enemy, who, let alone, may evacuate his positions
or weaken his force" (*OR*, vol. 12, pt. 3, p. 946).

This is exactly what happened. When news of Jenkins's daring raid
reached Union Colonel A. J. Lightburn, commander of the Kanawha Valley, he became concerned for the safety of his unprotected flanks and rear.
He then ordered several of his brigades to fall back and move out.

From the instructions given to Loring by Secretary of War Randolph, it
was obvious that General Loring's Army of Southwestern Virginia was a
part of Robert E. Lee's invasion plan of Maryland. In a lengthy letter to
President Davis dated 5 September, Lee ends his report:

> I am now more desirous that my suggestion as to General Lor-
> ing's movements shall be carried into effect as soon as possible
> so that with the least delay he may move to the lower end of the
> valley about Martinsburg, and guard the approach in that direc-
> tion. He should first drive the enemy from the Kanawha Valley,
> if he can, and afterwards, or if he finds he cannot accomplish
> that result, I wish him to move by way of Romney towards Mar-
> tinsburg and take position in that vicinity. (*OR*, vol. 19, pt. 2, p.
> 594)

Loring's army, made up of approximately 5,000 well-trained soldiers,
rapidly marched out of the vicinity of Giles Court House on 6 September
and went by way of Princeton and Flat Top Mountain. The enemy at

Raleigh Court House fled at their approach and concentrated their forces at Fayetteville, where Loring arrived on the 10th.

Due to the excessive heat of the day, their long, fatiguing march via a circuitous route, and several skirmishes with the Yankees as they approached Fayetteville, Loring's men were nearly exhausted upon reaching their destination on 10 September. After consultation among some of the officers, the Confederates took and held a position commanding the turnpike leading from Fayetteville to the Kanawha River to prevent the passing of enemy trains and, if possible, to cut off their retreat. But before the Confederates had successfully completed their deployments, they came under fierce attack by six companies of Yankee infantry. Three times the Yankees charged the knoll held by the Confederates, and after three hours of murderous and unequaled combat, serious losses were inflicted on men and officers of the Federal units.

The Confederate artillery then took position on an eminence 500 yards from the closest enemy fort. When they advanced to within 300 yards, they came under a scathing fire from Federal artillery and sharpshooters, who held the ravine and hill opposite them. As the battle raged, Colonel Lightburn ordered five companies of infantry to take position on top of Cotton Hill to be of assistance in the event of a retreat. Lightburn's troops posted in the vicinity of Gauley Bridge were ordered to pack everything and to destroy what they could not quickly save.

By then Fayetteville was surrounded by Loring's forces. The balance of the Federal army had no choice but to begin a retreat toward Cotton Hill and join their other forces. The next morning, they observed Loring's entire army, with colors flying in order of battle, deploying at the base of the mountain. The Yankees had no time to rest or regroup; quick action was necessary if they were to avoid being captured or killed. While five companies with a detachment of artillery remained behind to slow Loring, the rest of the army began a retreat toward Charleston.

Loring divided his force, sending half along the old Fayette Road and the other half directly up Cotton Hill along the new turnpike. Acting swiftly, the bluecoats opened on the Rebels with artillery and musket fire from behind a hastily prepared breastwork. While Loring's men regrouped, the Federals seized the opportunity to make good their escape.

A rapid, disorderly march was resumed, with the Federal situation growing worse as the withdrawal became more of a rout. The Confederates again took up the pursuit, and a running skirmish occurred across Cot-

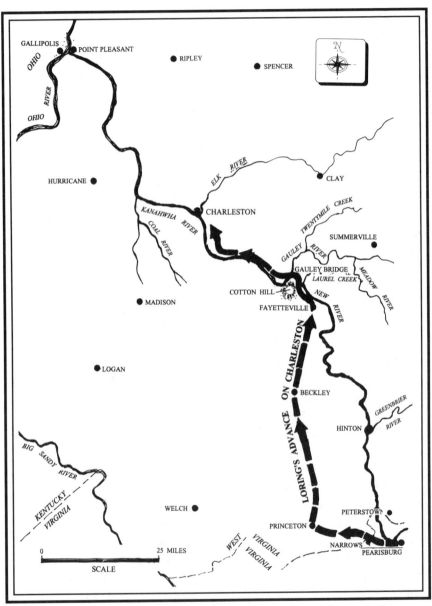

Kanawha Campaign in West Virginia, September, 1862. (Courtesy William R. Scaife)

ton Hill and down the western slope near Montgomery's Ferry, below
Kanawha Falls. Within a few hours, no Yankee soldiers were to be found
in Fayette County. Destroyed property along the retreat route afforded

Loring's men a rare opportunity to supply themselves with new guns, clothing, camp equipment, and food. They also captured 20,000 pounds of bacon, 425 wagons, 300 bags of oats, and numerous quartermaster stores.

Early on the morning of 13 September, Loring's advance units arrived on the south side of the Kanawha at Charleston. His artillery opened fire upon the town but later moved to Fort Hill and began a heavier bombardment. Union forces countered with a weak response from a six-pound gun near the north side of the river. Bewildered and frightened residents of Charleston thronged the streets, many of them hoping to leave with the Union army. Portions of Lightburn's bluecoats crossed the Elk River, cut down the suspension bridge, and took up positions in Federal entrenchments from which sharpshooters attempted to keep back the victorious Confederates. Again, Southern artillery made them abandon their positions.

About 5:00 p.m., Lightburn's train of more than 700 wagons, loaded with supplies, pulled out and headed toward Ripley, in western Virginia. With it went the Union army and hundreds of citizens and slaves. The army was to be reassembled at Point Pleasant on the Ohio River. General Loring's orders were to clear the Kanawha Valley; they said nothing about pursuing the enemy into Ohio.

On 3 October, the *Richmond Semi-Weekly* reported: "The bold step of our gallant Loring was appreciated. . . . Gen. Loring is fast gaining the confidence of all classes in this whole region by his mild and conservative course, and wherever the Stars and Bars have been unfurled they are flocking to its standard."

Once the Southern forces had established firm control of the Kanawha Valley, General Loring posted 4,000 troops at Charleston with detachments at Gauley Bridge and Fayetteville. The Kanawha Valley was now in the hands of Loring's Confederates. In this brilliant campaign involving a mountain march of 169 miles, the Rebels reported 18 men killed and 89 wounded; the bluecoats reported a loss of 25 killed, 95 wounded, and 190 missing. Colonel Lightburn was compelled to abandon all his stores, worth by Loring's estimate around $1,000,000, and did not have time to destroy the important Kanawha saline works. The defeat was the most serious of any suffered by Union forces in the western Virginia war to date.

On 17 September, just four days after Loring's victorious entry into

GENERAL ORDER.

HEAD QUARTERS,
DEPARTMENT OF WESTERN VIRGINIA,
Charleston, Va., Sept. 24, 1862.

General Order, No.

The money issued by the Confederate Government is secure, and is receivable in payment of public dues, and convertible into 8 per cent. bonds.   Citizens owe it to the country to receive it in trade; and it will therefore be regarded as good in payment for supplies purchased for the army.

Persons engaged in trade are invited to resume their business and open their stores.

By order of

MAJ. GEN. LORING.
H. FITZHUGH,
Chief of Staff.

Charleston, the bloodiest single day in the Civil War was fought at Sharpsburg, Maryland, between the Army of the Potomac and the Army of Northern Virginia. Before the sun went down, 4,710 lay dead, 18,440 wounded, and another 3,043 missing. During the night of 18 and 19 September, General Lee retreated across the Potomac and back into Virginia. It was his intention to recross the Potomac at Williamsport and move upon Hagerstown, but the condition of his army prevented the move.

Although the battle of Antietam has been examined for over 130 years, it has never been suggested that Loring's army in western Virginia was part of Lee's strategy. Nonetheless, when one examines the official records, it is not difficult to speculate that Loring may have been one of Lee's surprises.

On 25 September, while camped on the Opequon River, General Lee sent congratulations to Loring for his victory in the Kanawha Valley and offered for Loring's consideration an invasion plan of Pennsylvania:

> Great benefit would be derived if you could permanently destroy the Baltimore and Ohio Railroad, by taking down the Monongahela Valley from Weston, or any other point where it may be convenient to you to strike it, and destroy the bridges near Clarksburg and Fairmont, or, what would be better, blowing up the tunnels in their vicinity; both branches of the road would be disabled and the travel interrupted for the whole winter. You could then continue your course (if you thought it proper) through Morgantown into Washington County, Pennsylvania, and supply your army with everything it wants. (*OR*, vol. 19, pt. 2, pp. 625-626)

This was not an overambitious plan for Loring to follow since the Federals had pulled most of their forces from the area, but the trek would have been long without any turnpikes to carry the troops. Then General Lee mentions another route that Loring might take: use the Potomac River to come and join him — "probably a combined movement into Pennsylvania may be concerted" (*OR*, vol. 19, pt. 2, p. 626).

On the same day, Lee informed President Davis of his plans with Loring, and five days later, Secretary of War Randolph wrote to Loring about the matter:

The first object of the campaign (the recovery of the Kanawha Valley) being now accomplished, you will adopt measures for its defense, and proceed with as little delay as possible to pursue the plan of operations already indicated. Your first object will be to injure and break up the insurrectionary government in Northwestern Virginia, and then to effect a junction with General Lee. You must necessarily be invested with a large discretion as to the means of effecting these objects, and the Department can do nothing more than indicate in a general way what appears to be the best route for you to take. . . . You will . . . proceed . . . by the way of Clarksburg, Grafton, and Romney, to some point from which you can communicate with General Lee, and at which you can receive instructions from him. . . . Your departure should not be delayed longer than is absolutely necessary, as you have to march more than 200 miles and to accomplish a good deal, with not more than two months of good weather. . . . The highest estimate of the enemy's forces in Northwestern Virginia does not exceed 4,000. . . . You will have no difficulty, therefore, in dispersing them should they oppose your march. . . . Your speedy junction with General Lee is of the first importance. (*OR*, vol. 19, pt. 2, p. 638)

In a letter to General Lee, Jefferson Davis on 28 September wrote, "General Loring had not, when last heard from, left Charleston. His progress seems slow, but he may be, for good though unknown causes, detained in the valley" (*OR*, vol. 19, pt. 2, p. 634).

Loring responded to Randolph on 7 October and indicated his plans of complying with Lee's order to move out. But he mentions that "the route which [Lee] marks out for me (down the Monongahela River) is so long, difficult, and unsupplied with subsistence, that before I could reach the railroad the enemy . . . could . . . destroy my army and train." To attain essentially the same end, Loring proposed a much shorter route, with better supplies of subsistence, through Monterey: "I will, therefore, unless halted or ordered otherwise, proceed to comply with General Lee's orders in the manner above indicated, viz, by moving my infantry and trains to rear and thence through Monterey, &c., while with my cavalry I will sweep through the northwest" (*OR*, vol. 19, pt. 2, p. 656).

The next day, Loring left Charleston, moving south, eagerly looking to join with General Lee. On 11 October, Loring was 25 miles below Charleston at the Falls of Kanawha. He ordered General Jenkins's cavalry, by then 1,500 strong, to move at once on the campaign marked out by Randolph. They attacked the enemy at Bulltown, killing eight men and capturing 32 prisoners.

The day before, while General Jeb Stuart was crossing the Potomac at McCoy's (between Williamsport and Hancock, Maryland) on his way to his famous raid on Chambersburg, Pennsylvania, he learned that a large force of Union troops had encamped the night before at Clear Spring. These were Ohio troops under General Cox and were en route for the Kanawha Valley to reclaim the important salt mines at Charleston, that Loring recently had captured.

With Loring coming out of the mountains and with Jeb Stuart moving on Chambersburg, the Confederate strategy still seemed to believe in an invasion into Pennsylvania. Suddenly, this all changed. Secretary of War Randolph acted on Stuart's report by writing to General Lee: "The Kanawha Valley is again threatened by the enemy. Is it not better to help Loring there?" (*OR*, vol. 19, pt. 2, p. 665). Lee also wrote to Loring on 15 October: "If you can retain possession of the salt works at Charleston, and keep the enemy out of that country, I think it probably the best service your army can perform. . . . The season is now so far advanced that I doubt whether an expedition into Western Pennsylvania, which I once proposed to you, can be now advantageously undertaken" (*OR*, vol. 19, pt. 2, p. 666).

On 15 October, Loring was back at the Dublin Depot. And on the same day, a most surprising turn of events occurred:

> Major-General Loring,
> You will turn over your command, together with the orders and instructions heretofore communicated to you, to General [John] Echols, after which you will, with the least delay practicable, report in person to this office.
> > S. Cooper,
> > Adjutant and Inspector General
> > (*OR*, vol. 19, pt. 2, p. 666)

Why this sudden change in command? Actually, a problem had been festering for months between Loring and Virginia governor John Letcher and his State Line troops. Letcher, eager to please his constituents who disapproved of his quick subordination of state power to the Confederate authority, had issued a call for 10,000 men to be employed chiefly in the defense of western Virginia. The Confederate draft motivated many to volunteer for such state service. After all, who wanted to risk going to the killing fields when local garrison duty beckoned? Loring, who had been convinced he could double the size of his army once he got to northwestern Virginia and Charleston, had not expected to have his efforts sabotaged by Letcher. Loring complained frequently to Secretary of War Randolph and others that the governor sought to detain volunteers forcibly in a corps whose service was local and temporary rather than letting them serve in the Regular army.

As Loring's success at recruitment fell off, his sharp language became even more adamant. On 22 September, he wrote a lengthy letter to Randolph:

> I observe in the late message of the Governor of the State certain wanton and unfounded charges, that, exceeding my authority as a Confederate officer, I had improperly and mischievously interfered with the non-conscripts in Southwest Virginia and demoralized the militia. Deprecating a controversy with the Governor, and disclaiming accountability to him for my official acts, I deem it proper to lay my action on the subject before you. . . . There is certainly nothing to warrant the misstatement of the Governor that I "issued orders to stop the enrollment in Monroe, Giles, and perhaps other counties." . . . I have been seriously interfered with in collecting conscripts for the army by the officers of the State Line, who have, by the written testimony of my recruiting officers, heretofore sent to you, openly received these persons into their ranks, and from it up to this time I have received no aid in expelling the enemy from this section. . . . I deeply regret that the libel of the Governor on my conduct and motives constrains me now to depart from the preferable policy of silence, and to beg you, if in your judgment it is consistent with the public interests, to suffer this letter to be published in the papers, or presented to the State legislature for my justification. (*OR*, vol. 19, pt. 2, pp. 616-617)

One-armed Major General W. W. Loring, CSA. (Courtesy, Library of Congress)

Earlier in the month, Loring had already sent Captain Myrick, a member of his staff, to Richmond to request 5,000 more troops. Events would suggest that Myrick carried more than a request; he might have also carried an ultimatum from Loring about Letcher and his treacherous recruiting. If Letcher was not to be corrected, Loring would resign — which is exactly what happened. The separation from command had nothing to do with the campaign.

Undoubtedly, Loring was disgusted with the Richmond politics. Believing that no further action would occur in West Virginia before winter closed in, he decided to ask the government to transfer him to some other point of need and danger.

In his acknowledgment to Randolph about being relieved from his command, Loring acted neither surprised nor irritated about it. This further suggests that Loring was well aware of what was taking place. On 27 November 1862, Jno. Withers, Assistant Adjutant General, indicated that Loring was relieved from the command of the Department of Western Virginia "at his own request": "Maj. Gen. W. W. Loring, having been relieved from the command of the Department of Western Virginia at his own request, will proceed to Jackson, Miss., and report for duty to Lieut. Gen. John C. Pemberton, commanding" (*OR*, vol. 21, p. 1036).

George Randolph, Robert E. Lee, and W. W. Loring had worked together harmoniously from the beginning of their associations in March of 1862 throughout Randolph's tenure as Secretary of War. But although amicable decisions had been reached between President Davis and Randolph on many occasions, there was a certain subliminal difference or irritation at each other that was growing.

On 27 October, just nine days after Loring's resignation, Randolph issued an order to General Theophilus Hunter Holmes, giving him authority to cross the east bank of the Mississippi River to reinforce General Pemberton. President Davis rebuked him and asserted that Randolph did not have the power to delegate or appoint without consultation with Davis. Had Randolph done this with Loring, accepted his resignation without conferring with the President or Robert E. Lee? The official records confirm that General Lee continued to send dispatches to Loring, apparently unaware he had resigned. Randolph's response to Davis's admonishment was to submit his own resignation on 13 November 1862.

In a letter dated 28 December 1862, Loring gives the whole story to his good friend Dr. Charles Todd Quintard, who was now with the Army of Tennessee.

> I had a brilliant campaign in Western Virginia as long as it lasted; we took the Kanawha Valley and waters and levees in the Ohio; I, but for the interference of Randolph with matters of which he was ignorant, and as I am informed, without the knowledge of the President, would have had a campaign which would have been of great service. As it was I saw no prospect in Western Virginia this winter but monotonous inactivity — I applied to be relieved and ordered to an army in the field. It resulted in me coming here [Meridian, Mississippi]. (William R. Perkins Library)

One must wonder what would have taken place if Loring's army had been given the extra 5,000 men and moved up the valley into the rear of the Federals while Jeb Stuart was raiding Chambersburg. General Lee may have been presented with a new opportunity to strike back across the Maryland line and into Pennsylvania.

But Loring's days in Virginia and western Virginia were over. He was ordered to Mississippi to be second in command to General John C. Pemberton. Robert E. Lee and his army returned to Virginia; the invasion of Pennsylvania would be rescheduled for July 1863, at a place called Gettysburg.

With General Echols in command, the Army of Southwestern Virginia reversed its direction on 17 October and began its movement back into the Kanawha Valley. Overwhelming Union forces were being massed against it. General Cox had been returned to the department with 9,000 men. Within ten days, the bluecoats advanced from Point Pleasant and Clarksburg in great numbers, compelling General Echols to withdraw and give up all of the territory that Loring had won. By 1 November, the country was in the hands of the Federals. Because of lack of subsistence, Echols withdrew to the Princeton and Lewisburg lines, and on 10 November, Echols was succeeded by General J. S. Williams.

In western Virginia, 1862 ended about the same as it had begun.

Chapter 8

"Old Blizzards"
at Fort Pemberton

*T*HE LAND MASS *of the Confederacy was one of staggering proportions, involving a military frontier that stretched from the Virginia tidewater westward across the Appalachians, the hills and rivers of Tennessee and Kentucky, and the Mississippi River to the Great Plains beyond. Besides this, a coastline of several thousand miles had to be guarded against the enemy, whose naval superiority gave them the potential of descending in force on any point of the coast.*

The Southern forces, south and west of Richmond, because of the enormous tract of country to be defended, were obliged to keep large bodies of soldiers and departments unemployed, and at great distance from each other, awaiting the sudden invasions or raids of the Union troops, to which they were continually exposed. It was difficult to join them together for aggressive purposes — thus no one large army, such as Lee had in Virginia, could be maintained for any long period of time in the West.

The bickering of the Confederate Congress and the obstructionism of governors made the Western front, especially, dangerously weak. Although President Davis cherished the prospect of directing all Confederate military operations, the conflict had grown to such gigantic proportions and had spread to such remote areas that he recognized the need for a modern command system. After deliberation with Secretaries of War George Randolph and his successor, James A. Seddon, he decided to create a large command in the West.

On 1 October, adding to the overlapping commands and personalities, President Davis established the Department of Mississippi and East Louisiana and placed General John C. Pemberton in command of the second Army of Mississippi (the first Army of Mississippi, under General P. G. T. Beauregard, had been absorbed into the central army). Unification was needed.

The Southern command system in the West suffered from instability, complexity, and cumbersomeness. Department boundaries and responsibilities varied. General Pemberton's new department took charge of the east side of the Mississippi River, while General Theophilus Hunter Holmes headed the Trans-Mississippi Department on the west side of the river. The father of all rivers, the Mississippi, now became an invisible dividing line and prevented cooperation between the two commands since each department reported directly to Richmond; they were not controlled by one single commander. The task of ensuring quick interaction by either department rested on Davis's shoulders.

No sooner had General Pemberton been assigned to command than President Davis recommended him to be promoted to lieutenant general and to assume the command of all forces intended to operate in southwestern Tennessee in addition to the command just assigned. The promotion, confirmed by the Senate on 14 October, was a poor move on the part of Davis as it stirred the already hot soup of who was in charge. The result was wholesale unrest among the independently minded generals already serving in the Western theater.

Pemberton's promotion may have been due solely to the backing of President Davis. Whatever Davis's reasons were, Pemberton, a transplanted Pennsylvania Confederate whose dedication and morals were admittedly above reproach but who could not inspire soldiers, was clearly underqualified for such high rank and the important department that he was assigned. "A nervous man, Pemberton was unsure of himself and incapable of furnishing bold, aggressive leadership. . . . Pemberton's subsequent discomfort was primarily due to his own indecision" (Ambrose 6, 13). General Loring himself, in a letter to Dr. Quintard dated 28 December 1862, said, "I do not think much of the officer in charge" (National Archives). Loring, who had entered the service as a captain without the advantages of a West Point education, was undoubtedly piqued at having another Military Academy graduate placed over him. In the old Army, Loring had been a full colonel while Pemberton was still a captain, and Loring never let him forget it.

On 28 November, Pemberton learned that the Union forces that had landed on the Mississippi riverbank opposite Helena, Arkansas, were striking inland for a possible flank attack on General Earl Van Dorn who was guarding the northwest approach to Vicksburg. This crisis of Grant in the front, a potential flank attack from the Delta, and the rumor of a powerful amphibious expedition led Pemberton to abandon the powerful defense line of the Tallahatchie River and to withdraw behind the rain-swollen Yalobusha River where soldiers, reinforced by large numbers of slaves, were at work throwing up redoubts and digging rifle pits. In the driving rain and cold weather, General Van Dorn gave ground and retreated toward Coffeeville, Mississippi. On 5 December, Colonel T. Lyle Dickey of the Union XIII Corps cavalry, in pursuit of Van Dorn's rear guard, hit Van Dorn's skirmishers at Coffeeville. With a screened front, the Confederates — with cannon and infantry and Colonel William Jackson's 700-strong cavalry — stopped Dickey's pursuit, forcing him to return to Grant's lines.

Although Loring's transfer by the Adjutant and Inspector General's office is dated 27 November, there is an absence of written evidence to indicate when he actually left western Virginia and arrived in Mississippi. In his letter to Dr. Quintard, he mentions that "I have Charlie & Joe Mathews, Hanson Thomas and Henry Robinson with me, the rest of my staff including Fitzhugh who I miss very much, remain in Western Virginia."

Loring is mentioned in several sources as being at Coffeeville on 5 December.

> Here [Holly Springs] we found Col. T. C. Standifer . . . when we joined the 12th T. M. Scott was colonel; Boyd of Columbia, La. was Lt. Col., and Noel Nelson of Claiborne was major. It belonged to [Villepigue's] brigade and Loring's division, then an independent command. We retreated from Holly Springs to Grenada and at Coffeeville there was a hot fight. . . . (Bond 462)

> The 3rd Kentucky regiment was organized by Col. Lloyd Tilghman; after the exchange of prisoners at Vicksburg, he was part of A. Buford's Brigade, Loring Division, and [was] in the campaigns from Holly Springs, Coffeeville, Grenada, Canton, Big Black and Baker's Creek. (Anderson 597)

Richmond, recognizing the increasing gravity of the situation in the West, assigned General Joseph E. Johnston on 24 November to take over the complete region, naming it the Department of the Confederate West. It was a geographical department rather than a command. Johnston would then oversee General Braxton Bragg's Army of Tennessee, General E. Kirby Smith's Department of East Tennessee, and Lieutenant General Pemberton's Department of Mississippi and East Louisiana. He would be headquartered at Chattanooga, Tennessee.

On 4 December, word was received in Richmond that Pemberton, the new commander, was falling back before a superior force led by General Ulysses S. Grant. At this time, President Davis decided it might be helpful to visit the Western theater personally to see for himself what the situation entailed and to raise morale. He visited General Pemberton's army near Grenada on Christmas Eve. Here Davis found General Loring in command; General Van Dorn, with his 3,500 cavalry, had gone to raid

Holly Springs, leaving Loring commanding the 1st Corps, Army of Mississippi, newly named on 7 December.

On the same day, the troops were reviewed by President Davis, which Loring mentions in his 28 December letter to Dr. Quintard: "I was in command a few days of this army at which the President and General Joe Johnston were present. The army presented a fine appearance."

As the Confederates were celebrating Van Dorn's victory at Holly Springs on 20 December, Major General William T. Sherman was operating with 32,000 troops as a right wing of Grant's XIII Army Corps. On Christmas Day, Sherman had his forces at the mouth of the Yazoo River. Before concentrating there, he had sent out detachments to destroy the railroad running west from Vicksburg into Louisiana. On the 26th, Sherman's fleet moved up the Yazoo, preceded by the gunboats; and on the next day he landed his forces at Johnston's and Lake's plantations. The Confederate line confronting Sherman was about 14 miles long; the right consisted of strong fortifications at Snyder's Mill and Drumgould's Bluff on the Yazoo.

At Snyder's Mill, a stationary log raft spanned the Yazoo River, blocking river traffic and preventing Union gunboats from ascending the river past Snyder's. Heavy cannons were emplaced on the high bluffs overlooking the river, and the area was honeycombed with trench lines and rifle pits for the sharpshooters. Electrically rigged torpedoes were placed downriver.

Davis returned to Jackson on Christmas Day, and on the 27th, information was received from Loring that General Grant's army, which had been advancing, was now retiring as a result of the destruction of the depot of supplies at Holly Springs by Van Dorn's raid. As soon as Grant's troops started to fall back behind the Tallahatchie line, Pemberton took advantage of his interior rail lines and started shifting troops from Grenada to Vicksburg, situated on the Mississippi River near the southwestern end of a long series of hills running inland from the water. Most of the ground in this area was low and marshy, cut by lakes and bayous and heavily wooded with dense undergrowth.

The new year of 1863 opened with Generals Grant and Sherman moving toward Vicksburg with their ruses and plans to take the town at any cost. Whatever it would take, Grant would willingly try it.

The first phase of Grant's Vicksburg campaign had been an amphibious war involving hundreds of steamers, rams, transports, and gunboats and tens of thousands of men. By January 1863, the Confederate Mississippi navy had been wiped out except for two ships that had been removed from the tactical area. Only a 150-mile segment of the Mississippi River, between fortresses at Vicksburg and Port Hudson, remained under Confederate control. Should these two forts fall, the Mississippi would be lost, the trans-Mississippi Confederacy would become isolated, and Union forces would have access to the interior of west Louisiana and east Texas via the Red River, thus dividing the Confederacy into two parts.

At this time, General Grant resumed work on the Williams Canal that had started the summer before. The Federals sought to cut a nine-foot canal across De Soto Point on the Louisiana side of the river, in order to enable Grant's troops to get below Vicksburg without traveling on the river. When Sherman saw the canal, he remarked that it was no bigger than a plantation ditch. Grant's folly continued on through February and March until the fire of the Confederates' cannon compelled the Federals to withdraw their dredges from the canal. Grant gave up on the ditch.

The death toll was high for this part of the Delta campaign. Dreary, wet swamps, wretched sanitary facilities, flood-plain drinking water, and swamp creatures left many Northern boys sickened with fever, and large numbers died. Without ever firing a shot at the Rebels, these young men were buried in levees and shallow graves.

On 2 January 1863, Loring took command of the 1st Division of the Department of Mississippi and East Louisiana, composed of General Lloyd Tilghman's brigade, Colonel Albert Rust's brigade, and Colonel Thomas N. Waul's Texas Legion. Loring and his troops remained at Grenada and held the Yalobusha River line. Beginning 21 January, Confederate pickets posted at Terrapin Neck on the Mississippi River, 46 miles above Vicksburg, counted 107 steamboats and 15 gunboats as they passed during a 72-hour period. The combined onslaught by Grant and Sherman was about to begin.

For many years, the small boats traveling from Memphis to Vicksburg would use the Yazoo Pass as the shortest route. The pass was located five miles below Helena, Arkansas, and led into the Coldwater, Tallahatchie, and Yazoo Rivers, and then to Snyder's Mill above Vicksburg.

General Grant, aware of the pass, sent Lieutenant Colonel James H. Wilson, his topographical engineer, with a 500-man fatigue party to begin

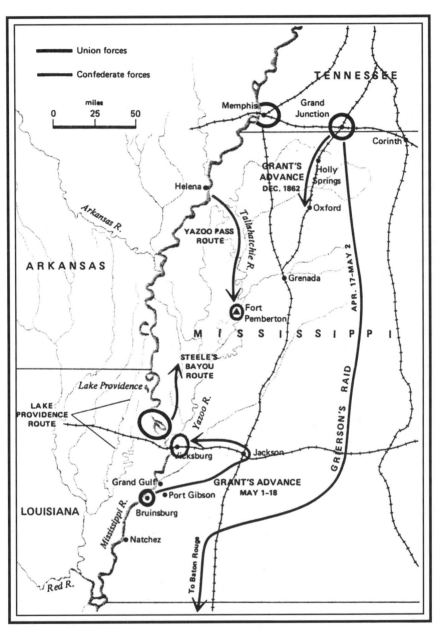

The Vicksburg Campaign, December 1862-May 1863. From Steven E. Woodworth, *Jefferson Davis and His Generals* (Lawrence: University Press of Kansas, 1990). Used by permission.

reopening the six-mile stretch of the pass that had been blocked by the Confederates. On 9 February, General Pemberton was apprised of the situation at the Yazoo Pass, and on the 22nd, General Loring received dispatches of the enemy's activities.

With one enemy force operating on the Tallahatchie River, north of Greenwood, Mississippi, another trying to dig a canal across the peninsula opposite Vicksburg, and yet another active at the mouth of the Yazoo River, Pemberton shifted Loring to Yazoo City, 45 miles north of Vicksburg, to take command of the Confederate forces charged with checking the Federal advance on the Tallahatchie. By now, the Union forces had reached the mouth of the Coldwater in their quest to bypass the Confederates and reach Vicksburg. Pemberton also ordered Waul's Texas Legion, already at Yazoo City, to wait for Loring, and he directed General Tilghman to move his brigade from Jackson to Loring's support.

General Loring hurried to Greenwood by boat. Upon landing, Loring was conducted to Beck's Ferry, the site for projected fortifications. Employing gangs of soldiers and impressed slaves, the engineers had started work on the defenses. Loring approved the location of the fort, named Fort Pemberton, which was two and a half miles by land and about four by water west of and upstream from Greenwood.

The site for fortifying the line was a neck of high land scarcely a half-mile wide on Clayton's Bayou, lying between the Yazoo River on one side and the Tallahatchie River on the approaching side. The work on the fort was pushed with all possible dispatch, including the mounting of several heavy guns and a few lighter field pieces.

As was customary in the battles in the cotton states, bales of cotton, when available, would be confiscated and piled up to create a defensive cover for the Confederates. Loring adopted the same strategy. Breastworks were made by putting three to five bales of cotton on top of one another, some four or five bales wide. Dirt was then thrown on the bales. The parapets of the stronghold were built of cotton bales, logs, and mud. The engineers staked off the ground in a zigzag way for the breastwork.

Troops were transferred from Grenada to Loring and Fort Pemberton. Additional troops from Haynes' Landing, Snyder's Mill, and on the Yazoo River above Vicksburg were also rapidly transferred to the fort. The garrison was composed of about 2,000 men in all, including Waul's Texas Legion, the 2nd Texas Infantry, the 20th Mississippi Infantry, and the Pointe Coupee Artillery, plus Loring's cannoneers.

If driven from the fort, General Loring promised to backtrack throughout the length of the Yazoo Valley. Consequently, he directed that an additional fortification be thrown up on the right bank of the Yazoo, south of the fort. These earthworks were designated Camp Loring.

With a view to obstructing the Tallahatchie and Coldwater Rivers, General Loring proceeded up the Tallahatchie for 70 miles where he learned of the breakthrough by the Yankees. He hurried back to Greenwood and immediately ordered General Tilghman to rush one infantry regiment and a battery of field artillery to Greenwood and at the same time to move his cavalry to the Coldwater to harass the Federals.

By the beginning of March, news that the enemy task force was en route down the Coldwater caused the soldiers to redouble their efforts to put Fort Pemberton into a defensible condition. Loring ordered the USS *Star of the West*, a captured Union steamer, to be towed on the Tallahatchie to the site of the fort where it was swung squarely across the channel and sunk, blocking the channel. Rifle pits extended from the fort to the bank of the river at the point where the vessel lay in silent determination to stop Grant's approaching fleet.

Moving with the river's current, the ten-boat Union task force took three and a half days to move over Moon Lake to the Coldwater. By 6 March, the vanguard of the convoy anchored 12 miles below the confluence of the Coldwater and Tallahatchie. On 10 March, the warships were 32 miles above Greenwood, and on the 11th, as the ironclad *Chillicothe* rounded the next-to-final bend leading down to the Yazoo, she was struck hard twice on the turrets by high-velocity shells from Fort Pemberton, which was dead ahead. Loring noted the progress of the expedition by the smoke of the steamers above the treetops, eight or ten miles upriver.

Five guns had opened fire on the *Chillicothe*. This first attack on Fort Pemberton lasted about 30 minutes before the *Chillicothe* backed upstream until hidden behind the bend. Federal scouts then reported that the Rebels were driving their cattle and carrying gear from the fort. This convinced their officers that Loring was preparing to abandon the works. To verify this report, the *Chillicothe*, followed by the ironclad *DeKalb* and the ram *Lioness*, started down the river again. At 4:15 p.m., the Confederate cannon reopened fire, and within seven minutes the ironclads had had enough and backed out of range. Loring had tricked them, and they knew it.

But the Yanks, led by Lieutenant Commander Watson Smith, were not

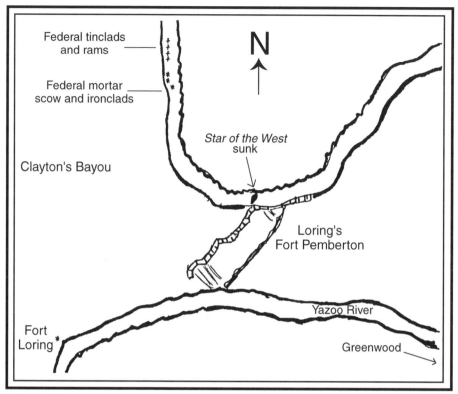

General Quinby's attempt to take Fort Pemberton from Loring — March 23 to April 4, 1863.

to be denied. On the night of 11 March, a cotton-bale battery was erected by a fatigue party on the edge of the woods about 700 yards from the Confederate 32-pound rifle. Since the Federals had no siege guns with them, one of the 30-pound Parrotts — a rifled, muzzle-loading cannon — from the Union *Rattler* was landed and moved into the emplacement.

Throughout the next day, Union sailors toiled away, reinforcing with bales of cotton the bows and bulwarks of the *Chillicothe* and the *DeKalb*. A second 30-pound Parrott was landed and placed in the battery that night. During the buildup of Fort Pemberton, Loring had repeatedly begged for more ammunition, and several of his reports stated that if he did not have enough, he would lose the engagement. This ammunition shortage kept the Confederates from opening fire on the Yanks while they were constructing their land battery.

On the morning of the 13th, the guns of Fort Pemberton began the day's fight. By 11:25, the Federals, on the water and in the land battery, returned fire on the Confederate fortifications. The *Chillicothe* remained in position until 1:03 p.m. when, after firing 54 11-inch projectiles, she withdrew to fill shells and cut fuses. While thus engaged, the ironclad was hit by 38 projectiles. Six sailors were wounded and cotton bales were ignited, but these were extinguished.

The *DeKalb* held her position and fired on the Rebels at 15-minute intervals. She in turn was struck six times, suffering three dead and three wounded. The 13-inch mortar vessel had lofted 49 shells into Loring's position during the day, exhausting its supply of 200-pound shells.

The two ironclads were unable to maneuver in the narrow stream and took a terrible pounding. All they could do was bounce their big projectiles off Fort Pemberton's resilient parapet of cotton bales and earth.

It was on top of these cotton bales, throughout the heaviest fighting of the day, that one-armed General Loring pranced back and forth, shouting and cursing purple oaths, his spittle flying, encouraging his men, "Give them blizzards, boys! Give them blizzards!" And blizzards of shot and shell the Confederates gave the Yankees until they retreated back up the muddy river. Loring's nickname "Old Blizzards" was thus earned in battle.

Throughout the night of 13 March, Loring kept his men busy repairing the fort's damaged parapets. The Federal ironclads, badly crippled and needing repair, were also running low on ammunition.

The Federals resumed their attack on the 16th. It was decided that the ironclads would close rapidly on the fort and smother the defenders under a storm of grape. But close quarters and quick work, the time-honored principle of gunboat warfare, did not succeed. As the *Chillicothe* closed within 1,100 yards of the fort, the Rebel gunners registered eight hits within 15 minutes, sealing both gun ports so neither could be opened. Both the *Chillicothe* and *DeKalb* retired while the land battery pounded the Confederate fortifications. Federal sharpshooters advanced to within 450 yards of the Confederate rifle pits, but they failed to reach either the right or left flanks with troops, owing to dense woods, cane, and river overflow.

Loring was then informed that the steamboats carrying Union General Isaac F. Quinby's men, who had been ordered by General Grant to Moon Lake, had entered Yazoo Pass. To slow the passage of Quinby's troops down the Coldwater and Tallahatchie, Loring ordered the Southern sympathizers operating on these rivers to build fire rafts and attempt to burn the enemy transports.

After Commander Watson Smith's humiliating failure to defeat the Rebels at Fort Pemberton, he turned over his command to Commander James P. Foster. The new naval chieftain called a council of war among the officers of his boats to decide what course of action the expedition should follow, and they later decided to remain at Fort Pemberton until ranking Quinby arrived. From the 16th to the 20th, the Yankee infantry vainly scoured the area in an effort to discover a feasible approach to the fort. Finally, Foster agreed to an immediate retreat. The sunken *Star of the West* ensured that it would be no easy task to clear the river. At the same time, General Loring ordered a pursuit upon the Federals' rear and both flanks.

The battle of Fort Pemberton then became a siege. As the task force withdrew with the intention of returning to the Mississippi, they encountered General Quinby and his division on six transports heading for Fort Pemberton on 21 March, 40 miles below the confluence of the Coldwater and Tallahatchie. Quinby, the ranking officer, deemed it best to order the troops back to Fort Pemberton. After much difficulty, the boats were turned about and headed back downstream, arriving on 23 March.

The aggressive Quinby established headquarters in a farmhouse and believed his men would be able to reach the Yalobusha below Fort Pemberton by building a pontoon bridge, allowing his force to land south of the fort. They could then attack it from the rear. However, by 28 March, the Rebels had thrown up new field works that covered the reach of the Tallahatchie where Quinby intended to cross the river.

During the Yankees' brief absence, Loring's men had greatly strengthened their fortifications. Several secondary strong points had been thrown up, and the number of defenders had been augmented by the arrival of General Winfield S. Featherston's and Brigadier General John C. Moore's brigades. The Confederates soon succeeded in building up a stronger force than the Federals. By 1 April, Loring's command exceeded 7,000 officers and men. On the 2nd, Rebel batteries shelled the Yankee camps. The Federal guns hardly replied.

Soon afterward, General Quinby came down through the Yazoo Pass with a corps, intending to get into the Yazoo River at Greenwood. Loring repulsed and detained him there until he could get to him with a force of 4,000 men coming from Vicksburg.

General Tilghman's brigade joined on the right. He proposed to try and break up the enemy's headquarters, about a mile away from the front. Tilghman had a county map showing the position of the farmhouse where Quinby had his headquarters. Tilghman trained his guns by the compass while a body of sharpshooters moved through the woods upon the enemy's right. At an appointed signal, they opened fire and broke up the whole camp. The Federals hastily began to retreat toward the Mississippi River by way of the Yazoo.

"Hit them on their way out!" ordered Loring. Detachments from the 26th Mississippi, 2nd Texas, and General J. Z. George's Mississippi State troops, posted along the Tallahatchie above Fort Pemberton, fired upon the retreating boats from an ambush position along the banks of the river.

After the battle of Fort Pemberton, it was decided that Camp Loring, roughly a mile and a half south of Fort Pemberton and located on a plantation, would be made into a fort because there was still a strong Union presence in the area. When Colonel Thomas A. Mellon's 3rd Mississippi Infantry arrived, the men diligently pitched in to transform the camp into a fort. General Loring remained at Fort Pemberton while the other officers set up headquarters at Fort Loring.

In January, General Joe Johnston had ordered General Earl Van Dorn to form a cavalry division out of the 6,000 troops stationed at Grenada and to move them to Tennessee to assist General Braxton Bragg. After preparing them for the field, which took to the middle of February, Van Dorn himself was directed to Columbia, Tennessee. He was thus out of Pemberton's department. The department had lost its eyes and ears. Pemberton wrote to Johnston on 21 March: "Have you separated the cavalry with General Van Dorn from my command entirely? If so, it very much diminishes my ability to defend the northern position of the State" (*OR*, vol. 24, pt. 3, p. 681).

Grant made five unsuccessful attempts to reach Vicksburg, which consumed four months and numerous lives. But despite the costly loss of time, he was slowly moving south, and though he was playing a cat and mouse game with the Rebels, he finally had them strung out, which reduced their effectiveness. Pemberton was on the defense as he moved units from one place to another. One of the only pillars outside of Vicksburg was Loring at Fort Pemberton; but with Quinby's withdrawal from the Yazoo Pass and the later stalemate in Steel's Bayou, six miles up the Yazoo from its mouth, Loring's value diminished, as did Fort Pemberton's.

By April 1863, the Confederates and the Yankees were almost on equal terms as far as supplying their respective armies. General Grant had to contend with a supply line several hundred miles long that started from Memphis. As the Confederates gave up control of their natural defensive posture along the river, the Yanks took over the river in order to move their men and supplies.

Unable to ship cotton freely on the river, the countryside was planted with corn, which the Confederate states needed. Forced off the river, Pemberton had to depend on haulage of all supplies by wagons over dirt roads. This region of Mississippi was limited to three railroad trunk lines, which quickly became overtaxed in attempting to supply over 60,000 troops, civilians, and the slave population.

Grant continued his amphibious movements by starting a new canal south of Milliken's Bend on the Louisiana side of the Mississippi. On 29 March, Major General John A. McClernand transferred his XIII Corps to Milliken's Bend and then to camps at New Carthage, Louisiana, where a staging area for the coming invasion was established. This was below the Vicksburg batteries and 32 miles upstream from Grand Gulf.

Chapter 9

Vicksburg and Champion Hill

*F*ORTRESS VICKSBURG was not as great as it was supposed to be. General Joe Johnston, when touring the town with President Davis in December 1862, had remarked:

The usual error of Confederate engineering had been committed. An immense entrenched camp, requiring an army to hold it, had been made instead of a fort requiring only a small garri-

son. The water batteries had been planned to prevent the bombardment of the town, instead of to close the navigation of the river to the enemy; consequently, the small number of heavy guns had been distributed along a front of two miles, instead of being so placed that their fire might be concentrated on a single vessel. (Johnston 152)

Alexander S. Abrams, an artillerist in the summer of 1863, grimly recalled: "The entire strength of the river batteries in November of 1862 did not exceed twenty-three guns, mounted along a space of several miles from near the Village of Warrenton, to a place called Mint Spring, above the city. This small number of guns was inadequate to prevent the passage of the enemy's boats" (Bearss, *Vicksburg*, 2:60).

The great guns of Vicksburg were not placed atop the bluffs; instead, they were situated at elevations from 30 to 40 feet above the main level of the river. If placed on the top, the greater range reduced the penetrating power of the projectiles, and the increased distance to the river made it more difficult to see the boats.

The main handicap of the whole defense was that the guns were muzzle-loading artillery, which had to be kept horizontal or else the projectile would slide forward in the bore away from contact with the powder charge. Thus, they could not be aimed down toward the enemy boats on the Mississippi. And with their slow rate of fire, it reduced the effectiveness of the guns.

On 16 April, the Federal flotilla of ironclads, cottonclads — boats that used cotton bales as protection from shells fired at them — and barges loaded with ammunition and rations swept past Vicksburg under the cover of darkness. By the 17th, they were safely below the town. General Grant decided to try it again by sending 12 barges with five stern-wheeled steamers to run past the fortress's defenses. By 23 April, five transports were still afloat and six barges had gotten through with cargoes undamaged. The survival of the transports was final proof that the Confederates had no hope of closing the river with guns alone.

General Pemberton, during the first ten days of April, paid little or no attention to Union activities across the Mississippi from Vicksburg, even though Major Isaac F. Harrison's cavalry had been skirmishing with General McClernand's vanguard since the last day of March. Pemberton was also undeterred by the warning of General John S. Bowen, who had sent reinforcements to Harrison, of an enemy drive southward from Milliken's Bend. Additional reports from Bowen reached Pemberton's headquarters in Jackson on 10 and 11 April, telling of continued clashes between the Federals and Colonel Francis M. Cockrell's Missourians on the Louisiana side of the Mississippi. Why wasn't Pemberton responding with quick action? The answer is that Yankee strategy and a bit of luck had succeeded, at the same time, in usurping Pemberton's judgment.

During the first week in April, Confederate scouts had reported almost 70 transports and gunboats, some loaded with troops, passing up the Mississippi River. Pemberton, letting wishful thinking prevail over his better judgment, had thought the Union generals were withdrawing troops from the Vicksburg area to be transferred back to Tennessee, when in fact General Grant had merely been releasing surplus vessels from the river. This maneuver had coincided with Major General Frederick Steele's division shifting from Young's Point to Greenville. Pemberton, misinterpreting these movements on the Federals' part, had determined on inadequate evidence that Grant was pulling back and so informed Richmond and General Johnston. Steele's move to Greenville, 50 miles north of Vicksburg, had been part of General Grant's and General William Tecumseh Sherman's plans aimed at diverting the Confederates' attention from McClernand's activities on the Louisiana side of the Mississippi.

And more was to come to confuse Pemberton. The Yanks designed a series of raids, in a combined operation, to sever General Bragg's major supply line, the Western & Atlantic Railroad, which would also draw most of the Confederate horsemen into Alabama, and to cut the Mississippi Central Railroad south of Grenada and the Southern Railroad east of Jackson, thus cutting Pemberton's supply line and reinforcements from Bragg's army.

At about this same time, Union Colonel Benjamin Henry Grierson, commanding three cavalry regiments and a detachment of artillery, was ordered to create a diversion in eastern Mississippi to draw off potential reinforcements and to cut the rail line to Vicksburg to interrupt supplies and thus throw Pemberton off balance. By the time Grierson's raiders reached New Albany, Mississippi, on 18 April, General Grant had at least three other well-synchronized movements underway, hoping to distract Pemberton.

As Pemberton received reports of a heavy force of enemy troops approaching Macon, Mississippi, he immediately decided, as Grierson had hoped he would, that Grierson and his raiders had turned toward Macon. This force was actually comprised of a maximum of 35 men.

Pemberton was adamantly opposed to sparing troops from Grenada, the strong point of Vicksburg's northern defense ring, where General Loring was in command. But he ordered hard-bitten Loring, along with the 15th and 26th Mississippi Infantry and Company C of the 14th Mississippi Artillery, to Meridian — where General Abraham Buford's infantry, en route from Alabama to reinforce Vicksburg, was bivouacked — with orders to take command of all troops to take action against the dangerous Union cavalry raid.

At Enterprise, Mississippi, on 25 April, Grierson advanced with his main force and demanded the surrender of the town, but Loring, having arrived with a sufficient force of infantry, frustrated Grierson's object. Lamentably, Loring was without any cavalry, and thus Grierson's mounted raiders escaped again.

As Grierson's men moved south, Pemberton dispatched messages all over Mississippi, hoping to prevent the escape of the cavalrymen, no matter which direction they took. So began the rapid draining away to the east of Pemberton's reserve strength, in pursuit of less than a thousand elusive horsemen, while Grant, across the Mississippi, was preparing to strike him hard on the west with a force of 30,000. The strategy was working. And Pemberton, without the eyes and ears of Van Dorn's cavalry, was hurting badly for communications.

The Union strategy of deception and diversion continued. Sherman's troops moved northeast of Vicksburg on 29 and 30 April, heading up the Yazoo River to make a demonstration against Confederate works at Haynes' Bluff and Drumgould's Bluffs, diverting General C. L. Stevenson's attention, who was defending Vicksburg. During these diversions, Grant and the Union army in force were coming down the Louisiana side of the Mississippi River, moving from Milliken's Bend south to a place called Hard Times.

General Stevenson was convinced that the Union push southward from Milliken's Bend was a feint. And in fact, General Sherman, in a letter some months earlier, had told Grant that by crossing the river south of Vicksburg, he would be putting himself voluntarily in a position — by dividing his forces — that an enemy would be willing to maneuver for a year to get him into. But Grant was moving with such speed that this point somehow did not matter.

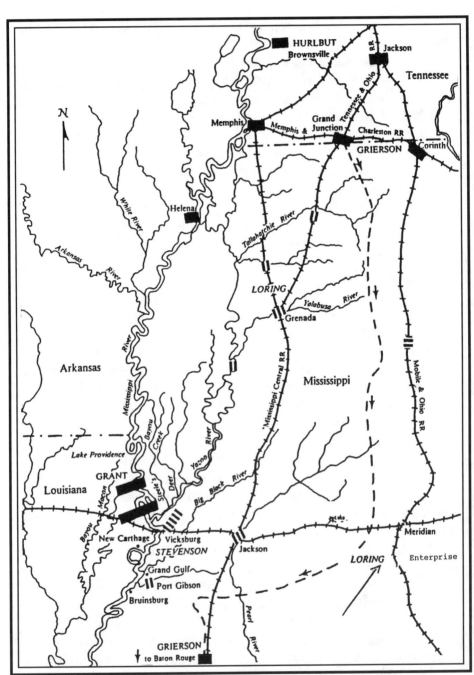

Grant was now determined to land his forces at Bruinsburg, Mississippi. The troops debarked at Hard Times at daybreak on 28 April and were ferried across the Mississippi to Bruinsburg, six miles away. The largest amphibious invasion since the Mexican War was beginning.

> In retrospect this was the critical moment of the Vicksburg campaign. Grant was still involved in an amphibious operation. His force was inevitably divided, with one of his three corps still on the west bank of the river and over half of another still engaged in disembarking and in unloading the transports. If Pemberton could have struck while Grant was thus off balance, with one foot in the water and the other on land, he certainly would have spoiled Grant's plans and he might have even destroyed his army. But Pemberton utterly failed to take advantage of the opportunity. Pemberton had five divisions scattered through the triangle formed by Port Gibson, Jackson, and Vicksburg. He had only one division and two brigades of another at the scene of the opening battle. He was in no position to prevent Grant from establishing himself on the east bank. (Ambrose 15)

When Pemberton wired General Johnston of the landing, Johnston fired a telegraph back on 1 May: "If Grant's army lands on this side of the river, the safety of Mississippi depends on beating it. For that object you should unite your whole force" (*OR*, vol. 24, pt. 3, p. 808). But as his force was spread out over the state of Mississippi trying to control Grant's every move, Pemberton never did so.

With General Grant on the east shore of the Mississippi, which direction would he move? His orders were to head south after crossing the river and join with General Nathaniel P. Banks to move against Port Hudson, Louisiana. After this combined operation, the two would undertake to move northward against Vicksburg.

But Grant learned that Banks was otherwise engaged in the Red River campaign at Alexandria, Louisiana, and would not be available until May or later to move on Vicksburg. Against the advice of his subordinates and in violation of orders, he then made the decision to move on the capital of the state, Jackson, and from there would go to Vicksburg.

On 30 April, a desperate General Bowen at Grand Gulf, situated in the thick of things at Hard Times, Bruinsburg, and Port Gibson, at the mouth of the Big Black River, and faced with two Union corps, telegraphed Pemberton for reinforcement. The Federals seemed to be moving on all fronts, and all toward the direction of Grand Gulf. General Loring, first ordered by Pemberton to leave Meridian immediately and move on to Jackson with two regiments, was ordered the next day, 1 May, to leave Jackson at once and take command of the troops at Grand Gulf. Pemberton had moved to Vicksburg with his headquarters.

> But the value of Vicksburg was now gone, for Grant could cross over below the city. When this happened, General Stevenson immediately ordered every man to march at once below Vicksburg and defeat Grant's landing. General Pemberton countermanded the order, permitting only [General Edward D.] Tracy's brigade and Cockrell's Missouri brigade to meet him. These fine troops under General Bowen detained Grant only a day. With Stevenson's whole army they may have driven Grant back into the river. (Maury 189)

Pemberton threw away a chance of a lifetime.

Generals Loring and Tilghman arrived at Grand Gulf close to midnight on 2 May. Bowen briefly filled them in on the strategic situation, and Loring agreed that it was necessary to evacuate the area.

Once everything of military value in Grand Gulf had been destroyed and the troops were on the road, Loring then assumed command of the retreating columns. Rear Admiral David D. Porter's gunboats took possession of Grand Gulf on 3 May. The Mississippi was one step closer to being fully opened for north-to-south egress.

Grant, knowing that Confederate reinforcements were being assembled at Jackson, 45 miles east of Vicksburg, avoided the error of moving straight on Vicksburg without first defeating the forces in the field that could come to Pemberton's assistance. So he moved on Jackson while Pemberton assembled his troops to defend Vicksburg, thus getting between the separated wings of Pemberton's forces.

General Loring and his troops were retreating from Grand Gulf toward Hankinson's Ferry on the way to Edwards Depot. The Federals were forming to the east of him beginning their feint to move him toward Edwards Depot, not knowing he was already heading in that direction. Loring's army and its large supply train tactfully withdrew from its proximity to the

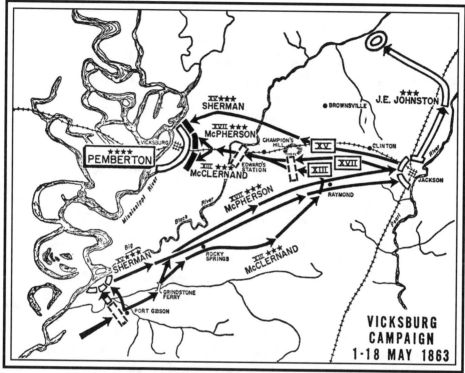

From *The Civil War Dictionary*, by Mark M. Boatner, III. (Copyright © 1957 and renewed 1987 by Mark Mayo Boatner III. Reprinted by permission of David McKay Co., a division of Random House, Inc.)

foe at Hankinson's Ferry on 4 May and established its headquarters three miles south of Mont Alban on the Baldwin Ferry-Mont Alban Road, west of the Big Black River. No sooner had Loring abandoned Hankinson's Ferry than Grant established his headquarters there.

Grant had selected Edwards Station as the army's next objective, so he determined to attempt to confuse the Confederate leaders as to where the next blow would fall. General James B. McPherson was told to have patrols reconnoiter the approaches to Warrenton, while General McClernand's troops scouted the roads leading to Fisher's and Hall's Ferries, which were held by Loring's division.

Loring's line of defense at this time was fronting on the Big Black River and in the direction of the road which led to the Big Black Bridge from near Baldwin's Ferry, to the left of General Stevenson's line, on Hall's

Ferry Road. Scattered over this six-mile distance, Loring had 6,500 fatigued men.

The differences between General Pemberton and General Loring became more obvious as the hours moved ahead in early May. General Pemberton had been put on the defense by General Grant. In fact, the first six months of the campaign in Mississippi had been all defense. Loring had other ideas: he wanted to go on the offense.

Headquarters Loring's Division,
Near Lanier's, Baldwin's Ferry Road, May 9, 1863-9:30 p.m.

Maj. R. W. Memminger,
Assistant Adjutant-General:
. . . The enemy are reported fortifying positions along the road leading to the railroad and toward Jackson. They will not attempt to pass the Big Black or move upon the railroad until this is done. Is it not, then, our policy to take the offensive before they can make themselves secure and move either way as it may suit them? . . . I believe if a well-concerted plan be adopted, we can drive the enemy into the Mississippi, if it is done in time. They don't expect anything of the kind; they think we are on the defensive. (*OR*, vol. 24, pt. 3, p. 849)

General McClernand informed Grant on 11 May that Loring was preparing to throw a force on their rear. On 12 May, sharp skirmishing ensued with Loring's troops and McClernand's XIII Corps. Grant ordered McClernand to disengage his force along the Fourteen Mile Creek, even though they were within three miles of Edwards Depot, their goal.

Meanwhile, McPherson's Union corps collided head-on with Brigadier General John Gregg's brigade at Raymond. In a furious fight with Union General John A. Logan's division, Gregg was finally forced to fall back toward Jackson. General Grant then decided to take first the capital of Mississippi. He ordered McPherson to move at daylight from Raymond toward Clinton and Jackson. Sherman would leave in the morning in the same direction, while McClernand would contain Loring's front.

At the capital, General John Adams and Governor John J. Pettus were doing their best to arm the city. A few days earlier, a concerned President

Davis had wired General Joe Johnston at Tullahoma, Tennessee, to proceed at once to Mississippi and take chief command of the forces there, giving to those in the field, as far as practicable, the encouragement and benefit of his personal direction.

On 13 May, 50 miles east of Jackson, General Johnston received word that elements of the Union corps were moving rapidly toward Jackson to cut the railroad leading west to Vicksburg. When Johnston arrived later in the day, Gregg told him that only 6,000 Confederates held the town.

Although earthworks had been thrown up around the city for its protection, Johnston deemed them not suitable and complained that they were poorly located. Having just arrived in Jackson with limited scouting reports on the enemy and the absence of promised troops, Johnston quickly decided to retreat before any pressure would be put on him to do battle. Gregg was ordered to hold the town until evacuation was complete. He then composed a message to Pemberton, who had moved his headquarters to Bovina:

> I have lately arrived, and learn that Major-General Sherman is between us, with four divisions, at Clinton. It is important to re-establish communications, that you may be re-enforced. If practicable, come up on his rear at once. To beat such a detachment, would be of immense value. The troops here could co-operate. All the strength you can quickly assemble should be brought. Time is all-important. (*OR*, vol. 24, pt. 3, p. 870)

This message was made out in triplicate and given to three couriers in the hope that one would get through to Pemberton. These instructions did reach Pemberton on 14 May, but at about the same time they were also delivered to Union General McPherson — one of Johnston's couriers was a Northern spy. The information was dispatched to General Grant.

McPherson's XVII Corps column marched southeast from Clinton while Sherman's XV Corps traveled northwest from Mississippi Springs. They soon ran into stiff Confederate opposition outside of Jackson in the pouring rain. In brisk fighting lasting over three hours, Sherman's batteries drove back the Southerners from the bridge to the trenches in the rear, requiring the Confederates to move closer to Jackson. Between 2:00 and 3:00 p.m., word from Johnston reached Gregg that the bulk of the men and materiel had cleared Jackson and were on the road to Canton, Mississippi, north of town on the Mississippi Central. Gregg ordered his men to disengage and follow Johnston north. At 4:00 p.m., Grant and Sherman entered Jackson and held a victory celebration in the Bowman House Hotel, a block north of the abandoned state capitol building.

Grant determined that Joe Johnston was retreating north to Canton and then would swing over to the Big Black River and come down the "Mechanicsburg corridor" — the ridge separating the watersheds of the Big Black and the Yazoo Rivers — to join Pemberton. Grant immediately alerted his commanders.

Since Grant was operating at the end of his supply line, he could not leave an occupying force at Jackson. He directed General Sherman to handle the dismantling of the state capital, which in effect meant to destroy all public property that might contribute to the Confederate war effort. This was the first Confederate capital to fall to the Union.

General Pemberton had been moving from Bovina to Edwards Depot to assume command of his forces when he received Johnston's order to move on Clinton. Pemberton delayed his departure from Bovina while he sent off dispatches to his key generals, alerting them to have the army ready to move forward at a moment's notice.

After these dispatches had been sent, Pemberton and his staff resumed their journey to Edwards Depot. Along the way, after weighing Johnston's orders, Pemberton began to have second thoughts regarding Johnston's wisdom. On reaching Edwards, and learning that Union General Andrew J. Smith's division was camped near Old Auburn, he decided to suspend his orders of directing a movement forward to Clinton. To the generals, officers, and men in the field, it looked like Pemberton was being true to form, changing his mind again.

He then called a council of war with his generals. After reading Johnston's orders to them and expressing his negative view of the situation, General Loring offered a counterproposal to advance and strike the Port Gibson-Raymond Road, which was Grant's line of communication. Stevenson and several other officers quickly seconded the plan. Pemberton, who wanted to sit tight and await attack, reluctantly yielded to those clamoring for battle. The badgered general adopted Loring's plan and rejected Johnston's orders, which he considered suicidal. He then sent a dispatch to Johnston informing him of the change in plans.

The movement on 15 May to begin to cut General Grant's supply line was surely not the quickest or the smoothest for Pemberton and the Confederate army. Then to complicate matters further in the midst of such turmoil, Pemberton took time to rekindle his feud with General Lloyd Tilghman, one of General Loring's finest officers.

> On the 15th of May, the day before the battle of Baker's Creek (Champion Hill), and not two hours in advance of the fulsome order to "prepare to meet the enemy," came an order from General Pemberton relieving General Tilghman of his command, and directing the senior Colonel of the brigade to take its command. . . . Here was a pretty kettle of fish. The whole army right close up, face to face, with Grant's army, twice or three times as strong, and our officers all in a stew. General Loring again cut the Gordeon knot.
>
> The next morning, even after the enemy had disturbed our early repast, this one-armed General rode squarely up to the pompous Pemberton and in language more forcible than elegant, more caustic than clever, informed the "General Commanding" that unless he then and there revoked the order of the day before in reference to General Tilghman that he might dispense with his services [Loring's] for that day's battle.
>
> And then it was that an order was hastily written — on the pummel of a saddle, I believe — restoring General Tilghman to his command. (F.W.M. 275)

This incident reinforces the charges that Pemberton was unable to direct men. His acquiescence to General Loring's demands shows that Loring was so much respected by all of the men and officers that Pemberton had no other avenue to pursue.

"Old Blizzards" Loring was somewhat stout but a vigorous man, about five feet, eleven inches tall. His thining black hair was beginning to show gray, and he combed it back and allowed it to grow very long for an officer. It hung down the back of his neck in ringlets and some of the men called him "Old Ringlets."

His anger could be terrible and his language inconceivable for an officer. In times of danger or excitement, he roared and chafed like a lion. He would roll out big oaths — when he found his artillery or wagons stalled, he cursed them out of the mire — and it almost seemed he could curse

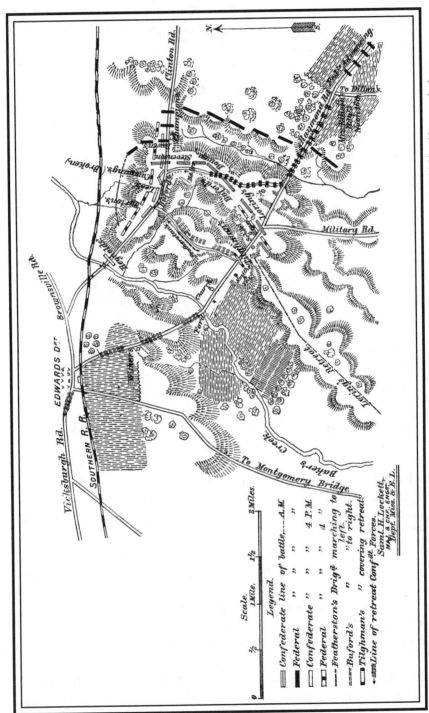

Champion Hill, May 16, 1863. (From *The Official Records of the Union and Confederate Armies*, vol. 24, pt. 2, 71.) Used by permission.

cannon up a hill without horses. There was no question that Loring could be a difficult subordinate; yet he was a benevolent superior to his junior officers.

On the morning of 16 May, the Confederate field army was strung out for about two and a half miles on two roads. It consisted of three divisions: Stevenson's (11,714), Loring's (6,300), and Bowen's (4,599) for a total of 22,971 strength. General Johnston was moving away from Jackson toward the north and west with 12,000 men, part of them just defeated in two engagements and part of them just arriving from the east as replacements. Thus, nearly 44,000 Confederate troops were scattered ineffectively over a territory 50 miles long and 20 miles wide and divided into three detachments, ready to do battle.

Lacking cavalry and adequate scouting, Pemberton's army was moving with scarcely any definite knowledge of the Union armies' positions. Conflicting messages that seesawed between Johnston and Pemberton and the general lack of leadership would bring things to a bad pass for the Confederates.

General Grant had five and a half divisions for a total of about 44,000 troops, all within ten miles of the railroad between Bolton and Edwards Station. All were within a few hours' march of each other and were located between the two principal Confederate detachments, greatly outnumbering each of them, although no more numerous than all of the Confederate detachments if combined.

The wisdom of keeping an army united and the folly of dividing it into detachments apparently never entered into Pemberton's plans. He seemed possessed to protect fortress Vicksburg, the Gibraltar of the Mississippi.

At 6:30 a.m. on 16 May, Pemberton received another order from General Johnston reiterating his command to move north of the railroad so that he could form a junction of the armies. He further told Pemberton his move southward against Grant would have to be abandoned.

Pemberton realized from the slow and poor move of the previous day that his plan had degenerated and decided he would obey Johnston's latest order. Pemberton at once gave instructions to reverse his order of march and to get back across Baker's Creek. The about-face movement meant that Pemberton's wagon trains, which on the advance had been at the end, were now at the head of the column. Field artillery and the ordnance wagons were unable to move because of the jam on this narrow road. General Carter L. Stevenson was to see that the supply train was driven as rapidly as possible to a point at least three miles beyond the Jackson road.

This retrograde movement had hardly begun on the morning of the 16th when skirmishing between Loring's cavalry pickets and that of McClernand's corps became brisk. When the skirmishing escalated into full-scale battle later that morning, a soldier of the 3rd Mississippi Regiment under General Loring reported that "we wuz the first to git it":

> Our skirmishers were out front firin'. Then we saw 'em runnin' back to our main line. Then they came, in the thousands. Over their heads came the artillery, blastin' all about us. . . . Then the Blue lines wuz seen comin' from the south. They wuz comin' at a double quick, bayonets fixed. . . . We unloaded at their cavalry and infantry, sendin' 'em rollin' back on their first charge. They kept comin' for more'n hour. . . . (Greenwell 56-57)

General McClernand, in front of Loring, was then admonished to move cautiously; thus, there was no advance by the Union columns posted on the Middle and Raymond roads.

Within a 24-hour period, 65,000 men, horses, and wagons from both armies would converge on and inhabit a two-and-a-half-mile stretch of countryside outside of Edwards Depot. No earthen levee had been erected, no trenches dug; only a smattering of unsurveyed ravines and land and bushes separated the tide of the Blue and Gray. This then became a huge, snakelike battle line two and a half miles long. Like a giant firecracker, when lit at one end it quickly spread down the line. When the firing on and skirmishing with Loring's troops early in the morning rapidly spread to the Clinton Road, it did not "hiss out"; instead, it let go with one big bang, and the battle of Champion Hill began.

Pemberton was directing his attention to the lethargic bluecoats on the Raymond and Middle Roads instead of staying in touch with Generals Stevenson and Stephen Lee, who had a disaster on their hands. "We stood in position for some time; the firing on the left grew in volume all the time, showing that the enemy was making his attack on our left and trying to cut us off from Edwards depot" (Greif 351).

A formidable attack had been precipitated on an unexpected line, at a right angle to the first line of defense that Pemberton had prepared. Three Federal divisions were moving rapidly, and Pemberton had found himself immediately outnumbered on the northeast end of the line.

To cope with the threat, he had quickly ordered General Lee of Stevenson's division to shift his brigade to the left. When Stevenson moved to confront the Federals on the Jackson Road, he opened a large gap in the Confederate defense line. This gap could be filled only if General Bowen and General Loring moved toward the northeast.

As the engagement at Champion Hill intensified, Pemberton ordered General Bowen, who was commanding the middle of the defense line, to send one of his brigades at once to the support of Stevenson. Neither Bowen nor Loring wanted to weaken their position lest the front cave in, but Bowen complied with Pemberton's order.

In Loring's official report, he points out that General Bowen was moved to the left without warning. Bowen's departure left Loring alone on the Coker House ridge of defense, with four blue divisions in plain sight. When the summons came for him to follow Bowen, he declined. It would be suicidal to move and permit McClernand to begin his offense. But he did close the gap as quickly as possible by moving General Abe Buford and his 2nd Brigade toward Bowen.

As the battle flared, so did the orders from General Pemberton. Loring reports:

> Soon a series of orders came, specifically and with great particularity, for two of my brigades to move to the left, closing the line as often as Bowen moved, and we in this manner followed him.
>
> During this time I received an order to retire, also one to advance, both of which were countermanded. My whole division, including reserves, was strung out in line of battle, mostly in thick timber. The enemy during these movements remained steadily in front in heavy force, being, apparently, a full corps, occupying a series of ridges, wooded, and commanding each other, forming naturally a very strong if not impregnable position, throwing forward a heavy line of skirmishers, and showing every indication of an attack in force upon my position, both in front and upon the right flank. (*OR*, vol. 24, pt. 2, p. 75)

It was at about this time, 12:35 p.m., that General Grant gave General McClernand instructions to attack Loring's front.

As the afternoon battle continued, the pressure upon Stevenson and Bowen at the northeast end of the battle line mounted. When General John A. Logan added the weight of his division to the Yanks' cause, the line at Champion Hill became unsupportable for the Rebels.

Pemberton asked for Loring a second time, and by 2:00 p.m., Loring was with his 3rd Brigade, commanded by General Winfield S. Featherston, moving to the left, following General Buford's movement. Loring, riding with General Thomas H. Taylor, Pemberton's provost marshal, had not followed the popular Plantation Road where his flank would be exposed to McClernand's forces. Instead, with the assistance of a guide, he moved on an unused road that led in a westerly direction and carried him through woods and over very rough ground a distance of two miles before reaching the scene of conflict. The march was as rapid as possible under the circumstances, and the troops moved at double-quick time most of the way.

But by this time, Pemberton, finding that the enemy's vastly superior numbers were pressing all his forces, believed it too late to save the day, even should Loring or Featherston's brigade come up immediately. When General Bowen personally informed him that he could not hold his position any longer, Pemberton then ordered a retreat toward Vicksburg.

Before this retreat order could be communicated, Loring had surfaced to the left of Stevenson. General Buford reports, "All the troops of our center and of the left wing were leaving the field in great disorder. I therefore threw my brigade back about a quarter mile from the negro cabins, and in the direction of Edwards Depot where I joined General Loring with General Featherston's brigade" (*OR*, vol. 24, pt. 2, p. 84). General Stephen D. Lee came up with a part of his brigade:

> My brigade was then rallied about half a mile from the Edwards Depot road and in rear of Buford's brigade, Loring's division, which had just arrived on the field at about 3:30 p.m. Major-General Loring soon after came up with Featherston's brigade, and recognizing him as the senior officer on the field, and not seeing my division commander (Major-General Stevenson), I reported to him for orders, and was placed on the left of Featherston's brigade. (*OR*, vol. 24, pt. 2, p. 102)

The 3rd Mississippi Regiment reported: "We made it to Champion Hill, with the rest of the division followin' close behind with General Lorin' leadin' from his mount. The old seasoned trooper we called 'im 'Old Guzzards' and he rode stiff and proud like someone out of a crusaders army in the old days" (Greenwell 58).

Loring, in the absence of Pemberton, and being the senior officer on the field, assumed command of this brave army:

> It was necessary, in order to save large numbers of men and guns, as well as to be able, in case the emergency should arise, to retire the army in safety and good order to the ford over Baker's Creek, along the only road open to it, that a vigorous and well-directed attack should be made upon the enemy. At this moment I met General Lee and Colonel [William T.] Withers, and was satisfied, from information obtained from them, that by such an attack upon the enemy's right during the panic which had befallen his center we could overwhelm it, retrieve the day, certainly cut him off from the bridge on our extreme left (of which it was highly important we should hold possession), and save our scattered forces. (*OR*, vol. 24, pt. 2, p. 76)

Loring had taken charge of the situation at the front. General Lee was told to reform his battered brigade on Featherston's left. As soon as Lee's Alabamans were in position, Loring would attack the enemy troops holding the Jackson road. Colonel Elijah Gates, 1st Missouri Cavalry, reported, "General Green sent me word that General Loring was preparing for a charge, and did not want his brigade to be behind in the charge" (*OR*, vol. 24, pt. 2, p. 118).

An aide then spurred up on a sweat-streaked horse with orders for Loring from Pemberton to retreat in the direction they had come. Loring thought, as did Featherston and Withers, that the day was not lost, and after hesitating a moment, Loring commanded, "Forward." Moments later, General Tom Taylor of Pemberton's staff rode up and preemptorily ordered the army to fall back on Edwards Depot.

General Loring's actions at Champion Hill were later approved by General Joe Johnston, much to the chagrin of Pemberton:

> General Johnston defends the inaction of my subordinate Lor-

ing who constituted himself . . . "the judge" of the propriety of the orders he had received and which were again and again repeated to him during the heat of the engagement. Johnston's excuses that officer's long delayed obedience, not because he considered that immediate obedience was impracticable, but because "Loring did not think it advisable to obey." (Pemberton 317)

But it was Loring's prerogative, as the field commander, and based on 20 years of active field service with the U.S. Army, to decide what was the proper thing to do at any particular time. This came from experience and not uncertainty. President Davis's orders had been to not go into a siege at Vicksburg, and General Joe Johnston had wanted Pemberton to join him at Canton. General Loring had acted in the best interest of the Confederate service.

Pemberton's army was forced back, step by step at first, but then the retreat to Vicksburg became a rout. Grant placed McClernand and fresh troops in charge of the pursuit. Major Samuel H. Lockett was sent by Pemberton to inform General Tilghman that "the position he occupied was one of vast importance in securing our retreat and that it must be held at all hazards" (*OR*, vol. 24, pt. 2, p. 70). Union General A. J. Smith moved upon Tilghman and attacked vigorously. With less than 1,500 men, Tilghman held Smith in check and kept open the only line left upon which the Confederate army could retreat. Tilghman gallantly lost his life in directing the fire of his artillery from Cotton Hill, where a long and spirited artillery duel took place. Tilghman had delayed the enemy.

By the time darkness was falling, the gateway to Edwards Depot, the Big Black Bridge, and Vicksburg was closed to General Loring. Quickly General Buford secured a guide who could lead the division to a ford on Baker's Creek, below the Big Black Bridge. Loring was still showing every evidence of following Pemberton into Vicksburg. But instead of being only three or four miles to the crossing, which the guide had led them to believe, it was 10 or 12 miles, and by then it was after midnight. The guide then informed Loring that it was impossible to lead the division to Big Black Bridge with the enemy in possession of Edwards Depot.

> I was ordered with my command to hold the rear, to enable the army to make good its retreat. . . .The enemy moved to a position commanding the ford in my front . . . necessarily forcing me to look to a ford lower down the creek, and to reach it had to pass through fields and swamps. . . . We lost what artillery we had. . . . My only means of preventing my division from being overwhelmed was to force my way through the enemy's lines under cover of night. (*OR*, vol. 24, pt. 2, pp. 73-74)

Loring's shrewdness, borne of years of military experience then came into full play. He decided that he would not join Pemberton in Vicksburg; that he would detach his three brigades there and then, not surrender them; and that he would march the distance to keep his force free and able to fight another day. "Gen. Loring came riding down our lines close up to us, and was encouraging the boys and told us that we had been sold, but he would be — if we should be delivered, and called on all to follow him and he would take us out" (Manahan 227). The men had fought all day, yet they had the stamina to begin moving southeast toward Crystal Springs, a village on the New Orleans, Jackson & Great Northern Railroad, 25 miles south of Jackson. What was remarkable about this movement was that it was done with not just a few men; it was done with three brigades numbering around 6,000 men, or about 27 percent of the Confederate field army. Loring managed to slip them around the Union divisions of Generals A. J. Smith and Francis P. Blair, who had set up camp for the night. "We passed so near the enemy on the night of the 16th that we could hear them talking. As we were approaching a road which crossed the one on which we were marching, General Loring learned that the enemy had a strong picket post at the cross-roads. He dressed a courier in a Yankee uniform and sent him around to come up the road and order the picket withdrawn. They obeyed the order promptly, as we had a clear road" (Greif 352).

The troops marched all night and all the next day, stopping frequently but briefly to rest, and after going 46 miles, they bivouacked near Crystal Springs late at night on 17 May. The worn-down brigades remained in camp at Crystal Springs until 10:00 a.m. on Monday, 18 May, when orders

were given by General Johnston to move to Jackson. To help prevent straggling, Loring purposely held down the pace of the march. The roadways
were rough and stony, and many of the men were barefooted. They
reached the recently torched capital on the 19th. Straggling had been
severe. Loring's division, on the morning of the battle of Champion Hill,
had mustered 7,800 officers and men; on 24 May, Loring reported that he
had 4,862 officers and men present and ready for duty. He had thus lost
nearly 3,000 men on his forced march.

While Loring had been marching to Crystal Springs on Sunday,
17 May, the situation outside of Vicksburg grew worse. Pemberton had
placed the army in position on the east bank of the Big Black River where
the Confederates hoped to stop the Union men.

But at daylight, General Sherman's fresh corps of bluecoats opened
with their Parrott guns and advanced against the left wing of the Confederate army. One of the brigades became panic-stricken and broke and fled
in confusion without firing a gun or striking a blow.

Pemberton, for the first time in his long military career, found himself
commander of a routed army. Under this terrific pressure, Pemberton gave
orders for the army to fall back to Vicksburg with Major General Stevenson conducting the retreat. Lockett was given instructions to destroy the
crossings. Loose cotton and fence rails, drenched with turpentine, were
piled at strategic places along the railroad bridge, and brimming barrels of
turpentine were set afire.

The Union generals were stunned by the unexpected ease of their
early movement and had difficulty in getting immediately organized to
pursue the fleeing army. But the bridges were blazing and no one would
follow on that morning. Pemberton was retreating into Vicksburg. General Grant remarked, "But for the successful and complete destruction of the
bridge, we should have followed the enemy so closely as to prevent his
occupying his defenses around Vicksburg" (Eisenschiml and Newman
445).

Had Loring's movement to Crystal Springs been counterproductive to
Pemberton's intention to defend Vicksburg at all costs? Pemberton had
probably been waiting for Loring while defending the Big Black Bridge

The William Wing Loring, CSA, bust in Vicksburg, Mississippi, located on Confederate Avenue, west of the battlefield. It was erected in 1912 at a cost of $1,200.

WILLIAM W. LORING
MAJOR GENERAL C·S·ARMY
COMMANDING DIVISION
MARCH 29-JULY 4, 1863

and was certainly hoping that Loring would show on the east side of the river on the morning of the 17th, but it had been impossible for Loring to join him. The importance of Champion Hill and its calamitous result finds its level of truth from many sources.

In reviewing the battle, while not condoning Loring's flagrant disregard of orders, it appears that the basic Confederate tactical mistakes were Pemberton's. In blasting Loring, Pemberton was looking for a scapegoat. Pemberton was not in a good position when he complained of his junior's failure to carry out instructions. Loring had for his guidance Pemberton's disregard of Johnston's May 13 order. (Bearss, *Decision in Mississippi*, 293)

If the evidence of all the events transpiring at this time could be laid before an intelligent jury, the verdict would not be flattering to the General of the Army of . . . Mississippi. . . . If common discretion had been exercised, the responsibility and the evils of the catastrophe that fell upon Pemberton afterward would have been averted. The whole series of fights from the time that Grant crossed the river until the surrender of Vicksburg was a fatal blunder, no matter who it was planned by or who sanctioned it. . . . There was one man of sense — General Loring. He absolutely refused to go into Vicksburg, and declared to General Pemberton that he would not obey his orders, and he did, with about 10,000 [*sic*] men, cut his way out in spite of General Grant's cordon. (Hogane 227)

During the day's fighting, Champion Hill and the crossroads had changed hands three times. In a one-hour climactic fight, Grant's 10,000 Federals routed Bowen's 4,000 Confederates, capturing over 1,700 men and 18 guns. By nightfall, Confederate figures showed 381 killed, 1,800 wounded, and 1,670 missing, for a total of 3,851 casualties. The Federal army had 410 killed, 1,844 wounded, and 187 missing, for a total of 2,441. It had been a bad day for both sides.

Chapter 10

The Army of Relief
in Mississippi

*A*T THE BEGINNING *of May, addi-*
tional troops had been ordered to
Mississippi to aid General Pember-
ton's army. By 24 May, when Gen-
eral Loring and his 4,800 men had traveled
from Crystal Springs to Jackson, the Army of
Relief, as it was called, numbered around
12,000 officers and men, with more on the
way. As the reinforcements arrived, they
wound up with Loring at his headquarters
north of Jackson.

When Johnston moved to join Pemberton he had but two
brigades — [Brigadier General John] Gregg's and [Major General William H. T.] Walker's — their aggregate strength being
six thousand men; and that was his army until the return to Canton. Here he was joined, on the 20th and 21st of May, by
[Brigadier General "States Rights"] Gist from [Lieutenant General P. G. T.] Beauregard, and [Brigadier General Matthew D.]
Ector and [Brigadier General Evander] McNair from Bragg. At
the same time Loring's division, happily separated from Pemberton during the rout of Baker's Creek, entered Jackson.
(Hughes 194-195)

These units numbered around 17,000 men.

The presence of Johnston's Army of Relief in the rear of the Army of
the Tennessee troubled General Grant. To meet Johnston, Grant placed
more than half of his army in a line facing east, which extended from
Haynes' Bluff on the Yazoo to the railroad bridge on the Big Black, being
thus guarded on each flank by a river.

General Loring at Jackson would have little time for rest and regroup-
ing. The Mechanicsburg corridor would soon become very active with
bluecoats.

On 30 May, General Johnston transferred General Loring's left wing
from Jackson to Canton to back up General H. T. Walker. On the 31st, Loring had 5,500 of his men above the break in the New Orleans, Jackson &
Great Northern Railroad; from there, the trains hauled the soldiers to Canton. The trains then returned to the Jackson area to shuttle the remainder
of Loring's division and Brigadier General Samuel B. Maxey's brigade
back from Port Hudson to the same destination.

The Confederacy continued to pour seasoned troops into Mississippi
to stem the Union tide of victory. By 1 June, Major General John C.
Breckinridge's "Orphan Brigade" of 5,200 men, from middle Tennessee,
reached Jackson. This force was augmented by the arrival of Brigadier
General Nathan G. "Shanks" Evans's "tramp" brigade from South Carolina. Evans's brigade was to remain at Jackson. Loring spread his division out in the countryside around the town, and the men settled into
their new environment. They were three and a half miles from the Big
Black.

Two days later, Brigadier General William H. Jackson's 3,000-strong cavalry division, riding 350 miles from Spring Hill, Tennessee, reached Canton. In a period of a few short weeks, the Army of Relief had grown much faster than General Johnston or the Department of Mississippi could handle. The troops arriving from the east were very tired from their journey on old trains. There was also a deficient supply of all size ammunitions, artillery pieces, field transportation, horses, mules, foodstuff, shoes, medical supplies, tents, and camp equipment. Pemberton had moved everything into fortress Vicksburg for his defense of the city. The re-equipping of the Army of Relief would take weeks. By the middle of June, Johnston would have the manpower but not the supplies to move on the Federal forces. This delay benefited Grant.

To organize the 31,000 officers and men ready to move on Grant, Johnston delineated divisions under Loring, Breckinridge, Walker, and Major General Samuel G. French in addition to the cavalry division. Johnston then marked time waiting for supplies and ammunition. When Grant learned that a strong force of Rebels commanded by Loring occupied Jackson, he expressed alarm and issued orders directing General Peter J. Osterhaus to put his troops and hired negroes to work demolishing the railroad east of the Big Black River. Osterhaus's men destroyed the railroad between the Big Black and Edwards Depot and systematically stripped the area of cotton, livestock, forage, and foodstuffs, making it more difficult for Johnston to subsist his army.

Communications between Pemberton's and Johnston's armies was utterly impossible. In appearance on the map, General Grant was caught between two large Confederate forces, but the fact was that the Confederates did not know where the other was or what they were doing or planning, while Grant knew exactly where both armies were. Grant treasured this fact and sealed off Vicksburg so that nothing came or went unless he said so. It doomed any meaningful dialogue between the two Confederate armies.

As the Yankees tightened their grip on the approaches to Vicksburg, couriers experienced increasing difficulty in slipping in and out of the beleaguered city. General Walker offered a reward of 30 days' furlough and a fine saddle horse to ride during the balance of the war to any man who would carry a dispatch to General Pemberton. Loring called for volunteers to carry percussion caps through Federal lines. Thirty volunteered, among them a Captain W. L. Gay of the 22nd Mississippi. Nearly all were killed or captured; only two reached Vicksburg. Captain

Gay, after remaining for ten days inside Federal lines, subsisting upon blackberries, was forced to return to Loring without reaching Pemberton's line.

Grant called for and immediately received 12 new regiments of reinforcements from Memphis. Based on new enemy activity, Johnston issued orders to Loring's division and Jackson's cavalry to move from Canton to Yazoo City at daybreak on 5 June. At this time, the hot weather became nearly unbearable. Private W. J. Davidson at Camp Yazoo City reported: "My Division arrived here after dark last night. The troops suffered greatly from heat, thirst and fatigue. Two of our brigade men dropped dead, some fainted on the march, while more than half are straggling into camp this morning. We traveled all yesterday without water except what we could get through charity of the citizens on the route" (Bearss, *Vicksburg*, 3:1006). The troopers and animals were placed and stationed according to the supply of water, as a drought had created a scarcity.

Between 7 and 17 June, General Grant received an additional 21,000 reinforcements, which gave him numerical strength over the Rebels. On 11 June, General Johnston notified General Walker that preparations for a forward movement were nearly completed. Johnston was prepared to put his Army of Relief in motion: "I intend simply to examine the enemy's lines, and see if there [is] any prospect of breaking them in order to save the garrison" (Greene 193).

The Army of Relief, now 32,000 strong with 78 artillery pieces and hundreds of supply wagons, began moving out on 18 June from several staging areas in its bid to save Vicksburg and Pemberton. Breckinridge's combat-tested division tramped out of Jackson; French's division left its cantonment on Mrs. Carraway's plantation; and Loring's and Walker's divisions left Vernon. General Loring began the movement and crossed over the Big Black with his division.

On 3 July, Johnston and his Army of Relief were within musket shot of the enemy. Would the rescue of Pemberton be made in time to save his army and Vicksburg? From Confederate headquarters at Carney Creek, General French recorded: "I rode over to meet Johnston. Found Loring, Walker and Jackson present. We spent nine hours vainly attempting to get accurate information from the citizens respecting the road and streams but little could be learned of the country on either side of the Big Black that was satisfactory because it was so contradictory" (French 182).

While Johnston and his commanders dallied on the 3rd of July, Pemberton, who had had no communication with Johnston and did not know of the plans of Johnston's imminent attack, assembled his four division commanders for consultation within Vicksburg. The unanimous decision was for surrender.

At 10:00 a.m. on 4 July, the Confederate troops marched out of Vicksburg, stacked arms, laid their colors upon them, and then returned to the town. General Logan's division marched in to take possession. Johnston's well-planned but belated campaign to relieve Vicksburg had failed. Jefferson Davis lamented that the Confederacy had lost the "nail-head" that held the South's two halves together. With the surrender of Vicksburg went the trans-Mississippi, with all of its rich resources, as well as its much-needed army of over 30,000 men. They would not be able to cross the river and were effectively isolated.

On this same date, General Robert E. Lee began his retreat from bloody Gettysburg. The coincidence was tragic that two mortal blows struck the Confederacy on the same day.

With the news of a truce flag at Vicksburg, Sherman ordered up a striking force of 12 divisions to pursue and chase Johnston's forces. Marching orders toward the Big Black were issued immediately. On the afternoon of the 4th, scouts brought word to Johnston that the enemy was already crossing the Big Black at Messinger's Ferry.

Johnston was then forced to extricate his Army of Relief from its dangerously exposed position near the Big Black River. Long before daybreak on 6 July, Johnston's four infantry divisions had their gear packed and had begun the movement back toward Jackson. Again, the stifling Mississippi heat and acute shortage of water had the army strung out for miles on the narrow roads. With thousands of soldiers, horses, mules, and wagons trudging along, the dust became so intense that men and animals had trouble breathing. The Army of Relief retreated 25 miles in two days, arriving in Jackson on 7 July.

Jackson remained the only Confederate stronghold left in Mississippi. With the call of Champion Hill, the capital had been abandoned by Sherman within 24 hours, and the Confederates had returned to claim their city. But how long could Johnston hold it? The Jackson perimeter — an irregular crescent shape, about two and a half miles deep and two miles wide with both of the flanks well anchored to the Pearl River — would be defended by Loring, Walker, French, and Breckinridge.

Sherman's bluecoats reached Jackson the afternoon of 10 July. Two days later, he directed an order to open fire on the town and its defenses. The Union cannoneers sprang into action and sent 3,000 projectiles, both solid and explosive, into the designated area. The crossfire of shot and shell reached all parts of the capital, showing Johnston that the position he held would be untenable under the fire of a powerful artillery, which Sherman was readying.

In addition, the Confederates' supply line was still inadequate. Johnston, in a telegram to President Davis designed to prepare the commander in chief for the news that Jackson might have to be evacuated, wrote: "If the position and works were not bad, want of stores would make it impossible to withstand a siege. If the enemy will not attack, we must, at the last moment withdraw" (Bearss, *Battle*, 83).

From 10 to 16 July, Sherman's army poured lead, iron, and steel into Jackson but refused to make a frontal attack. Johnston wired Davis on the 16th, "The enemy is evidently making a siege which we cannot resist. It would be madness to attack him" (Howell 225). The abandonment of Jackson could not be deferred much longer.

Johnston then informed his officers to leave their positions and issued detailed instructions for a "secret" evacuation of the city that night. Preparatory to crossing the Pearl, Loring and Walker assembled their divisions on the low, level ground east of the capital. Loring's division, following Walker's, crossed the upper bridge at Carson's Ferry. Once on the Pearl's east bank, the divisions, accompanied by their trains, tramped rapidly eastward toward Brandon, Mississippi. "Once across the low-level river they silently wove their way over the narrow twisting road to Brandon, eleven miles away. Straggling was epidemic as the weary column marched eastward away from the former capital city. The governor and his staff once again fled to east Mississippi to establish a government in exile" (Howell 226-227). By the morning of the 17th, 30,000 Confederates and thousands of horses and wagons had slipped out of Jackson under the noses of a much larger army.

General Edward Ferrero's and General Blair's divisions of General Frederick Steele's corps entered the city. Sherman made his headquarters in the governor's mansion and dashed off a telegram to Grant reporting the fall of Jackson and explaining that the weather was too hot and the country too destitute for a vigorous pursuit. Grant, however, wanted Johnston's army to be chased, so Sherman ordered several brigades to go as far as

Brandon, Johnston's original destination. But scarcity of water at Brandon had forced the Army of Relief to keep moving eastward. The Rebel army was in retreat; Grant and Sherman had failed to destroy it.

A colorful report to Admiral David D. Porter from Sherman at Jackson states, "We must admit these rebels out travel us. . . . The enemy burned nearly all the handsome dwellings round about the town because they gave us shelter. . . . Jackson, once the pride and boast of Mississippi, is now a ruined town. The good folks . . . will not soon again hear their favorite locomotive whistle" (*OR*, vol. 24, pt. 3, p. 531).

The Army of Relief marched about 60 miles to the east over the next six days, first in heat and dust, then in torrential Mississippi rains. At Morton, Johnston established his headquarters, and the balance of the army strung itself out for miles along the Southern Railroad of Mississippi, with Loring settling at Forest Station. As Sherman pulled back to Vicksburg, the Big Black River became a rough frontier between Union occupied territory and the Rebel hinterland.

General Sherman had undoubtedly believed that the Rebels, after their defeat at Jackson, were demoralized to the point of desertion. There was no need for the powerful Union army to pursue and destroy them; they would most likely disband and disappear on their own.

But Johnston had been lucky. His casualties had been light: only 71 men killed, 504 wounded, and 25 missing during the entire Jackson campaign. And he had been blessed with a mature cadre of commanders rather than recent appointees. Johnston himself was 56 years old, and his four infantry division commanders — Loring, Breckinridge, French, and Walker — were all in their forties. It was this "old guard" that had held the army together at such a precarious time. Despite Sherman's predictions that the Army of Relief would disband, no such thing happened. On 30 July, they still had 30,000 aggregate present.

But by the middle of August, Federal threats in other parts of the nation led sections of the Confederate army away. General Braxton Bragg called for General Breckinridge's division to aid the Confederacy at Chattanooga, and General Walker sent two of his brigades to assist at Atlanta. Within a short period, Johnston had sent most of his army from central Mississippi, leaving Loring and General William H. "Red" Jackson with only 6,000 men to cover most of the state.

September through November 1863 found Loring's troops at Enterprise, Mississippi, to help in paroling and exchanging the Vicksburg army. Loring's division benefited as the conscripts and returning absentees reported at Enterprise. By 30 September, Loring's headquarters were at Meridian.

After the battle of Chickamauga on 20 and 21 September, Federal troops and cavalry began to appear in western Mississippi. On 15 October, Loring received word that 4,000 troops with 100 wagons had passed through Holly Springs going south. To meet this incursion, Loring hastened to Grenada with his division, making his headquarters at Canton.

In order to take the pressure off of Sherman's supply line at Memphis, General Grant ordered McPherson at Vicksburg to lead a task force of 8,000 men on 21 October against Loring at Canton. "Red" Jackson's cavalry repulsed the superior Union force, and they did not capture Canton. But the Union diversion was successful as it pulled many Confederate troops out of northern Mississippi, away from Sherman's supply line.

Once Sherman moved toward Chattanooga, the Vicksburg area quieted and Loring's division embarked upon a brief period when there was no fighting.

On 29 November, General Loring sent a long letter of introduction to General Jackson about Miss Mary, who was seeking help. Was this Loring's fiancée?

> This [letter] will be given you by Miss Mary Williamson, who you will be pleased to know. . . . I need not tell you that she is accomplished, sweet and pretty, this you will perceive upon seeing her. . . . Her Father & only brother are in the army, they are left at Edwards Depot without the means of subsistence & their necessities compel them to remain in the only home they have, the enemy destroyed all else & took away their negroes. She says that starvation is upon them unless they are allowed to pass into Vicksburg with five bales of cotton to get the neces-

saries of life. . . . I do not know whether pressing emergencies authorize you, if they did, I know the tear of beauty would never pass uncared for by you.

But far more eloquent than I, let Miss Mary tell her own story. If there is no authority in cases like this, there ought to be.

(William Hicks Jackson Papers)

Later, on 2 February 1864, a member of the 20th Mississippi Regiment penned home a letter: "It is said [General Loring] was engaged to be married to a very beautiful young lady, living near Port Gibson, who died a few weeks ago." This story has never been verified.

Chapter 11

The
Meridian Campaign

O N 15 DECEMBER, General Loring
gave a grand ball with the beauties
of Madison and Rankin Counties in
attendance. While the ball ushered in
the Christmas season in Canton, the Yankees
had a yuletide greeting of their own for the
general back in St. Augustine: "The 'Loring
House' property, recently owned by the min-
or children of Charles Loring [the general's
older brother], is sold for unpaid tax
charged thereon, under an Act entitled 'An

Act for the collection of direct taxes in Insurrectionary Districts within the United States'" (Commissioner of Internal Revenue). The old homestead property had been seized by the Federal government.

On 16 December, General Joe Johnston was relieved of command of the Army of Mississippi by President Davis and was ordered to proceed to Dalton, Georgia, to assume command of the Army of Tennessee. Lieutenant General Leonidas Polk, a personal friend of the President and an Episcopal bishop, was given Johnston's command. He established his headquarters at Meridian, Mississippi, and referred to it as the Department of the Southwest. His army would consist of two divisions of infantry commanded by Major Generals W. W. Loring and Samuel G. French.

Many of the officers and men took leave for the holidays, but after 1 January 1864, General Loring would find vigilance the order of the day as he was the outer defense rim of Jackson. He would be the first to learn of any Federal activity in the chess game that was being played with Sherman, who was returning from a victory at Lookout Mountain, Tennessee.

General Grant wrote on 15 January: "I shall direct Sherman to move out to Meridian with his spare force and destroy the roads east and south of there so effectually that the enemy will not attempt to rebuild them during the rebellion" (*OR*, vol. 32, pt. 2, p. 100). Sherman concurred: "The single track from Meridian to Selma is the only link that unites Mississippi to Alabama and Georgia, and . . . its destruction will do more to isolate the State of Mississippi than any single act" (*OR*, vol. 32, pt. 2, p. 114).

At Canton on 18 January, Loring "ordered works to be constructed at Deasonville (north of Canton) for the protection of the railroad, which, with that of the works to connect with Jackson, is of immediate military necessity" (Mississippi Department of Archives and History). News then came for General "Red" Jackson in the field that the enemy had been reinforced at Vicksburg on the night of 27 January by 15 transports of troops. General Nathan Bedford Forrest, one of Polk's cavalry commanders, in northwestern Mississippi next wired General Loring that the enemy had evacuated LaGrange and was reported moving from Colliersville in his direction.

This news was enough to convince Loring that Sherman would be moving quickly to drive the Confederates out of Mississippi. Loring wanted to stay and fight them; he was not interested in moving out. But his suggestions to General Polk, who was on his way to Mobile, Alabama, for an inspection, fell upon deaf ears.

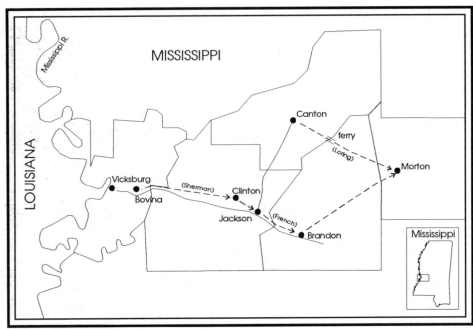

Loring's retreat toward Morton. (Map by R. J. Vreeland)

The road work and bridge at Deasonville would never be completed. Loring prepared to begin withdrawing toward Calhoun's Ferry. Sherman's Meridian expedition was about to begin.

Sherman's corps, some 25,000 men, left Vicksburg on 3 February in two columns, General Stephen A. Hurlbut's by Messinger's Ferry and General James Birdseye McPherson's by the railroad bridge, with a goal to chase the Confederates out of Mississippi and to capture the village of Meridian, 125 miles east of Vicksburg. The small town was a transportation center with all types of military stores stockpiled. To confuse the Rebel command, Sherman started rumors that the Federals were headed for Selma, Alabama, or even Mobile.

Reports began to filter into Loring's headquarters about Sherman's advance. At 10:30 p.m. on 5 February, Loring wired General French at Jackson: "I shall move my Division by daylight to Madison Station enroute for Morton" (*OR*, vol. 32, pt. 2, p. 674).

Because General Polk was in Mobile, he issued orders on 4 February placing General Loring in command of the operations on the Western front of the Department of Mississippi:

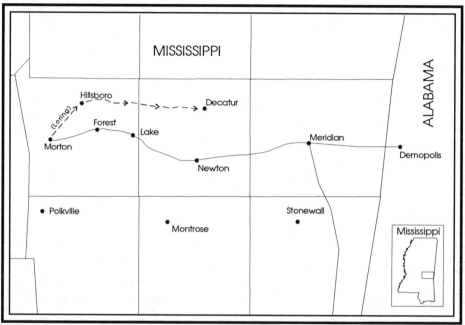

Loring's retreat continues to Newton using the Hillsborough Road. (Map by R. J. Vreeland)

You will take command of the military operations . . . until further orders. General Forrest has been ordered to leave a force sufficient to check the enemy on the Tennessee front and to move with the whole of the rest of his force to Grenada. General French has been ordered with his division to Jackson, where he now is. Generals French, Lee, and Forrest have been advised that you have been placed in command. (*OR*, vol. 32, pt. 2, p. 671)

The Confederates retreated to the southeast, toward Morton. Loring's division camped on the night of the 6th about 14 miles northwest of Morton. All during the frigid night of 7 February and the cold morning of 8 February, the Confederate army arrived at Morton. General Polk reported to General S. Cooper, the Adjutant and Inspector General, that "my infantry force in this part of the department consists of Maj.-General Loring's division, about 6,000 men, and French's 1,250, with 1,700 exchanged prisoners imperfectly organized — say 9,000" (*OR*, vol. 32, pt. 1, p. 335). Also arriving at Morton was General William A. Quarles's and General Francis M. Cockrell's brigades that had arrived from Mobile. Meanwhile, General Polk returned from Mobile and made his headquarters at Meridian, Mississippi. General Loring remained in command of the field forces.

On 5 February, Sherman's forces had surged into Jackson for the third time within six months and had chased General French and his limited forces toward Brandon. Sherman remained in Jackson long enough for the city to suffer, leaving it in flames as he began moving his army east towards Brandon.

The Union army now took on a unique appearance as it was joined into one long, blue, snakelike column of 25,000 men, wagons, mules, and horses. It became a Yankee juggernaut. The drums beat the tempo and the columns marched close together. Its firepower was so heavy that the Confederate cavalry could not get near it. "As the Union column converged on Brandon on the 8th, French cleared out leaving some of the buildings burning. After Sherman got into the area, it was no better than Jackson. The most exact summary of the affair was noted in the diary of Otto Wolfe of the 119th Illinois, "marched through Brandon, burned down most of Brandon" (M. Bearss 93).

At Morton on the morning of the 8th, Loring decided to stop and fight the bluecoats. He commenced moving his troops westward, back toward Brandon, to meet Sherman's column. A line was formed two miles from Morton. General French reported:

> This morning Loring placed the whole force at my command to face about, form line of battle, and give the enemy a fight. . . . Some skirmishing ensued. We held a good position and the troops were in fine spirits, but the enemy would not attack us. At a council held it was deemed best to continue to fall back and await the arrival of [General William E.] Baldwin's Brigade and [General Stephen D.] Lee with his cavalry, so we marched all night to Hillsboro. (French 189)

After sunset on the 8th, Loring wired General Polk and other officers that his troops were compelled to fall back to Newton Station, 33 miles east of Morton, but by way of the indirect Hillsborough road. Loring probably believed that this route would keep him in front of Sherman as the road was so bad. The shivering retrograde to Hillsborough during the night of the 8th found Polk waiting to meet with his generals. By this time, the enemy had very successfully spread the report that they were en route to Mobile, which could not be lost at any cost. On 9 February, Polk, meeting with his generals in the field, made the decision to split up the army. General French was ordered immediately to Newton Station with the brigades of Quarles, McNair, Ector, and Cockrell and from there to proceed to Mobile. Polk also ordered General Lee's cavalry, in the rear of the Yankees, to reinforce troops at Mobile. The army that Sherman was chasing thus shrunk to one division: Loring's. The cavalry of Colonel William L. Maxwell had been left to cover Loring's movement toward Decatur. Skirmishing went on fitfully all day on 10 February, at times obstinately, as Loring retreated through the Tuscalameta Swamp. Both armies were beginning to wear down from the 125-mile march from Vicksburg to Meridian in the dead of winter.

On the 11th, it became obvious to Polk that he had fallen for Sherman's lies that he was headed for Mobile. At this point, Polk decided that Loring had better fight a delaying action as he moved toward Decatur. If the Federals could be delayed, then stores could be evacuated from Meridian. Polk then headed for Meridian to direct the operations.

On the 12th, Loring indicated to Polk that he was 14 miles from Meridian and in a strong position. On the same day, Polk informed Loring of the plan for the next week:

> It has not been my intention to bring on an engagement with the enemy, the disparity of forces being too great to justify it. It has been of great importance to remove all the public stores here and at other points along the Mobile and Ohio Railroad beyond the enemy's reach. . . . I find I have succeeded in clearing the front sooner than I feared. All the stores will have been removed by the afternoon of tomorrow or earlier. I desire not to risk an engagement if it can be avoided, and you are instructed to regulate your movements with a view to that object. . . . My line of retreat will be toward Demopolis, Alabama. You can take up your line of march whenever you think it expedient. (*OR*, vol. 32, pt. 2, p. 723)

Sunday, 14 February, was a sad day for the Mississippians who had been fighting alongside General Loring for so many months. Meridian would not be defended, and Mississippi would be abandoned.

> The smaller, rural towns of Brandon, Hillsborough, Pelahatchie, Forest, Lake, Morton, and Decatur were given over to the enemy with hardly a shot being fired. The shivering Third Mississippi continued its hard trek as more stragglers drifted from the ranks and into woodland, bound for home. . . . The whole episode of the Confederate retreat was a painful experience for those who took part in it. It was a miserable, cold, leap-frog, tumbling backwards affair as far as the infantry was concerned. The cavalry sniped with Sherman's force as it pressed eastward but the few valiant horse soldiers alone could not hope to stem the blue onslaught. "Old Blizzards" Loring feared Sherman's numbers and was not up to a fight. (Howell 267-268)

Having halted Sherman's advance long enough for the supplies to be removed from Meridian and its confines, Loring and French moved dejectedly toward Alabama.

At midnight the regiment quick-stepped under overcast skies out of Mississippi into Alabama. Marching eastward via Alamutche and Gaston, the Confederates crossed the Tombigbee River at Moscow and proceeded as far as Demopolis, Alabama, before halting. The march had been far from easy as an ice storm had pelted the miserable columns with sleet and snow. So closed Loring's Meridian campaign. No other Confederate army had ever made a 150-mile retrograde in the middle of winter.

Because Sherman had also been waging war with the press, his Meridian expedition was just a blip in the Northern newspapers. When he returned to Mississippi in January 1864, he explicitly ordered, "No newspapermen on this campaign." His march to and from Vicksburg covered over 400 miles during the shortest month of the year. The railroad was destroyed from Jackson to Meridian, 100 miles. Every town was burned, 5,000 negroes freed, 400 prisoners brought away, plus 3,000 animals. All C.S.A. cotton, the cash crop of the Confederacy, was burned. By 28 February, Sherman was back in Vicksburg. The general stated, "Contemporaneous with these events was a diversion made on Mobile. Occurring at the same time as my movement, it completely deceived our enemy and caused the spread of great alarm in Alabama . . . whose time will come in due time" (*OR*, vol. 32, pt. 1, p. 178).

General Stephen D. Lee named the red-bearded general "Sherman the torch" and viewed Sherman as something of a war criminal. In a letter to Halleck, Sherman boasted that when Polk retreated across the Tombigbee it left Halleck to smash things at pleasure, and he thought it was "well done." He felt that if the raid had accomplished nothing else, he had at least scared the bishop "out of his senses."

The Southern newspapers were not kind to General Polk. Even Loring said to Polk, "I see that the papers are finding fault. If necessary I will come out with a statement showing that you did all you could with the force you had" (*OR*, vol. 32, pt. 2, p. 722).

Chapter 12

Fighting in Georgia — Resaca, Cassville, and Kennesaw Mountain

BY THE END OF *February, the war theater had moved to Alabama and Georgia. General Loring was at Demopolis, Alabama, a camp fashioned to receive the returning paroled Vicksburg army that had surrendered the past July.*

Although there was a lull in military activities in Polk's department after Sherman returned to Vicksburg, a movement of great and immediate concern was the reported

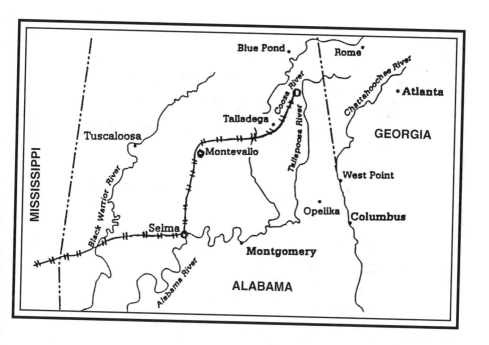

concentration of troops along the Tennessee River in north Alabama. By mid-March, Polk was receiving reports of a concentration about Decatur. On 2 April, Governor T. H. Watts reported the Yanks were fortifying at Decatur. Was an advance upon central Alabama being considered?

Upon receiving Watt's report, Polk immediately ordered General Stephen D. Lee's cavalry to Tuscaloosa. From there he would send out part of his command to Elyton (present-day Birmingham) in Jones Valley, and to scout the country northward to the Tennessee Valley. He also ordered General Loring to immediately move his infantry division to Montevallo, Alabama, which was on the railroad north of Selma. Polk believed his combined force of 8,000 men could block any advance into central Alabama by promoted Brigadier General Benjamin Grierson's and General Sooy Smith's Federal cavalry.

There would be no railroad cars for Loring's men to ride for this movement. Having just walked the breadth of Mississippi, from Vicksburg to Demopolis — over 150 miles — they now would begin to walk across Alabama. The grueling march over 90 miles of winding Alabama back roads took five days to complete. Sherman, through the reports of his scouts and spies and the Southern newspapers, knew everything that was

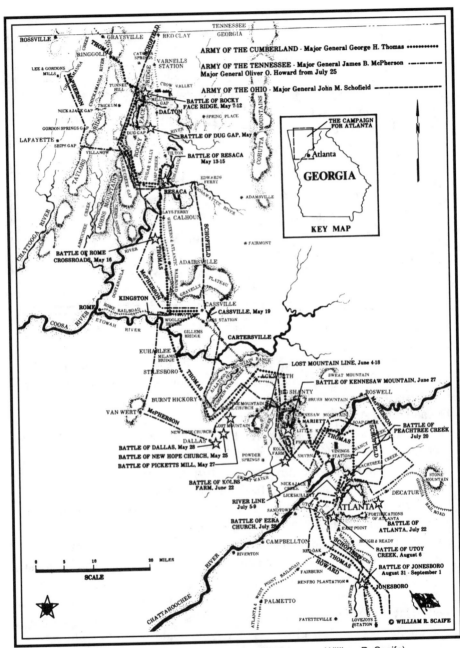

The Campaign for Atlanta, May 7-September 2, 1864. (Courtesy, William R. Scaife)

happening. Commanders of the outposts along the river and detachments on the railroad were alerted and on guard against any surprise moves by Loring.

On 4 May, Polk received a directive from President Davis to move Loring's division, and any other available force at his command, to Rome, Georgia, as quickly as possible and unite with General Joe Johnston's forces. The Confederate War Department was anxious for Johnston to make an offensive campaign into Tennessee and Kentucky that spring. However, Grant ordered Sherman to move against Johnston's army to break it up and move into Georgia. With the movement of Sherman toward Dalton, Polk immediately ordered Loring to prepare five days' rations and to move to Rome via Selma and Blue Mountain, Alabama, on the Alabama & Tennessee River Railroad.

Loring's move from Montevallo would take him 134 miles to the northeast to Blue Mountain, where the railroad stopped. General Johnston knew the move by Sherman was coming rapidly. As early as 5 May, he had ordered Loring to send his brigades on as they arrived at the terminus of the railroad at Blue Mountain and to not wait to assemble the division. Another message to Loring went out on 7 May: "The necessity of your troops reaching Rome, Ga at once is more pressing every moment" (*OR*, vol. 32, pt. 3, p. 675). On the same day, W. W. Mackall, Chief of Staff, sent an urgent message to General William T. Martin commanding at Rome: "Send a messenger to meet General Loring's brigades and have them make a forced march from Blue Mountain to Rome, and do not wait for wagons or baggage" (*OR*, vol. 38, pt. 4, p. 662). With Sherman's buildup in front of Dalton, Georgia, Joe Johnston needed all the troops he could get.

From Rome, all troops were hurried by rail to Resaca, Georgia. This small, rural depot town was very important to General Johnston because its defenses guarded the vital rail crossing of the Oostanaula River; if this was captured, it would cut off his rail linkage with Atlanta. Loring and his staff reached Resaca on the 11th; Buford's brigade had arrived the previous day, and part of Featherston's brigade would arrive on the next. Loring was ordered by Polk to take command of the town.

On 13 May, Union General McPherson's forces emerged in organized strength in front of Resaca. General Polk's Army of Mississippi — now the third corps of General Johnston's Army of Tennessee, with Loring's division as the advance element of Polk's corps — was placed in line just west of Resaca to meet the oncoming Yankees. Loring positioned part of his troops on the west bank of Camp Creek near its mouth, just below the Oostanaula River, because the high hills that he occupied covered and protected the railroad bridge at Resaca. This advanced position also enfiladed the upper part of Camp Creek and served as a bastion for the line of works along the east bank of the stream.

Loring's report of the day's battle describes the scene:

> [Colonel Thomas M.] Scott's brigade was moved forward and took position in line on Bald Knob, about a mile west of town. About 1 p.m. the brigade became warmly engaged, and held the enemy in check three hours and could have maintained its position longer, but was ordered to retire into our line of intrenchments [*sic*]. It drew off in perfect order and took position on the right of [Brigadier General Alfred J.] Vaughan's brigade, [General James] Cantey's brigade. [General John] Adams was drawn up on the right of Scott's with Featherston's in rear as reserve. . . . I ordered breast-works thrown up on both front and rear lines, which the men set about with great spirit and speedily accomplished. (*OR*, vol. 38, pt. 3, p. 875)

The early intervention by Loring and his division allowed the Army of Tennessee to squirm out of the trap being set by Sherman and gave Johnston time to fall back from Dalton. General Johnston said Loring's timely opposition allowed him to select the ground to be occupied by General Hardee's and General John B. Hood's divisions as they arrived from Dalton.

On the 14th, Union brigades pushed across Camp Creek and began to ascend the slope that the Confederates were holding. One bluecoat reported:

> The fighting was severe, and the whole heavens seemed to be split with bursting shells. . . . Scarcely had the regiment got into position, when our skirmishers were driven back by overwhelming numbers. . . . With a determination unequaled, came the Confederates, charging us in three lines of battle, of Loring's division, with shouts and yells. Six or seven stand of colors were seen, and as many regiments were confronting us. (*OR*, vol. 38, pt. 3, p. 214)

But by late evening, the morale of Polk's commanders was a good deal weakened by the knowledge that the Federal troops had made a foothold in the rear of their flank and had gotten over Camp Creek and were on the hill overlooking the railroad and wagon bridges into Resaca.

Sharp and heavy fighting commenced early on the 15th and continued until night, with both sides gaining little and losing heavily. With General McPherson threatening the railroad bridge in front of Loring at Resaca, and with General Thomas W. Sweeny now in a position to easily cut the railroad near Calhoun, Georgia, General Johnston decided he had better move quickly and withdraw toward Calhoun. By midnight on the 15th, the wagon trains of the Confederate army were heard crossing the wooden bridges at Resaca. Polk's and Hardee's corps crossed the same bridge they had been defending and moved south toward Calhoun.

But Johnston, unable to find a suitable defensive position at Calhoun, continued to move toward Adairsville. There, the consolidation of Johnston's army was almost complete. Hardee, Jackson, and part of French's brigades had rejoined. Unfortunately, the defense of Adairsville had been misread, and Sherman was flanking the Confederates again. A quick movement had to be made. At a council of the divisional officers the night of 17 May, it was decided to fall back immediately to Cassville, 15 miles south of Adairsville. Another midnight march ensued.

Johnston, with his years of military experience and wisdom, deliberately adopted the Fabian policy of carefully entrenched lines, as he knew he might be compelled to retire. One soldier in the trenches was equal to three or four on the attack of the enemy. This way Johnston constantly neutralized the numerical superiority of Sherman's forces. Sherman, with a totally different temperament, had to accept Johnston's game and play this Indian-type warfare in the woods, all the way to Atlanta.

On the morning of 18 May, the Federals at Adairsville again found Johnston gone. Correctly guessing that Sherman's army would use both roads to Cassville — the eastern road, which led directly from Adairsville to Cassville, and the western road, which followed the railroad south to Kingston and then headed due east six or seven miles to Cassville — Johnston saw an opportunity to strike the force on the eastern one when the two Federal columns were at the greatest distance from each other. To take advantage of this opening, he ordered Loring's division to confront the enemy on the direct road from Adairsville and contain his advance while General Hood was to swing off to the Confederate right and fall on the

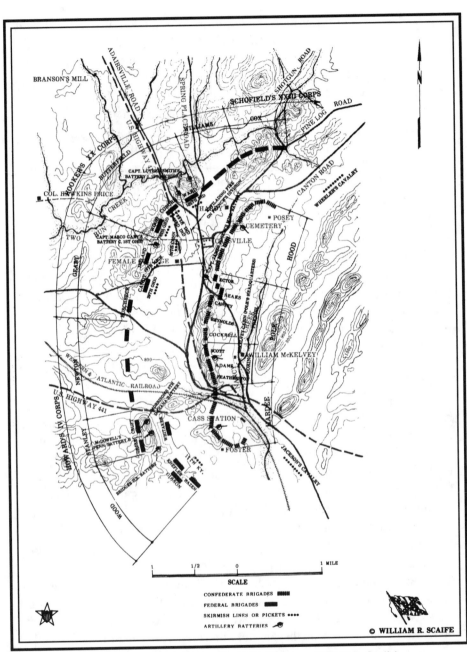

The affair at Cassville the evening of May 19, 1864. (Courtesy, William R. Scaife)

exposed left flank of the advancing Northerners. Hardee, meanwhile, was to slow as best as he could the other enemy column coming on from Kingston. At Cassville, Dr. P. F. Whitehead, a surgeon in Loring's division, wrote:

> Gen. Johnston today . . . announc[ed] that he had arrived to the point which was to be the battle ground. Skirmishing has been going on for several hours and as I write (2 a.m. in the morning) there is not a quarter of a minute that I do not hear a gun. I think that the battle will be fought tomorrow notwithstanding we have been retreating for days the troops are in fine spirits and confident that we shall whip the enemy. (Whitehead manuscript collection)

On 19 May, General Loring assumed command of the brigades of Featherston, Adams, Cockrell, and Scott until further orders. On this same day, as General Hood's brigades marched out to ambush Union General John M. Schofield's advancing XXIII Corps on the direct road to Cassville, Brigadier General Edward M. McCook's bluecoat cavalry division made an unexpected attack on the rear of Hood's division, causing Hood to order his corps to change fronts. The ambush on Schofield was thus called off, and by noon, Johnston decided to move the defense line to a stronger position, just behind Cassville. "Here, then, all agreed the stand would be made or an advance projected" (*OR*, vol. 38, pt. 3, p. 705).

Polk, Loring, and the whole Confederate front abandoned their positions and retired about a mile to a position on a ridge east of Cassville. The new line ran for about three and a half miles along the heavily wooded crest of the ridge overlooking a broad, open valley to the west, in which lay the town. Hood's corps was deployed on the right, Polk's corps, with Loring's and French's brigades, was in the center, and Hardee's corps was on the left, south of the railroad. Johnston felt that for the first time during this campaign, his flanks and communications were secure, and later he described the position as "the best I saw occupied during the war . . . with a broad, elevated valley in front of it completely commanded by the fire of the troops occupying its crest" (Scaife 46).

But by the time our artillery opened on them, that of the Union came into action in beautiful style, and selecting their positions

with great skill, opened fire on ours and soon showed an almost
overwhelming superiority. It must be remembered that they had
two guns to our one, and a great number of rifled pieces, which
also gave a great advantage in range and accuracy. I saw one
battery of ours knocked to pieces, and the gunners driven from
their guns in less than fifteen minutes. (Tower 187)

By nightfall, Generals Hood and Polk informed Johnston that the
line had been enfiladed by Northern artillery and that they would be
unable to maintain their position the next day. Hardee, on the other hand,
was confident that his corps could hold its ground, although he was not
in the middle of the battle. Johnston later lamented, "Although the position was the best we had occupied, I . . . yielded [to Hood and Polk] —
a step I have regretted every since" (*OR*, vol. 38, pt. 3, p. 705). Orders
were given for an immediate retrograde toward the Etowah River, eight
miles south of Cassville. Another all-night movement of the army followed.

Once over the river, the bridge was burned and the wagons moved
toward Allatoona on two roads. The night retreat impaired the confidence
of the men. Johnston retired his Army of Tennessee into the rugged Allatoona Mountains, 11 miles south of the Etowah River. Here he fortified a
strong position at Allatoona Pass, where the Western & Atlantic Railroad
penetrated the mountain range through a deep rock cut.

But Sherman was thoroughly aware of the strength of Allatoona Pass
and decided to turn Johnston's position and compel him to give up Allatoona by moving the Federal army south from Kingston, with his object
being Marietta, Georgia, and regaining the use of the railroad. In consequence of Sherman's flanking movement, Johnston was forced to vacate
his almost impregnable position and move his army southwestward away
from the railroad pass to counter Sherman's movement.

Late in the afternoon on 23 May, Johnston ordered Hardee's corps to
march by the crossroad town of New Hope Church to the Stilesboro and
Dallas road; Polk's corps of Loring, French, and Cantey was to move in
the same direction but a little farther south; and Hood's corps was to follow Hardee the next day. On 25 May, the whole Confederate line was in
position: Hardee across the Stilesboro, Dallas and Atlanta road; Hood
upon the right of Hardee, his center at New Hope Church and his line in
front covering the road leading from Dallas to Acworth; and Polk's corps

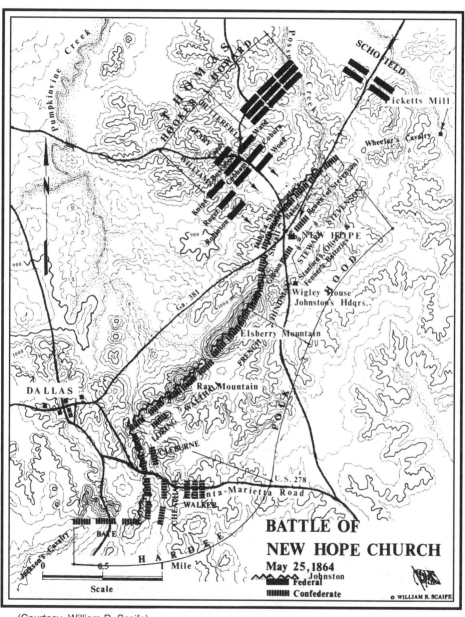

(Courtesy, William R. Scaife)

closed up upon Hood's line and camped on the Marietta and Dallas road. The whole of Johnston's line was admirably chosen for defense, occupying a series of ridges and being entrenched. The conflict begun on 25 May was called the battle of New Hope Church. The intense engagements at New Hope Church, Pickett's Mill, and Dallas were just a part of the heavy fighting along the New Hope-Dallas line that continued for ten days in heavy rain.

While firing and skirmishing continued during the first few days of June, Sherman extended his line of troops eastward, back toward the railroad and his supply line. On 4 June, Loring found that the enemy had abandoned his front. On this same day, he was ordered to withdraw his line and move eastward, toward Lost Mountain, with the rest of Johnston's army.

The corps' wagons and artillery pulled out first, followed by his infantry at 11:00 p.m. Johnston's entire army was shifting to block Sherman's flanking movement toward the railroad and Marietta, Georgia. The defense of Atlanta was getting tighter. The retreat through the mud, rain, and darkness was horrible. General French wrote, "Mud, mud, everywhere, and the soldiers sink over their shoe tops at every step. It took seven hours to move six miles" (French 201). The constant fighting, entrenching, and marching severely punished the men and animals.

Sherman established his headquarters at Big Shanty and described the scene:

> Kennesaw, the bold and striking twin mountain, lay before us, to our right Pine Mountain, and beyond it in the distance, Lost Mountain. On each of these peaks the enemy had his signal station, the summits were crowned with batteries, and the spurs were alive with men busy felling trees, digging pits, and preparing for the grand struggle impending (Scaife 61).

And it continued to rain.

On the morning of 14 June, Generals Hardee, Johnston, and Polk rode forward to Pine Mountain to examine the ground. Down below, 600 yards away, Generals Sherman and Olive O. Howard spotted the group of Confederate officers on the mountaintop. Sherman ordered Howard to have Knap's Pennsylvania Battery fire three volleys at this evidently high-ranking party. The first shell missed but prompted Johnston to order the soldiers around him to scatter. A second shell hit and killed Major John B. Pirtle's horse under him, but the major arose, unhurt. General Polk, the Episcopal bishop, who was dignified and corpulent, rode back slowly, not wishing to appear too hurried or cautious in the presence of the men. Another shell then rocketed across the intervening ground and struck Polk. He was dead before he toppled from his rearing horse.

General Loring was not present when this momentous event occurred, but because he was the senior officer in the corps, he assumed command of the Army of Mississippi. Johnston swiftly issued the orders:

> Maj. Gen. W. W. Loring assumes command of the Army of . . . Mississippi. . . . In assuming command of this army the major-general commanding cannot refrain from an expression of deep regret at the untimely and unexpected death of its late commander, and shares in common with all officers and men of the command grief at the loss of the patriot general, the memory of whose valor and virtue will be long cherished by his troops. (*OR*, vol. 38, pt. 4, p. 776)

At age 46, one-armed "Old Blizzards" Loring was well prepared for the new command, having headed it many times in Polk's absence. Brigadier General Winfield S. Featherston took over Loring's division.

The Federals then attacked the Pine Mountain salient, attempting to drive a wedge between the main Confederate line, but failed. On the 15th, Johnston ordered Pine Mountain abandoned. Heavy shelling fell on Loring's line position for the next two days. Recognizing the vulnerability of General French's position, after three Federal divisions had converged on his salient, Johnston withdrew during the night of 18 June some two miles to the south where he formed the Kennesaw Mountain line, permitting Union commanders General George H. Thomas and Schofield to gain two miles of difficult country without even having to fight for it. Johnston was running out of time and terrain.

Kennesaw Mountain, about four miles northwest of Marietta, had twin crests, one slightly higher than the other, with a "saddle" connecting the two peaks. Little Kennesaw, being bald and without timber, afforded a commanding view of the surrounding country as far as the eye could see. The view from this elevation embraced Lost Mountain, Pine Mountain, and the beautiful cultivated plain, extending to the Allatoona Mountains.

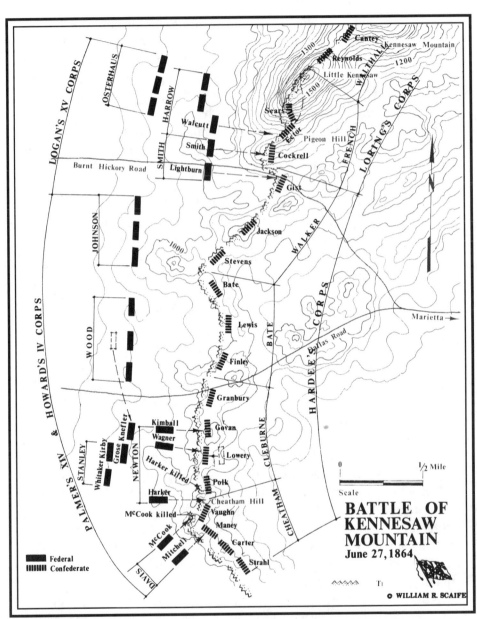

The Battle of Kennesaw Mountain was Loring's greatest victory in the Civil War. This is the only time he is shown as Corps commander. (Courtesy, William R. Scaife)

On 18 June, Loring ordered General French: "It will be necessary for you to march up the mountain in single rank and meet General James Cantey, who marches in the same order" (*OR*, vol. 38, pt. 4, p. 780). Hauling the artillery up the steep rocky and wooded slopes was accomplished by tow lines, hooks, toggles, and hundreds of infantrymen. The heavy guns were pulled from tree to tree up the slope. Finally, on the lower hill, French had planted nine cannons that had been dragged up that night.

Veteran D. J. Wilson of Era, Texas, recalled: "On one occasion I was standing on the roadside watching the artillerymen trying to get one of the cannons out of the mud, when I heard someone behind me say, 'Put your shoulder to the wheel.' I looked around to see who gave the command and saw General Loring. Well, we all got to the wheels and moved it right out" (Wilson 281).

On 19 June, the Confederate army was in its new position on the Kennesaw Mountain line, which, when including the thin lines of cavalry on its flanks, formed a semicircle about Marietta on the west and to the north and extended eight miles long. The mountain itself was occupied by Loring's corps with French's division holding the southwestern slope and part of the crest, General Edward C. Walthall's division the line along the ridge, and Featherston's division reaching down the northeastern slope to the railroad. From the crest of the mountain, the signal corps and general officers could look down and witness the duel between the batteries and follow every movement of Sherman's army. Sherman, posed in front of Kennesaw, had an army of 100,000 men, 28,000 horses, 32,000 mules, 5,000 wagons, 850 ambulances, and over 250 pieces of artillery. Heavy fighting on the 19th and 20th ushered in the ongoing battle of Kennesaw Mountain.

During the month of June, north Georgia had been subjected to the heaviest rainfall in years. It had rained 19 days in a row, and the roads were quagmires of mud, which made the marching and flanking tactic difficult for Sherman's forces.

By late June 1864, Sherman's three armies had spent the first seven weeks of the Atlanta campaign employing essentially one mode of offense, a continual movement toward the flanks of Johnston's Army of Tennessee. But the wily Johnston had slipped away every time, digging in behind new and formidable earthworks. Frustrated by two recent stalemates on both flanks of the line, Sherman decided to try a massive direct

assault on the Confederates' Kennesaw Mountain line when the weather
would permit.

Early morning on Monday, 27 June, there appeared great activity
among the Federal staff officers and generals all along the eight-mile line.
Precisely at 8:00 a.m., 200-odd Union cannons roared into action simultaneously, pounding the Rebel line on the mountainside and across the flats
beyond in their pits and ditches. The defenders marveled at the volume
and intensity of the fire.

General French, in order to observe the activities, scrambled to the top
of the mountain and placed himself on a large rock that rested between his
guns and the infantry that was farther down the mountainside.

> Artillery-firing was common at all times on the line, but now it
> swelled in volume and extended down to the extreme left, and
> then from fifty guns burst out simultaneously in my front, while
> battery after battery, following on the right, disclosed a general
> attack on our entire line. Presently, and as if by magic, there
> sprang from the earth a host of men, and in one long, waving
> line of blue the infantry advanced and the battle of Kennesaw
> Mountain began. (French 208)

Brigadier General Arthur M. Manigault added:

> The cannons bellowed like so many mad bulls, sent shot and
> shell plowing the ground, scattering rocks, dirt and everything
> movable, cutting down trees and felling limbs . . . then a spas-
> modic end. The cannoneers stepped from their pieces. The blue
> infantry started to assail the Confederate line in masses . . . our
> musketry played upon them cutting them down like grass
> before the sickle. O what a slaughter here. (Tower 176)

General Loring's military report on the action stated:

> About 10 o'clock a.m. it was discovered that the enemy was
> moving in heavy columns towards our position, evidently con-
> templating a combined attack along our whole line. Three
> Corps moved rapidly toward my position and for sometime
> were exposed to a heavy & destructive fire from all our artillery

posted on the mountain. They soon came within range of our musketry. . . .

The attack upon the two slopes of the mountain was made with great vigor and was met with determined & deadly resistance. The batteries of Featherston posted on the ridge east of the mountain which up to this time had been masked, now opened furiously upon the enemy at short range, which in conjunction with the galling fire kept up by the sharpshooters, caused him to reel and fall back in confusion, leaving many of his dead on the field.

In less than two hours the enemy was repulsed with great slaughter along our entire front and retreated in confusion, leaving a number of prisoners and many dead and wounded in the field. . . . Yankee reports estimate their loss in our front between 2,500 & 3,000 killed, wounded, missing which is a low estimate. (*OR*, vol. 38, pt. 3, p. 869)

Loring's men reported action until sundown. In the first major victory by the Confederate army in the move on Atlanta, General Loring's corps performed well for the veteran. General French, while perched on his hilltop, wrote:

We sat there perhaps an hour enjoying a birds-eye-view of one of the most magnificent sights ever allotted to man, to look-down upon a hundred and fifty thousand men arrayed in the strife of battle below. Twere worth ten years of peaceful life, once glance at their array! Better an hour on this mountain top than an age on a peaceful plain. . . .

Seldom in war have there been instances where so many guns have been trained on a single spot. But it was only in the darkness of the night that the magnificence of the scene was displayed — grand beyond imagination, beautiful beyond description. Kennesaw, usually invisible from a distance at night, now resembles Vesuvius in the beginning of an eruption. (French 208)

How these generals loved war.

Sherman, still searching for a weak link in Johnston's superior position, decided the time had come to make a different movement. He wired Washington that he was accumulating stores that would enable him to cut loose from the railroad for a time and avoid Kennesaw, which was giving the enemy too much advantage. Sherman prepared to move south toward Atlanta with another flanking movement.

On 2 July, the Yankee artillery opened up at 4:15 a.m. and kept up the cannonade until 6:00 a.m. This was the usual action Sherman took when he was beginning to move his army, hoping to check the Rebels.

Loring was given orders to withdraw that night. Kennesaw represented the last of the mountain barriers before Atlanta. For 26 days, the two armies had confronted each other near Marietta; now the Confederate army would have to come out of the mountains to defend Atlanta. Johnston would have to hurry to cut off the flank movement.

By the morning of the 3rd, Johnston's weary army was in motion toward a ridge behind Nickajack Creek, which crossed the Western & Atlantic Railroad near Smyrna Camp Grounds, about four miles south of Marietta and only ten miles northwest of Atlanta. Here double-line entrenchments, nearly six miles long, had been hurriedly put up by the Confederate engineers with the assistance of the Georgia militia. This became known as the Smyrna line. Loring's corps and General Joseph Wheeler's cavalry manned the right of the line, east of the railroad. Hardee's corps was west of the railroad, and Hood's corps was next to Hardee, with "Red" Jackson's cavalry. Supporting Hood's corps was a division of 3,000 Georgia militia under General Gustavus W. Smith.

When Johnston stopped his retrograde at the Smyrna line, Sherman quickly seized the opportunity to rapidly move all of his corps directly toward Smyrna. On 3 July, the cavalry was already being driven in by Sherman's bluecoats. On 4 July, heavy shelling occurred across the whole front. Johnston soon realized his forces were insufficient to hold the Federals in check.

The Smyrna line lasted only 48 hours. Sherman was now maneuvering in force and with determination against Johnston's troops. He had advanced his men from around Marietta to such an extent that Johnston decided to withdraw his troops once again to the Chattahoochee River.

Here, General Francis A. Shoup, chief of artillery, had assembled an innovative defense system of rifle pits, log forts, and rifle and artillery parapets, covering six miles on the north bank of the Chattahoochee. This line was large enough for the entire Confederate army to take refuge in.

The massive earthen structures could readily absorb the impact of artillery fire and were virtually impregnable. On 5 July, Loring's corps was placed east of the railroad bridge that crossed the river. Sherman admitted it was one of the strongest field fortifications he had ever seen in the war.

The swollen Chattahoochee River and its tributaries provided few places for the Federals to ford and get to the south bank behind Johnston. On 8 July, Sherman began an exploratory probing of the line to satisfy himself as to the strength of Johnston's position. While General James B. McPherson's army threatened to cross at Turner's Ferry, six miles downstream, General Thomas, in support of this move, began demonstrations on the front line, thus bottling up Hardee's, Hood's, and Polk's corps. On 9 July, Sherman's skirmish lines appeared and heavy artillery began shelling for hours, which meant Sherman was ready to move again.

Upstream, on 8 July, General Schofield's bluecoats made a surprise crossing at Soap Creek using 20 pontoons to cross to the other bank. By the 9th, a strong bridgehead had been established. The crossing of the Chattahoochee River line had begun. Faced with Thomas's ponderous army in his front with two well-established bridgeheads across the river on his right flank at Roswell and Soap Creek, Johnston had no choice but to order the evacuation of his strong position on the night of 9 July.

That night, from his hill near Vining's Station, Sherman was able to see a good deal of flutter in the Confederate camp and the movements of troops eastward in preparation for a new position. Sherman at a later date censured Johnston for lying in entrenchments on the river "comparatively idle while he got control of both sides of the river above him" (Horn, *Army of Tennessee*, 340). Just how far would Johnston's retrograde movement take him in Georgia? What had happened to the plan to divide and conquer? Why, with Sherman's forces divided and while he was waiting for supplies, didn't the Confederate army attack?

Loring and his brigades had been 74 days in the immediate presence of the enemy, laboring and fighting daily. There had been rain and mud and, lately, excessive heat. Exhausting marches, day and night, had been forced upon them. All month long they had been subjected to an almost continuous cannonading. During this time, both sides had suffered heavy casualties. But despite all of these hardships, the Rebels remained loyal to the cause.

Chapter 13

The
Atlanta Campaign

O N 14 JUNE, when General Polk was
killed and General Loring was appointed commander of the Army of
Mississippi, General Order No. 1
had read, "Maj. Gen. W. W. Loring assumes
command of the Army of Mississippi."
Though the word "temporary" was not used,
the Richmond government would have to
approve the promotion.

   On 17 June, when the army was near Marietta, Georgia, Dr. P. F. Whitehead noted in a

letter, "Much speculation in regards to the promotion of Gen. Loring who is now in command of the corps; he has not taken any of his staff with him yet, they remain with General Featherston who commands Loring's division" (Whitehead manuscript collection).

The Southern trooper going into battle required constant inspiration. The need for a professional soldier to be around to reassure the men was shouldered by the old line officers — men such as Loring, who was naturally fearless and combative, harsh of tongue, and carried a reputation for toughness. As one Confederate put it,

> The only way in which an officer could acquire influence over the Confederate soldiers was by his personal conduct under fire. They hold a man in great esteem who in action sets them an example of contempt for danger; but they think nothing of an officer who is not in the habit of leading them. Every atom of authority has to be purchased by a drop of blood. (Patterson 50)

With these accolades, the officers of the Army of Mississippi, on 22 June 1864, high atop Kennesaw Mountain, put together a petition to Jefferson Davis in Richmond requesting Major General W. W. Loring be appointed lieutenant general and permanently assigned to command the Army of Mississippi.

> We, the undersigned officers of the army of the Mississippi, feeling a deep interest in the appointment of a successor to the command made vacant by the death of the lamented Lieut. General S. Polk, and believing that the Government will lend a listening ear to the earnest wishes of its soldiers when properly expressed and when compatible with the public interest, beg leave to request that Major General W. W. Loring be appointed Lieutenant General and assigned to the command of this army.
> Many of us have long served under the command of General Loring & all have seen his courage, skill and ability as a commander well tested; and the able and gallant manner in which he has borne himself through all, has inspired us with the most implicit confidence in his leadership & the earnest desire that the request herein made be granted. (Joseph F. Siano private collection)

Election of officers was common from the beginning of the war. In the case of a commander, this had to be approved by Richmond; thus, 26 high ranking officers as well as eight brigadier generals signed the petition requesting "Old Blizzards" Loring be appointed as their commander.

With Loring's corps perched on the top of Kennesaw Mountain and fighting one of the ablest Confederate victories of the war, this important petition was delayed in being forwarded to Richmond until they came off the mountain on 30 June. In the interim, Davis, without any consideration of Loring, issued the following on 23 June: "Major-General Stewart has this day been appointed lieutenant-general to command the corps recently commanded by Lieutenant-General Polk" (*OR*, vol. 38, pt. 4, p. 787).

The scholarly A. P. Stewart, who had never led anything larger than a division, came from Lieutenant General John B. Hood's corps, and Hood, another West Point graduate, had long been the darling of Richmond society and a favorite of President Davis. The Old Guard was being shuffled out, and Loring — not from West Point and not from a privileged state — was passed over.

On 4 July, Dr. Whitehead wrote, "Lt. Genrl. Stewart will assume command of our Corps this evening. General Loring returning to the Division; the latter is deeply chagrined" (Whitehead manuscript collection).

> "Old Blizzards" Loring, a soldier by profession for twenty years, a warrior from the wild west frontier who had a fair claim to having been under fire more times than any other living man was not a man to bear deep resentment and nursed no grudge.
>
> But he was sensitive, as a soldier should be, of his honor, his valor, and his judgment, and certainly the leaders of the Confederacy had not accorded him the responsibilities and the opportunities that an officer of his experience and accomplishments could rightly expect after three years, non-stop warfare for the "cause." (Hesseltine and Wolf 10)

On the evening of 9 July, Loring's division was given orders to withdraw toward Atlanta and to cross the Chattahoochee River. The retrograde movement took the Southern army to a new position along what was called the Peachtree line, which had been previously constructed. This was the eleventh entrenchment of the retreat.

The weather had turned intensely hot. Sherman, finding all of the regular crossing places destroyed, decided that instead of attacking Atlanta directly, he would make a circuit of the city and destroy all of its railroads.

On Sunday, 17 July, Sherman's bluecoats began the general movement against Atlanta. By the next day, the city was being surrounded. On this famous Monday morning, when Sherman's army was in motion, a spy brought to Sherman an Atlanta newspaper. The news was startling: General Joe Johnston had been removed from command by President Davis. The spirit of West Point and the brotherhood of the corps put aside the old reliable guard.

After the Confederate army had fallen back across the Chattahoochee, Jefferson Davis, with the help of secret letters from General John B. Hood, rapidly began to lose what little confidence he had had in Johnston. He believed that military miracles were brought about by assuming and sustaining the offense, and Hood promised to do this. In his desperation, Davis wanted a miracle to happen in front of Atlanta. He wanted a gambler and a visionary to turn the tide against Sherman.

The apprehensive President had decided to send General Braxton Bragg, now his military advisor, to Atlanta to review the situation. Here, Hood had extensive conversations with Bragg, without consulting Johnston. Johnston had never liked Bragg, having once remarked, "I know Mr. Davis thinks he can do a great many things other men would hesitate to attempt, i.e. try to do what God failed to do. He tried to make a soldier of Bragg but it couldn't be done" (Horn, *Army of Tennessee*, 343).

Nevertheless, the President had pretty well decided before Bragg ever got to Atlanta that Johnston would be relieved. On 17 July, Hood took over the Army of Tennessee. Before leaving Atlanta, Johnston dispatched a caustic message to General Cooper in Richmond calling attention to the fact that General Lee's retreat in Virginia had been quite as rapid as his own and quite as far. "Why, then, should I be condemned for the defensive while General Lee was adding to his great fame by the same course?" (Maury 147). Johnston had fallen back skillfully, losing fewer men in the first month of the Atlanta campaign than Lee lost at the Battle of the Wilderness in Virginia in two days.

On the 18th, General Hood came to Johnston's quarters, and in the evening, Johnston retired from the command and quickly left Atlanta to go to Macon, never returning to help Hood.

On hearing about the change of command, the soldiers in the ranks were shocked and dismayed. Was this the death knell of the Army of Tennessee? This act of the War Department threw a damper over the army; "Ole Joe" was their idol. On the other hand, the private soldier of the army looked upon Hood — at the age of 33, the youngest lieutenant general to be commanding a Confederate force — as an overrated general.

They were not the only ones who held Hood and his promotion in low regard. Senator Louis T. Wigfall commented, "[Davis] has removed General Johnston and put Hood in his place. He has thus ruined Hood, and destroyed the last hope of the Southern Confederacy" (Maury 149). General Manigault believed that "the removal of General Johnston from the command of the Army of Tennessee, was one of those hasty and ill-judged steps on the part of Mr. Davis, which, I believe, contributed materially to the downfall of the Confederacy, and possibly caused it. . . . [Hood is] incompetent, and entirely unfit for the responsible position he occupied" (Tower 200).

Johnston's removal and Hood's appointment as commander of the forces defending Atlanta was welcome news to Sherman and his generals. They feared Johnston, but not Hood. Sherman himself said, "No officer or soldier who ever served under me will question the generalship of Joseph E. Johnston" (Wingfield 90). With the exception of Robert E. Lee, Johnston was unquestionable the ablest general officer of the Confederacy in the summer of 1864, and Davis made a mistake in removing him.

At the end of the war, General Johnston sent Loring a warm letter from Greensboro, North Carolina, on 30 April 1865 pertaining to Loring being promoted to lieutenant general:

> As our official relations are about to terminate, it may not be inappropriate on my part, to offer the only evidence I now can of my appreciation of your military character.
>
> When removed from command, in July last, it was my intention to urge strongly your promotion to the first vacant Lieut. Generalcy. . . . The services to which I should have referred, as having earned those promotions, were in Mississippi and Northern Georgia, under my own eye, as undoubted proof or competency, I should have pointed to your command of Polk's corps after his death. . . .
>
> I rejoined the army with the same intentions; but they were

frustrated by the great reduction of the army, which by making consolidation necessary, rendered it impossible to find adequate commands. (U.S. Army Military History Institute)

Atlanta's irregular circle of fortifications made it one of the best-protected cities in the world at that time. Sherman did not entertain the slightest notion of sacrificing his forces in a gamble to force the ten-mile circumference of high breastworks, redoubts, cannon emplacements, and rifle pits that for a year had been prepared for just such an eventuality. His plan was to invest Atlanta as quickly as possible. He sent Generals Schofield and McPherson toward Decatur, east of Atlanta, while General Thomas, with the bulk of the Union forces, moved toward Peachtree Creek, where Loring's division was positioned.

The Peachtree Creek, which empties into the Chattahoochee just above the railroad bridge, was a narrow and muddy stream, about 40 feet wide but very deep, varying from 4 to 12 feet, and impassable, except by bridge. The valley was narrow, about 200 yards wide with hills beginning gradually from the south. Here, Loring was on high ground, looking down into the valley of the creek.

The morning of 20 July found Thomas's army crossing south of Peachtree Creek, comparatively isolated from the other Federal corps. This is what the Confederate high command had been waiting for — one of Sherman's armies to be divided. It would be an even fight for the butternuts with 30,000 bluecoats on the other side of the creek.

General Hood embraced the opportunity to strike the divided Federal army. On that morning, Hood called together his corps commanders — Generals Benjamin F. Cheatham, Hardee, and Stewart (who headed up Loring's division) — at his headquarters in Atlanta to explain the day's battle plan.

At 1:00 p.m., Hardee would open the attack by searching out the left and rear of the enemy that had crossed the creek, while Stewart's corps would advance against the enemy in echelon from right to left, crushing Thomas's left flank. Cheatham would maintain his position on the right, facing Schofield and McPherson.

Developments soon arose, however, that would hinder Hood's first sor-

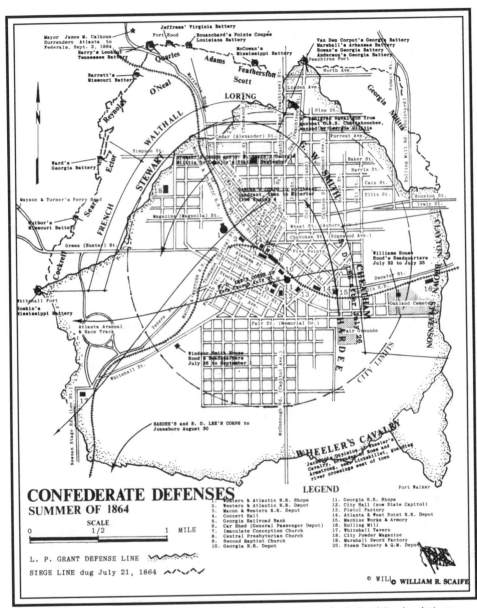

The Battle of Atlanta, 1864. The battle was not fought within the city limits of the day, but several miles outside the city. (Courtesy, William R. Scaife)

tie. Schofield and McPherson were approaching Atlanta from the east faster than Hood was aware of at the time of the meeting. This meant that all of the divisions would have to shift to the right, which necessitated a change of orders, and any such change in the stiff-jointed Confederate command system very often resulted in failure to execute the plan properly. Stewart, believing that the attack should be made at once, attempted to obtain orders from Hood for an immediate advance. He was instructed to continue to move to the right and keep in touch with Hardee's corps. When it was time for Stewart's forward movement, he sent into the field the divisions of Loring on the right and Walthall in the center with French on the left, held in supporting distance.

Loring had but two brigades, Featherston's and Scott's, numbering 2,700 men. He quickly ascertained that beyond the thick forest in his immediate front, several large fields opened out through which his men would be compelled to charge, giving his division the most exposed position on the whole line. The orders given to him stated that as soon as the division on his right had gained a distance of 200 yards, he was to follow in single line of battle and that he must not stop for any obstacle. If he came to breastworks, he should fix bayonets and charge the enemy. Each division was to incline gradually to the left as it advanced and press toward Peachtree Creek.

At 4:00 p.m., the enemy was in plain view about 700 yards distant on the opposite side of the field, occupying a ridge running east to west. The division halted until Cheatham's division on the right began advancing through the woods. Finally, after a long delay, Loring was ordered forward.

As Loring's division advanced, the men moved with confidence and resolute step in the face of the enemy's works. These gallant troops, moving in two lines of battle, received a terrible fire from the Yankee batteries when arriving within 400 or 500 feet of the Federals' line, and soon small arms opened upon them. With a quickened step and a deafening Rebel yell, the command moved forward and drove the enemy from their positions, not stopping until the colors were planted on different points of the breastworks from right to left in a distance of half a mile. Loring had moved so quickly and boldly that he had unexpectedly entered the angle between Brigadier General W. T. Ward's and Brevet Major General John W. Geary's Union divisions, sustaining comparatively small losses. As the Yanks fled in confusion from their works, the steady aim of the Mississippi, Alabama, and Louisiana marksmen of Loring's command resulted in a great slaughter of the enemy's ranks.

It was at this high point that Loring realized that the cooperating forces had not yet engaged the enemy as Hood had planned. This allowed the bluecoats to begin to enfilade from both directions, which thinned Loring's ranks quickly and enabled the Federal forces to rally, finally compelling Featherston and Scott to fall back 250 yards under cover of a ridge, where the fight was continued.

Dale Greenwell of the 3rd Mississippi reported:

> I found we wuz runnin' into a wall of fire from cannon and musketry. It wuz so thick that men fell like flies, and began to drop back. Even the bark wuz flyin' all over the place.
>
> The firin' wuz comin' from the area where Hardee's left division wuz suppose to be, but they wuzn' there. To our left wuz the division under General Walthall, and on past him wuz French's division. They had gone over the works to their front and wuz chasin' the Yanks, but we had to fall back cuz our right flank wuz bein' turned for lack of support there. . . .
>
> If General Cheatham's division had stayed in battle order joinin' us, we wouldn't have had all the fire from the right he wuz supposed to face. (Greenwell 91, 93)

Having fallen back, Loring requested Stewart to strengthen his command for a counterattack with one brigade to replace Adams, who was on detached duty. Loring then held his position until dark. Orders were received to remove the dead and wounded from the field and to fall back into the trenches, which was accomplished by 9:00. Loring's losses at the battle of Peachtree Creek were 1,062. The Confederates had given Thomas a few bad hours but in the end gained very little. This was Hood's style of fighting.

General Manigault wrote, "This battle of the 20th proved a complete failure, altho a success as far as mere fighting was concerned. We gained no substantial advantage and it did not delay the enemy twelve hours" (Tower 224). The failure at Peachtree Creek now demanded urgent measures by Hood in order to save Atlanta.

At daybreak on the 22nd, General Thomas discovered that the Confederate works on the Peachtree line in front of him had been abandoned to a new entrenchment line around the city — the twelfth and last one. Thinking Hood was evacuating Atlanta, Sherman ordered McPherson to pursue south and east while the other two Union armies closed in on Atlanta from the north and east.

Cheatham's and Stewart's corps, reinforced by 5,000 Georgia militia under General Gustavus W. Smith (but without Loring's troops, who were recuperating from the Peachtree battle), held the Atlanta entrenchments while Hardee was ordered to make a night march to get behind McPherson's army and Wheeler's cavalry was to attack Decatur. The battle occurring on this day — usually called the Battle of Atlanta, though it took place outside the city — covered fully seven miles. Again, the disjointed offense plan was badly miscalculated by Hood. By 3:00 p.m., just as Hardee's attacks were being brought to a halt, Hood ordered Cheatham and Smith to attack Union General Logan's corps frontally. After a series of successes, Cheatham's advance was stopped by a strong counterattack. Sherman then massed artillery fire to restore order to the main Union battle line. By nightfall, the Federal line was restored to essentially the same position it had held 24 hours earlier. Federal casualties were 3,722, and Confederate casualties numbered 8,000. General Hardee's opinion was that this battle was "one of the most desperate and bloody of the war" (Boatner 30).

Major James Connolly, of the Army of the Cumberland, wrote his wife on the next day: "The rivers are all crossed and the mountains all scaled, and nothing now remains between us and the doomed city but the ridges of red clay thrown up by the rebel army" (Brown 56). The siege of Atlanta had begun.

General Sherman was not a man to fight unnecessary battles; he preferred to destroy his enemy's ability to make war. He decided to vary his siege operations with slashing cavalry raids on the Confederate railroads feeding the city.

On 27 July, General Hood was presented with another chance to destroy an isolated portion of Sherman's army. General Stephen D. Lee, who had just been promoted to lieutenant general, was brought from Alabama to take over Hood's old corps. He arrived on the 26th, and on the 28th he was ordered westward through Atlanta out the Lickskillet Road to occupy a position from which he could block General Olive O. Howard's extension of the Union right and set him up for a flank attack by Stewart, who would bring his corps out the Sandtown Road that evening. Stewart would follow

Lee's advance and then circle the head of the bluecoats and strike from the southwest of Howard's unguarded flank the next morning.

General Hood's orders to Lee were simple: hold the enemy in check on a line nearly parallel with the Lickskillet Road. But finding the Federal army in its assigned position, General Lee neither informed Hood nor waited for Stewart's flanking force to get into position. Instead, without pausing even to arrange a coordinated attack with the whole corps, he immediately threw forward whatever unit first came to hand. The result was a piecemeal attack.

The Federal forces being engaged were comprised of at least 10,000 men with repeating rifles. They were on the crest of a continuous ridge with three sets of battle lines. In the terrible July heat, the Rebels rushed on the bluecoats behind their piles of rails, logs, and rocks, and within 30 minutes two spirited but foolish attacks had been repulsed by the Union men, inflicting tragic losses. Confederate artillery was finally brought up, which opened heavily upon the Federals for 15 minutes. Again, Lee ordered another attack.

Meanwhile, Stewart's divisions headed by Loring and Walthall, marching from Atlanta, soon heard the noise of the battle and hastened toward Lee's position, thus abandoning their own plans. Finding Lee in dire need of assistance, Walthall moved his division forward into the battle left of Lee's shattered men, but achieved nothing but disaster for his troops.

The slaughter of Walthall's division in a short period of time indicates the intensity of the fire power of the Union army. Walthall's brigades headed by Brigadier Generals Alexander W. Reynolds and James Cantey lost 152 officers and nearly 1,000 men, considerably more than a third of the division's strength. Quarles's brigade, the reserve, lost 514 men and all the regimental commanders but one.

Walthall was then directed to withdraw to the rear of Loring's division, which had been hastily drawn up adjacent to the Lickskillet Road. Walthall was given instructions to hold the position on Lickskillet Road until Loring's line was complete. Loring's veteran division was exposed to heavy incoming fire from the Federals as they formed for their attack. Well-calculated Union volleys from their repeating rifles were intense and took their toll. Men fell by the score without ever being within range to deliver an effective return fire.

General Lorin' came up in a hurry and ordered us to the left of Lee's corps and to try and drive the enemy off a hill that they had dug into. The division spread into battle rapidly. The Yankees had us like sittin' ducks on a pond, in the open, and we could only see the smoke from their guns and muskets. They poured shot down on us (Greenwell 95).

And then it happened:

As we were movin' into regimental battle lines, General Lorin' wuz shot and toppled from his horse. (Greenwell 95)

Loring was down with a wound to his left breast.

At the same time, Stewart came galloping onto the field, waving Loring's men forward — and then he was struck in the forehead by a spent bullet. The two generals were quickly moved to the field hospital. Stewart was out of action for ten days, but Loring was absent for 43.

This battle of Ezra Church, 28 July 1864, was an unsettling, bloody, three-hour affair that brought no benefit to Hood's army and cost him nearly 5,000 casualties versus 700 Union casualties. In addition to Loring and Stewart, Generals Stephen D. Lee, John C. Brown, and R. L. Gibson were wounded and Matthew D. Ector had been wounded the day before and had his left leg amputated.

Union General Cox later related a frequently repeated story that reflected Hood's impetuous tactics of always attacking. After the fighting, one of Logan's pickets called out across the lines at twilight, "Well Johnny, how many of yours are left?" A despondent Confederate replied, still maintaining a semblance of the sense of humor so essential to a soldier, "Oh, about enough for another killing" (Cox, *Campaigns*, 186).

During the scorching month of August, it seemed as though everything was in limbo. Grant was stuck in front of Petersburg, and now Sherman was stuck in front of Atlanta. The Southern and Northern press both recognized the hopelessness of the war. May, June, and July had brought casualties into the tens of thousands for both sides. And there was talk that Lincoln may not be reelected if things did not change — and quickly.

The Federals began to erect forts and mount siege guns within easy range of Atlanta. After Sherman received the bad news of his cavalry's failures, he decided to try and wear down Atlanta from the air. On 1 August, he told Schofield, Thomas, and Howard to fire 10 to 15 shots from every gun they had in position that would reach any of the houses in Atlanta. On 7 August, he ordered Thomas to telegraph Chattanooga and have Parrotts sent down with 1,000 shells and ammunition. Eight four-and-a-half-inch rifled siege guns were brought down and began firing continuously into the city at an average of one shell every 20 minutes.

The first signal that Sherman's army was ready to move again and give up on the siege of Atlanta was when Sherman sent Slocum's corps back to the abandoned Confederate works on the Chattahoochee River. On the 25th, the cannons ceased firing. The Rebels inside the city must have wondered what was to happen next.

Sherman was moving his 65,000-man army south toward the West Point Railroad. When he reached it on the 29th, he spent the next day wrecking and destroying it thoroughly.

On 31 August, Sherman seized Rough and Ready, a village on the railroad halfway between Atlanta and Jonesboro, and cut the telegraph lines linking Hood and Hardee. The Union army in great strength crossed the Flint River, and by 1 September the Yankees had maneuvered Hood out of Atlanta and had split up his weakened army into three distinct bodies.

On that day, "everything indicated that Atlanta is to be abandoned now that the railroad has been cut. And before noon the orders came" (French 222). The campaign for Atlanta by Sherman had lasted exactly four months, during which time scarcely a day had passed without an engagement of some kind.

On 1 September, the day Atlanta was abandoned, the luck of the Confederates took a turn for the better when General Sherman lost one of the most favorable opportunities ever to destroy and eliminate his antagonist, the Army of Tennessee. He decided to let the shattered Confederate army go unmolested as he began to move his weary and exhausted army north, back toward Atlanta, to give them a rest and to claim his prize.

Sherman entered the city on 8 September. He then proposed an armistice of ten days between the armies to give rest to the men, to reorganize and recruit, and also to exchange prisoners. This was agreed upon by both commanders.

At Lovejoy's Station, 20 miles from Atlanta, the weakened Confederate army began to regroup and took respite from the past four months of moving and fighting. Several thousand men had no shoes, food was scarce, and ammunition was dangerously low. Worst of all, the men were deserting, believing this was the end of the war.

On 10 September, General Loring returned to command his division. "We were passed in review yesterday by Uncle Billy Loring," wrote one soldier. "He has just returned to command the division having entirely recovered from his wound of the 28th of July. . . . I would rather be reviewed by General Loring than any other general" (Howell 353).

Before the armistice had half expired, the greater part of Hood's army moved out on 18 September, marching in a northwesterly direction toward a point on the Atlanta & West Point Railroad called Palmetto Station, near the Chattahoochee River. Here, Hood's army could be conveniently supplied and could control the railroad and country where most of its supplies came from. But this movement left the door wide open for Sherman to enter central Georgia, southeastern Alabama, and, if he wished, Florida.

Palmetto Station became the summit for a meeting between President Davis and General Hood. Their strategy of the hour was to checkmate Sherman with an offensive on his communications and supply line north of Atlanta. Draw him out of Atlanta, select a position on the Alabama line in proximity to the Blue Mountain Railroad, and fight.

On 30 September, the army marched to near Brownsville Post Office, and on 1 October they bivouacked near Dark Corners, Georgia. Here, all division commanders were invited to Hood's headquarters, and the object of the move was discussed with Generals Loring, French, Stewart, Lee, Walthall, Stevenson, and Henry D. Clayton. Hood announced that the winter campaign was to begin.

Chapter 14

Hood's Fall Campaign —
Georgia, Alabama, and
Tennessee: Columbia,
Spring Hill, Franklin,
and Nashville

*HE OPEN-FIELD assaults around
Atlanta had taken a massive toll on
Hood's army. The number of prisoners and deserters was heavy, and
the Federals had captured at least 13,000
men. Over 12,500 had been killed or wounded; thousands of soldiers lay in makeshift
hospitals. By early September, the Army of
Tennessee could muster scarcely 23,000
effective infantry; on 20 September, Hood's*

rolls listed over 62,000 men absent. Far from the magnificent force it once was, it was now a ghost army.

Hood's divisions began their march through Georgia on 2 October. In silence the column moved toward Big Shanty, a depot on the Western & Atlantic Railroad vital to General Sherman's supply and communication line. Hood's specific orders to General Stewart indicated that he and his entire corps — led by Loring, French, and Walthall — were to "move against Big Shanty . . . and, should you be able to take possession of the place you can then send a division to Acworth and Allatoona" (Howell 361). This was a tall order for Stewart's men.

> At Big Shanty, Ga. our brigade wuz called out front. General Lorin' galloped up to General Featherston, stood up in his stirrups, pointed towards Big Shanty Station, took his hat off and moved about sizin' up the situation, returned a salute to his junior, and trotted back towards the artillery and the first brigade.
>
> The drummer wuz beatin' out the thump, thump, thump as we neared the village. Everything wuz quiet and peaceful there. Soon we saw the Yankee troops hightailin' it for the depot and lockin' themselves up. We wuz on them before they saw us. They had cut loopholes to fire from and commenced to fire wildly on our skirmishers. But we returned such a volley on the depot that they soon put out their white flag and gave up. They had suffered about a dozen killed and wounded. Another sixty wuz rounded up and sent to the rear to the provost marshal for questionin'.
>
> Then we regrouped and headed north for Acworth which wuz occupied by a small garrison. On the morning of the 4th of October, Adams's brigade wuz ordered on the village and after a short skirmish the garrison surrendered. (Greenwell 97)

These raids by General Loring's division on the Chattanooga-Atlanta rail supply line at Big Shanty, Kennesaw Water Tank, and Acworth in early October involved far more than killing a few bluecoats or capturing some supplies. Loring in fact was laying waste to the railroad itself, much in the manner Sherman had been doing all over Mississippi and Georgia. "The whole line or railroad from Big Shanty up to Allatoona (full fifteen

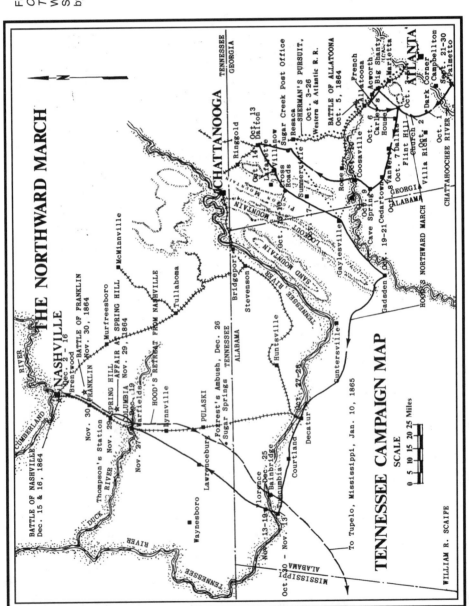

miles) was marked by the fire of the burning railroad," Sherman noted from his Kennesaw Mountain observation point (Sherman 2:147).

Sherman was surely damning himself for not putting an end to Hood's defeated army a month earlier. Now they were tearing up his supply line and moving rapidly away from his massive army sitting in Atlanta. When the telegraph line from Marietta was cut, Sherman needed some quick action to stop Hood's ghost army on their northward movement.

General Hood was elated that Sherman would come out to fight him in the mountains of Georgia.

> In truth, the effect of our operations so far surpassed my expec-
> tations that I was induced to somewhat change my original plan
> to draw Sherman to the Alabama line and then give battle. I
> accordingly decided to move further north and again strike
> Sherman's railroad between Resaca and Tunnel Hill, and then
> move in the direction of the Tennessee, via Lafayette and Gads-
> den, with no intent, however, to cross the river. (Hood 258)

On 9 October, General Sherman himself arrived at Allatoona. His scouts began to complain about the rough and wooded country that masked Hood's movements. They had reports that Hood was at Cedartown and Villa Rica, south of Rome, Georgia. In a complete turnabout in strategy and temperament, Sherman issued his famous edict: "It will be a physical impossibility to protect the railroads now that Hood, Forrest, Wheeler, and the whole batch of 'devils' are turned loose without home or habitation" (Sherman 2:152). Loring, of course, was one of those devils.

On 12 October, Hood's whole army — 25,000 men — emerged from the woods onto the tracks of the Western & Atlantic Railroad north of Resaca, Georgia, which was held by the Federals. A soldier in Loring's division records: "We reached the R.R. at Resaca . . . and tore it up as far as Tunnel Hill above Dalton. We stayed all night at Dalton on the night of the 13th. We burnt all the ties and bent iron, and destroyed a great deal of new ties and bridge timber that they had collected at Tilton, the depot of construction, which is below Dalton" (Howell 364).

Sherman was at Rome, Georgia, when he learned of Hood's appearance at Resaca, 25 miles away. Sherman immediately ordered three of his infantry divisions to the small town, which they reached on the morning of the 13th. By that time, Hood's whole army had passed up the valley toward Dalton. Sherman could not catch the fast-moving butternuts or the elusive commanders, who by snaking in and out of the Georgia mountains were laying waste to much of the railroad as well as to the countryside. Sherman did not take the detour into the mountains to chase Hood's army. He telegraphed Grant: "I propose that we break up the railroad from Chattanooga forward, and that we strike out with our wagons for Milledgeville [the state capital of Georgia at the time], and Savannah. Until we can repopulate Georgia, it is useless for us to occupy it. By attempting to hold the railroad we will lose a thousand men each month and will gain no results. I can make this march, and make Georgia howl" (Sherman 1:152).

Since it was evident that Hood's army would have no opportunity to do battle with Sherman's bluecoats, Hood designed a new plan for the Army of Tennessee. He proposed first to destroy the railroad and communications leading into Chattanooga and to attack and defeat General Thomas's and General Schofield's divisions and capture Nashville, the Federal base. He would then cross the Cumberland River and march to Richmond, Kentucky, from which point he would threaten Louisville and Cincinnati and at the same time recruit men for his army. It appears that all of Hood's commanders — Loring included — believed this was a viable plan that could be executed to a successful victory. At the heart of the Confederate army was a cult of patriots. Their movement would never be arrested; they would go on until silenced by death.

On 16 October, General in Chief H. W. Halleck, Chief of Staff, wired Sherman and intimated that the authorities in Washington were willing for him to undertake a march across Georgia to the sea. On 19 October, Sherman replied to Halleck, "Hood has retreated rapidly — I shall pursue him as far as Gaylesville, Alabama. I will go down the Coosa River until I am sure Hood has gone to Blue Mountain" (Sherman 2:158).

The game was over. Hood and Sherman would no longer seek one another out. To the contrary, both armies began moving in opposite directions, as though they could not wait to get away from each other and seek yet a new foe. Sherman, now like a tornado, chose his path toward Savannah.

Hood's campaign in northern Georgia had been an arduous one. Fatigue and exposure were taking their toll on an already weak army. On 19 October, Hood moved his troops across the rough terrain of north Alabama and encamped at Gadsden. In the pouring rain, the army next crossed the

Black Warrior River and trekked over Sand Mountain, moving 19 miles toward Decatur, Alabama.

Although garrisoned by Federal troops, Decatur was thought to be vulnerable to attack and was a strategic crossing point over the Tennessee River. Upon arrival in front of Decatur on 26 October, Hood found 2,500 Federal infantry defending an entrenched line that included two forts and 1,600 yards of rifle pits and defensive parapets. By early afternoon, "Old Blizzards" Loring had taken up a position near the fort and commenced firing his batteries. He met stiff resistance from Union General Robert S. Granger's bluecoats, and Loring was recalled after sustaining casualties. On 28 October, in a dense fog, Loring's skirmishers were pushed forward to a sheltered ravine within 800 yards of the main fortifications.

By midday, a Federal sortie drove Loring's mixed line of sharpshooters and skirmishers out of the ravine, resulting in a loss of 120 men and five officers captured. Granger had put up a vigorous defense that convinced Hood it would be too costly to force a crossing of the river, even though there was a bridge in place. Hood drew off with his ragged army, following the railroad tracks moving toward Courtland. They encamped at Leighton on 30 October.

At the same time, Sherman resolved to leave General George H. Thomas, "The Rock of Chickamauga," at Nashville to deal with Hood's army. Sherman said, "I know that the country about Decatur is bare of provisions, and inferred Hood would have to move westward to draw his food and stores. His men are all grumbling; the first thing the prisoners asked for is something to eat" (Sherman 2:163).

Hood resumed moving westward toward Tuscumbia, Alabama. Once there, Loring's shivering men huddled around campfires. Autumn was growing wetter and colder as winter rapidly approached. The army lay on the south side of the Tennessee River, opposite Florence, Alabama. Straggling on this long march reached enormous proportions. The combination of bad weather, scanty supplies of food and clothing, and waiting for the forgotten portable pontoons detained Hood's army in the vicinity of Florence for three weeks.

On 13 November, General Hood crossed the Tennessee River and established his headquarters in Florence. Loring's veterans — down to 3,575 from 9,301 — crossed a week later. Hood beseeched his army in "to endure any privation in rations and let the privation be to us not a cause of murmuring, but an incentive and an occasion for the exhibition of a most determined patriotism" (*OR*, vol. 45, pt. 1, p. 1227). Most of the common soldiers, however, were not deluded one bit by Hood's empty oratory.

The Federal forces in Tennessee were not united, being scattered all over the middle part of the state, and thus they were vulnerable. It became Hood's strategy to interpose his army between Thomas at Nashville and Schofield in his advance position at Pulaski, Tennessee, 30 miles south of Columbia, and to cut off and destroy Schofield.

On 21 November, Hood's Confederate legions, marching in three columns, with General Nathan Bedford Forrest's cavalry operating in front, began skirmishing with Major General James H. Wilson's cavalry on their march to Columbia, 70 miles to the northeast. Their object was to secure the bridge that crossed the Duck River at Columbia. "We started this morning through mud from four to twenty inches deep, and then through snow that the keen wind blew in our faces" (French 290). The wet weather, bitterly cold most of the days and nights, made the ill-clad army suffer terribly as they advanced.

When General Schofield learned of the Confederates' intent, he quickly began to head toward Columbia. The two armies were racing for the bridge there. The Confederate columns were moving on country roads roughly parallel to the turnpike on which Schofield was marching. At Lawrenceville, General Edward Hatch's cavalry had a brush with Loring's and Stewart's infantry and were driven out of town. But the Federal infantry under General Jacob D. Cox came into Columbia in time to check General James R. Chalmers's advance, part of Forrest's cavalry, thus gaining the town for Schofield.

On 27 November, the two armies faced each other, but neither side made any charges.

> Hood then left Lee with Clayton's and Stevenson's divisions, together with all of their artillery, on the south side of the river to demonstrate heavily in Schofield's front, while Hood would lead his main force in a secret crossing of the river above the town and move by country roads to bring it behind Schofield, eleven miles north of Columbia at Spring Hill, TN. Here the Columbia-Nashville turnpike was intersected by several other roads, and a Confederate force in control would have Schofield in a trap from which he would not easily extricate himself. (Horn, *Army of Tennessee*, 384)

During the night of the 28th, pontoon bridges were laid at Davis's Ford on the Duck River, five or six miles east of Columbia. At the head of the column to begin crossing was General Hood and his staff. General Patrick R. Cleburne's division was the first across the river, followed by Cheatham's and Loring's divisions. Walthall's division was rear guard for the crossing. The army then moved toward the town of Spring Hill.

Schofield, divining Hood's intentions but under the severe fire of Hood's artillery, crossed the Duck River on 27 November, destroying the railroad bridge and also his pontoon bridge. On the 28th, he started moving his long wagon train of supplies and ammunition northward toward Spring Hill on the Columbia-Franklin Turnpike. This five-mile-long wagon train was accompanied by two divisions under the command of General D. S. Stanley.

At noon on 29 November, General Abraham Buford's cavalry force, another division of Forrest's cavalry, approached Spring Hill from the east; at the same time, Stanley came up from the south, forming a line of battle on the run. Stanley parked the wagon train and artillery on the pike between the town and the railroad station.

General Hood, at the head of Cleburne's division, rode into the vicinity of Spring Hill about 3:00 p.m. Cleburne formed a line of battle off the Rally Hill road by 4:00 p.m. A hot engagement quickly sprang up, between Cleburne and Stanley's advance troops on the pike. About sundown, Schofield's army began to arrive in Spring Hill and General Bates was personally directed by Hood to engage the lead division. As daylight grew shorter by the minute, there began the most controversial event of the entire war: the Spring Hill affair.

And now a series of blunders, misunderstandings, and changes in orders among the Confederate commanders in the field allowed the day to get dark without a Rebel victory.

About dusk, Hood ordered Stewart's corps to move on and place his troops across the turnpike beyond Spring Hill. Wading across the creek in full darkness, they began the march to the assigned position. General Stewart headed north but took the wrong road and proceeded to get lost. A courier from Hood soon rode up and told him of his error.

With the help of a guide, Stewart retraced his steps but soon discovered more confusion in Hood's orders: "If Stewart's command were to take position, as directed on [General John C.] Brown's right, it would require all night! Stewart, not satisfied with this contradiction of orders and con-

vinced there was a mistake, halted his troops and directed that they be
bivouacked, while he himself rode to get further instructions from Hood.
. . . It was now 11 p.m." (Hay 91). Hood then told Stewart to go ahead and
bivouac his corps for the night.

Loring and French were suffering from this misguided adventure. As
French recorded, "What did we come here for? . . . Cheatham's Corps
went into bivouac near the pike, and so in comparative silence the long
night wore away. Hood slept. The head and eyes and ears of the army, all
dead from sleeping. Ye gods! will no geese give them warning as they did
in ancient Rome?" (French 291).

While these two Confederate corps slept, General Schofield, apprised
of his situation of being trapped, frantically moved his force from Columbia and escaped northward on the turnpike. Twenty-two thousand men,
800 wagons, and thousands of horses would have to pass Hood's weary
and sleeping army. Thus, on the night of 29 November began the "eyelash
escape" of the Union forces. With different fortune or better management,
the battle of Spring Hill might have been a decisive Confederate victory.

Rarely in the whole war was a commander to have such an opportunity
as was Hood's that November afternoon, with his troops in position to
close and bar the way to Schofield and to crush or capture his divisions as
they came marching northward, strung out along the pike. But the opportunity was lost. What really happened?

A veteran of General Forrest's cavalry, Judge J. P. Young, studied this
campaign for many years and determined that General Brown, who commanded Cheatham's old division, either lacked nerve on that day or was
drunk. Brown, extremely popular in middle Tennessee, had been given "a
great many presents of liquor" from grateful Southern sympathizers.
While Brown "was not habitually intemperate," at Spring Hill he was "too
much intoxicated to attend to his duties" (Losson 210).

He was not alone. "Cheatham was accused of being drunk in bed,
allowing Schofield's Army to pass by unscathed" (Simpson 66). Residents
around Spring Hill explained that night's fumbling in blunt terms and with
a grave charge: Hood was under the influence. (It must be said that Hood,
a badly maimed man, suffered constant pain from his withered arm and his
barely-healed stump of a leg. He used laudanum, a tincture of opium, as a
pain killer. Having fallen from his horse on the march, he may have turned
to this medicine early.) Hood's guide, John Gregory, was at Hood's headquarters — Absalom Thompson's farm — on the night of 29 November

and stated that the Thompsons "spread a big feast" for the Confederate officers that lasted until midnight. He observed a good deal of drinking among the officers during the march and that it continued at the Thompsons'. Stewart's divisions — Loring, French, and Walthall — were bivouacked two miles north of Spring Hill along the turnpike and were not involved in such misconduct.

Colonel Henry Stone, Assistant Adjutant General on Thomas's staff, wrote: "There were queer doings in the rebel lines among some of the leading officers. . . . There was music and dancing and feasting, and other gods than Mars were worshipped. During the sacrificing at their shrines, the whole of Schofield's force moved silently and fearfully by. . . . But in the morning there was much swearing . . . [for having] given themselves up to the charms of society the night before" (Crownover 10).

The next morning a feeling of guilt pervaded the Confederate high command, despite later protestations of innocence by everyone. Hood was as wrathy as a rattlesnake. The game had gotten out of the trap. The truth was that Hood had been outgeneraled.

General French reported that the next day, "We were up before the morning star" and quickly put back on the Columbia-Nashville Turnpike on a double-quick march to pursue Schofield's retreating army. "Well, General French, we have missed the great opportunity of the war," exclaimed Hood. "Yes," replied French, "the Yankees passed along all night and lit their pipes at our camp fires" (French 292).

All along the Nashville pike, the road and ditches were littered with the debris of Schofield's night march. Although the Union general had nearly cleared Spring Hill by dawn, he had no headstart whatsoever on the Confederates. With 800 wagons, many loaded with the Union's ammunition, spread out over five miles, plus 22,000 troopers and animals, the movement of the wagon train was very slow. Forrest's cavalry finally caught up to Schofield's weary rear guard, who had been marching for 24 hours, and began to harass them as much as possible as they approached Franklin. By noon, the Confederate advance had arrived in a small valley some three and a half miles south of Franklin. Schofield then turned over the defense of Franklin to General Jacob D. Cox, while he devoted his own energy to improving the fords at the Harpeth River and helping the army retire toward Nashville.

An elaborate system of earthworks had been established at Franklin in 1862. They consisted of an inner ditch, or trench, surmounted by a breastwork of earth and head-logs in front, overlooking a deep outer ditch or moat on the south side of the town. This was a semicircular line laid out in a sawtooth plan. These earthworks were supported by 28 well-dispersed guns. Ten of these guns were placed on the knoll overlooking the railroad cut and the Harpeth River.

Two and a half miles south of town, the Columbia-Nashville Pike crossed a ridge known as the Winstead-Breezy Hill range. This high ridge formed the southern border of the plain of Franklin. The terrain from that point northward was generally an open plain up to the line of these earthworks. There were obstructions on this plain. East of the Columbia-Nashville Pike was a hedge of Osage orange trees, and west of the pike was a thicket of locust trees. On the commanding heights across the river to the east, which the bluecoats occupied, artillery had been placed to deliver an enfilading fire to the plain in front of the earthworks. Also on a hill north of town was Fort Granger, an earthwork from which artillery could command the railroad and bridge to the south. By 1:00 p.m., the Federals were in place for the defense of Franklin.

On the slope of Winstead Hill, less than two miles across the open plain from the Federal fortifications, General Hood, with his crutch strapped to his saddle, rode up the eminence to study the Federal position through his field glasses. After the muddle at Spring Hill, he was consumed with a burning impetuosity and desire to ravage the bluecoats. He would not wait for anything, not even for Stephen Lee's artillery to arrive from Spring Hill. And worst of all, he would not heed the advice of his line officers. Hence, on this bright and warm Indian summer day at the end of November 1864, John Bell Hood with reckless audacity, ordered the last great charge of the Civil War. Hood, the ardent advocate of attack, thus repeated his commitment to direct assault despite the dramatic failure of this policy in fighting for Atlanta. There would be no generalship — it would become a soldier's fight to see who could endure the killing the longest.

He fixed his headquarters on the field at the old Neely House, not far from the foot of Winstead Hill, on the Columbia Turnpike. The position was not one from which he could view the coming engagement, and he had to rely upon the reports of his subordinates for his information on the progress of the battle.

All through the morning, Stewart's and Cheatham's corps had come up from Spring Hill in double-quick march. Stewart's mission was to march his advance as far as the Lewisburg Road and then to turn the entire column northward through the fields to force Union General George D. Wagner from his ridge on the Columbia Pike. This flank movement worked, positioning Stewart roughly one and a quarter miles southeast of Franklin. His division was aligned in the grove behind John M. McGavock's place. Loring's division was on the right, Walthall's in the center, and French's on the left. By then it was 3:00 p.m. Hood had to attack soon; the sun would set at 5:00.

In the thickly forested and sparsely inhabited Southern states, it was a rare thing to have a battlefield on which the contending armies could be seen. Usually, they fought in tangled woods and thickets, where the extent of the engagement was measured by the sound of the distant artillery and the crash of musketry. At Franklin, both sides could see the field and follow the movements.

A witness to this great epic, Dr. G. C. Phillips, surgeon for the 22nd Mississippi Regiment, recounts: "It seemed as if we were on the rim of a great bowl. Franklin in the bottom, with a low semicircle of breastworks towards us . . . during this time while the lines were forming it was perfectly still; no sound jarred upon the ear to disturb the beautiful and peaceful scene. I do not like this quietness. It is ominous, and I fear our men are going to be annihilated" (Phillips 261).

At about 4:00 p.m., a staff officer from the commanding general brought Stewart the order to advance, and the word "Forward" was shouted. Then the flag dropped, and the lines advanced. With a front two miles or more in length, and the widest open field approach over which any Confederate army ever charged, Hood's army surged up out of the hollow in which they had formed. They, the ghost army, moved down into the valley below. In a short time the whole Confederate line could be seen, stretching in battle array, from the dark fringe of chestnuts along the river bank to far across the Columbia Pike. Reaching the open field at its base, each division unfolded itself into a single line of battle with as much steadiness as if forming for a dress parade. Flags were flying, and with a quick step they moved forward to the sound of stirring band music.

The 18,000 Confederates marched in a straight line, parade fashion, across the Franklin plain in full view of the whole Union army. It is documented in many Federal staff officers' reports that for a moment, the Federal force was spellbound with admiration in seeing this tidal wave of gray marching at them. For a brief minute, 20,000 bluecoats peered down their

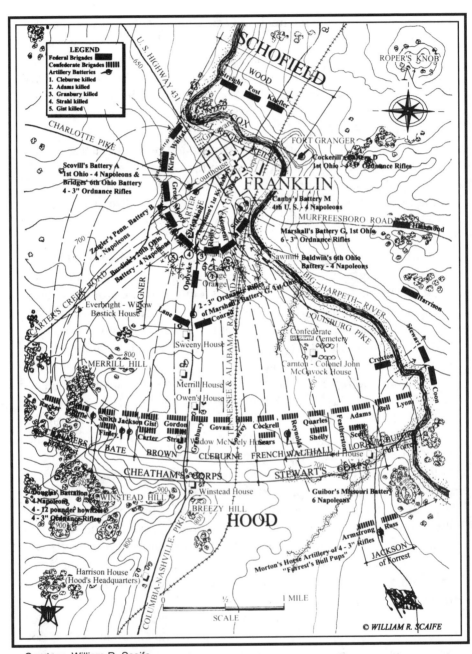

Courtesy, William R. Scaife.

gun barrels to behold the gallant Confederates moving proudly over the open plain to the attack. It was a glorious and imposing sight.

Then, when within 300 yards of the Yanks' breastworks, a cannon boomed from Fort Granger across the river. This seemed to be the signal waited for as additional cannons from east of the river began firing.

Then suddenly, a sheet of flame and smoke burst forth from the entire crescent-shaped Union breastworks, and the air was filled with grape, shell, and rifle bullets that ended with a thump as they crashed into a body. This barrage was answered with the Rebel yell and musketry from the charging Confederate troops as they made their grand assault on Franklin.

Actually, three separate and disjointed battles were being fought this day at Franklin, although they occurred in the same time frame. The Confederate army's advance started, as it were, from the circumference of a wagon wheel, with each brigade marching toward the hub, which was the enemy's works. Hence the brigades, as they advanced, began to overlap with one another as they got closer to the hub.

The advance of Loring's and Walthall's divisions — part of Stewart's corps on the right wing of the advance — had been slowed by the curve of the Harpeth River, which flowed northwestward until it reached the flank of the Federal works near the railway cut at the Lewisburg Pike. Because of the course of the river, the width of the plain contracted rapidly as Stewart advanced, necessitating readjusting and changing the direction of his lines on the center and right. And, undetectable from two miles away were two natural defenses to hamper Loring and Walthall in their attack. Thirty feet in front of the Union line was a thick, almost impenetrable thorny hedge of Osage orange. It was strongly supported by sharpened branches made into an abatis and deeply imbedded in the earth. Other clumps of these immovable hedges were also on the plain.

The second obstacle occurred where the river and the Lewisburg Pike ran parallel to a deep railroad cut in the Nashville & Decatur Railroad. This cut made it necessary for the charging brigades to change direction and to be enfiladed by artillery posted at the end of the Murfreesboro bridge site on the Franklin side of the Harpeth River and from Fort Granger.

Nothing was going well for General Stewart on this afternoon. The first assault by French had been a disaster, and part of Walthall's division had become disorganized when passing through a thicket of Osage orange bushes and was then torn apart by Union General John Casement's repeating rifles. On Stewart's right, near the Lewisburg Pike, Loring's division — comprised of Scott's, Featherston's, and Adams's brigades — was encountering every conceivable obstacle to be found on the plains at Franklin.

After the first line of attack had moved forward, some units of Loring's and Walthall's commands had become intermingled because of the obstructions presented by the railroad cut and the Osage orange. As Loring's men scrambled around the railroad cut, they were struck by a murderous fire from Brevet Major General Thomas J. Henderson's battery of guns that were placed at the Murfreesboro bridge site. Loring's brigades swung to the left, exposing their entire flank to enfilading fire, which caused them to begin overlapping with Quarles's brigade of Walthall's division. Adding to this was a severe bombardment from Fort Granger.

Struggling forward, Loring's troops met the massive abatis in front of the Federals' parapets. Upon charging, they were dismayed to find them impassable. As soon as Loring's lines came into view, they were met with destructive fire from Brevet Brigadier General Israel N. Stiles's and Casement's Union forces. The small, tough trunks of the trees, thinned out as they had been, did not protect Loring's brigades from the destructive fire of Stiles's line.

The first assault of Loring's men met a bloody repulse. Loring ordered his second line forward, and they soon came on and reached the works in front of the 128th Indiana. But the intense fire from the musketry and the cannons was dismantling Loring's division by the minute. One bluecoat said, "They were coming up to our works on their hands and knees" (Cox, *Battle of Franklin*, 125). The fight was bitter and stubborn.

With Scott's brigade blown to pieces, Featherston's moved up to the front of the division. Featherston's and the remainder of Scott's brigades began to overlap and partially consolidate as they pivoted sharply toward the northwest. Within 800 yards there was terrific fire of shot, shell, grape, and canister. Near the enemy lines they came upon the cut in the railroad, and when they changed their direction, the consolidated firepower from three Union positions intensified. Huge gaps were torn in the lines as bloodied mobs of soldiers toppled down the embankment or fell across the tracks. The line was stacked deep along Loring's front. Both brigades meshed and crammed together against the obstacles. From the railroad to the ditches immediately in front of the Union breastworks, the brigades left their heaviest trail of casualties and scattered war debris.

"The fight was furious, and the carnage awful beyond anything I ever observed," said Colonel W. D. Gale, Stewart's Adjutant General (Gale 4). The men of Loring's division were mown down en masse by enfilade and reverse fire on their front, right, and rear. Charge after charge was made, and as fast as one brigade was shattered and recoiled, another bravely went forward into the very jaws of death and came back broken and bloody, again rallying quickly with their heroic officers and again going forward to do what seemed impossible, or die. Loring was quickly reforming his broken brigades as best as he could out of the range of the most severe combat.

One Union soldier noted: "We had been watching Loring's division as it reached the river. We stood still waiting for it to come within the range. The 'field and staff' were all mounted, and we could see them ride their lines and dress them up, just as though they were on brigade drill" (Stevens 166).

At one point during this first attack, an entire brigade faltered when it encountered the heavy fire and abatis and began to fall back. An eyewitness recorded General Loring's actions under this galling fire:

> Loring rode to the front amid a hail of bullets raining through the abatis. He tried to hold the frightened brigade in place as they fell back.
>
> Loring shouted for them to stand fast. Once he cried out in anguish, "Great God: Do I command cowards?" Then Loring turned alone on the horse and faced the enemy fire for over a minute.
>
> He was in full Confederate uniform. A sword belt encompassed his waist; sword and scabbard were polished and shone brightly. A large dark plume of ostrich feathers drooped over his hat. Loring was a perfect target for some Union sharpshooter who dreamed of felling a Rebel general.
>
> He stood alone, however, in one last defiant act by the Army of Tennessee. Then Loring turned and galloped to the rear to regroup the unit. (McDonough and Connelly 146)

After the first attack failed, the next four hours were a nightmare for Loring's command. Some of his units had worked through the abatis to cling to the outer side of the Federal earthworks, pinned down. Others lay behind the abatis, dodging the awful fire. Loring's brigades had become broken up into smaller bands that scattered on the battlefield because of the heavy cloud of acrid cannon smoke and the approaching darkness.

Hood remained at his headquarters on the Winstead Hill range, and the accounts available indicate that he knew virtually nothing of what was happening to his army. Even in the daylight hours he could not see anything due to the fierce cloud of smoke covering the ground.

The Battle of Franklin had been the bloodiest five hours of the Civil War and it became the grave for the Army of Tennessee. "I never saw the dead lay near so thick. I saw them upon each other, dead and ghastly in the powder-dimmed star-light," said Union Colonel Emerson Opdycke (*OR*, vol. 45, pt. 1, p. 241). "The annals of war may long be searched for a parallel to the desperate charge of the Army of Tennessee at Franklin, a charge which has been called 'the greatest drama in American history'" (Horn, *Army of Tennessee*, 402-403).

Of the 27,000 Federals engaged, there were 2,326 casualties, of whom 1,104 were missing. Of 27,000 Confederates engaged, 6,252 were lost, of whom 702 were missing. Five Confederate generals were killed this day — Cleburne, Adams, Otho F. Strahl, Gist, and Hiram B. Granbury. Who would lead the army to Nashville? With five generals killed and six more wounded, and six colonels killed and 15 wounded, Hood's cadre had been drastically reduced.

Despite the bloody holocaust of the day, General Thomas in Nashville was convinced that the Confederate army outnumbered him by far both in infantry and cavalry. Thus, he decided to evacuate Franklin and instructed Schofield to do so immediately. All during the night, the Union army crowded onto the Nashville Pike and moved as quickly as they had done at Spring Hill the night before. By the dawn of 1 December, Schofield had escaped Hood's net one more time: his force was safe within the fortifications of Nashville and was added to General Thomas's 70,000-man army.

Hood had come this far and was determined not to be denied Nashville. To him, Franklin was just another stepping stone on the way north. He immediately issued a special field order congratulating the army upon what he termed the success achieved the day before over the enemy: "The commanding general congratulates the army upon the success achieved yesterday over our enemy by their heroic and determined courage. The enemy have been sent in disorder and confusion to Nashville, and while we lament the fall of many gallant officers and brave men, we have shown to our countrymen that we can carry any position occupied by our enemy" (*OR*, vol. 45, pt. 2, p. 628). Jefferson Davis was heard to observe that "one more such victory and there would not be any Western army left" (Morgan 224).

Loring and other division commanders were ordered to have details sent on the field to gather up and stack the arms found there and hold their commands in readiness. Stewart's corps was directed to move at daylight on 2 December and follow General Lee on the pike toward Nashville. The undaunted Hood ordered the army forward as fast as they could make the trip.

Probably no city in America, with the exception of the capital cities of Washington and Richmond, was more strongly fortified than was Nashville in 1864. The line of Union works, carefully laid out and heavily constructed, followed commanding hills looking down on the southern face to the valley of Brown's Creek, which flows into the Cumberland above the city, and on the west into the valley of Richland Creek. The whole bend of the Cumberland River was completely enclosed. Regardless, Nashville was the prize, and Hood meant to have it.

Loring's division made reasonably good marching time, despite more of Schofield's military refuse that littered the Franklin Pike. The division arrived in the hilly woodlands several miles south of Nashville on 2 December. On the following day, it was moved westward through deadened woods and fields and across the Granny White Pike to a hill near the Hillsborough Pike. Here the division scooped out entrenchments a mile in length. Loring's depleted front was stretched out to man the ditch; it almost looked like a skirmish line rather than the main line of defense. Stewart's corps held the left flank of the army, Lee's the center, and Cheatham's the right. On 4 December, Loring celebrated his 46th birthday.

Up until 8 December, fatigue parties from Loring's division assisted in throwing up five detached redoubts, or strong points, on either side of the Hillsborough Pike and strengthened their own positions near the Granny White Pike. On the 8th, the temperature dropped to 12 degrees, and on the next day it began sleeting. The whole Confederate army suffered greatly as they huddled in their shallow, unfinished works. Many were thinly clad

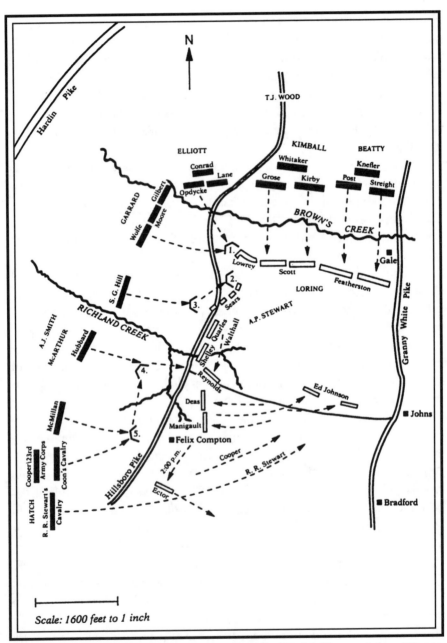

Assault on the Confederate Left, December 15, Nashville. Reprinted by permission of Harper-Collins Publishers, Inc. From *Embrace an Angry Wind (The Confederacy's Last Hurrah)*, by Wiley Sword. Copyright © 1990 by Wiley Sword.

and barefoot. Shoes, hats, blankets, and clothing in general were in short supply because Hood had not taken any time to order them. General Hood, a terrible administrator, seemed to concern himself with only one thing, and that was to attack.

During the first two weeks of December, Union General Thomas had been constantly badgered and pressured by General Grant to attack Hood. But Thomas would not be hurried into battle; he waited until he and the weather were ready. On 15 December, with a break in the weather, Thomas decided to come out from behind Nashville's mighty fortifications. The word soon spread that the Union army was moving, and many civilians came out to such vantage points as hills and rooftops to watch the coming battle.

General Thomas's plan was a simple one, calculated to take maximum advantage of his superior numbers. A continuous line of battle would be maintained across the entire front so that as Hood's thin line was stretched, it would, at some point, succumb to the pressure of the Union advance.

At 1:00 p.m., Schofield's XXIII Corps was ordered to swing around the rear of General A. J. Smith's advancing corps, thus establishing a continuous alignment two miles long with Generals Thomas J. Wood, Smith, Schofield, and Wilson's cavalry, all advancing relentlessly toward the Confederate left flank and rear. Stewart soon perceived that his position was the immediate objective of the attack.

Stewart ordered Walthall to place his men under arms and positioned a company of infantry and a battery of artillery in each of the redoubts in his immediate front (nos. 4 and 5). The remainder of his command was put in position behind a stone wall along the eastern side of the pike, extending for the distance between redoubts 3 and 4. Stewart's line on his extreme left flank was still not long enough to cover redoubt 5. To the right, Loring was holding the salient embracing redoubts 1 and 2.

After three hours of intensive fighting, redoubts 4 and 5 fell, and the men of Smith's corps poured through the interval between the two forts and drove across the Hillsborough Pike. Federal artillery was brought forward and began pounding Walthall's thinly stretched line at close range, then began a massive assault with his entire corps. Little could be done to stem the Federal juggernaut advancing across the Hillsborough Pike on Walthall's front.

Shortly after 12:30, Loring's pickets looked out from the all but abandoned trenches along the crest of the hill, midway between the two main lines of battle, and saw Wood's infantry coming toward them. General Wood's assault had no sooner been launched against Stewart's front than Schofield joined in the attack, bringing the total to just under 50,000 attacking Stewart's corps of 4,800. It seemed like the whole Union army was heading for Loring's position in redoubt number 1.

The artillery pounded the Confederate line, particularly the salient where the line turned southward at redoubt 1. This salient acted like a hinge between Walthall's and Loring's divisions. Impressed with the importance of carrying this hill, the Rebels' center, two Union batteries were ordered up and so placed as to bring a converging fire on the crest of the hill. But the Federals could not shake Loring's division in the main line. The salient it held seemed impregnable to direct attack.

By 4:00 p.m., the enemy, who had passed the Hillsborough Pike a full half mile, completely turned the flank and gained the rear of Walthall and Loring, whose situation by the minute was becoming perilous in the extreme. Finding their positions untenable, Loring and Walthall would have to retire quickly or be captured and taken prisoner. "The collapse of the left flank around 4:30 PM was so sudden that many of Walthall's and Loring's soldiers were trapped in the blue pocket and forced to surrender. Many troops were wounded while scores of others were simply too tired and cold to run. In the following hectic withdrawal many casualties were sustained by Stewart's Corps" (Howell 398).

As the Federal troops pushed down the road after Loring and Walthall, Loring's soldiers gallantly formed a new line along the Granny White Pike, nearly at right angles to their former position, to check the anticipated rush of the Federals from Loring's and Walthall's fronts; this was successfully done. Loring's winded command continued falling back through the hilly, wooded countryside in relatively good order to a position roughly one mile southeast of the position they had vacated.

All of Stewart's corps were ordered to retire to a position between Granny White Pike and Franklin Pike, lying midway between Brentwood, four miles to the south, and the Nashville fortifications. The diminished corps took position and began to prepare for the resumption of the battle on the next day.

Loring spent the night moving about in the darkness and getting his depleted division into battle position. "Our brigade (3rd Mississippi) took up a position behind a stone fence several feet high. Our army was strung out along an east-west line which had a gap in the middle, where all the main road or pikes went through. We wuz to hold it and would withdraw through it if necessary" (Greenwell 111).

The new line was shorter than the previous one; it was about three and a half miles long and much more compact and defensible with its flanks turned back at Peach Orchard (present-day Overton's Hill) in the east and at Shy's Hill (present-day Compton's Hill) in the west. Most important, it covered two of the eight spoke-like turnpikes coming out of Nashville, the Franklin and Granny White roads.

General Cheatham's corps was shifted to the left at Shy's Hill while Lee's corps formed the right flank at Peach Orchard. Stewart, with Loring's and Walthall's battered divisions, was in the center of the new line. Along Loring's and Walthall's front, the center of Hood's line, the Federals approached at an early hour on 16 December, placed artillery in position, and opened a heavy fire that continued almost incessantly through the day.

> They began their attack on our section (Loring's) pourin' heavy artillery into our lines all day. With an occasional break in artillery, their troops of riflemen came stormin' our way. We poured volley after volley into their ranks, chasin' 'em back to the wood; but before long, here they's come again. With our muzzle loaders we had to work fast against their repeatin' rifles.
>
> We took losses and had gaps in our lines. When a trench was dug, it wuz just a muddy hole, unfit for hogs . . . and we pumped lead into their ranks fast enough to drive 'em back again and again. (Greenwell 111)

From morning until afternoon, superior Union artillery bombarded the entire Confederate line.

These battle-wise Confederate veterans knew when the odds were insurmountable. It was now a matter of survival and escape from death or from one of the Northern prison camps. The break had come quickly and decisively, and Hood's entire line soon gave way. "As the drizzle of cold rain turned to ice the Third Mississippi (Loring's division) and her sister regiments battled fiercely to hold their positions. Massive Union columns, many armed with new repeating carbines, found the going tough and took a severe mauling as they struggled through ankle-deep mud uphill to grapple with Loring's men" (Howell 400).

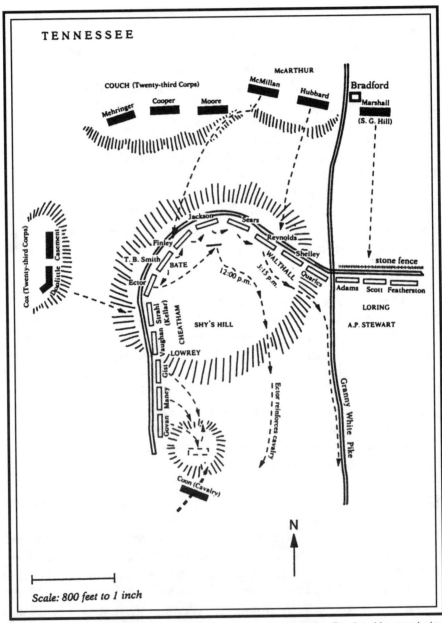

Assault on the Confederate Left, 4:30 p.m., December 16, Nashville. Reprinted by permission of HarperCollins Publishers, Inc. From *Embrace an Angry Wind (The Confederacy's Last Hurrah)*, by Wiley Sword. Copyright © 1990 by Wiley Sword.

After the lines of Loring's and Walthall's divisions were pierced, the men gave way and broke apart at many points and began fleeing toward the rear with Federal soldiers chewing them up in hot pursuit. Loring and Walthall rode up and down the broken lines, encouraging and exhorting the men to steady themselves and make a stand, trying to form a line, "but it was like trying to stop the Duck River with a fish net" (Horn 644).

The once proud Army of Tennessee had degenerated into a mob. This was the only rout of a major Confederate force during the entire war.

Finally, beyond Brentwood, the fragments of the command were in some measure united and bivouacked in groups for the night. The Yankees had captured four generals as well as almost 6,000 prisoners. General George H. Thomas became the third of the triumvirate, joining Grant and Sherman, who won the war for the Union. Loring had fought all three of them and was still afoot.

For the next two weeks, the Northerners maintained a most vigorous pursuit. General Thomas would make a persistent effort to smash the remaining part of the Army of Tennessee as it retreated southward toward the Tennessee River.

General Stephen D. Lee and his cavalry had kept the Franklin Pike open for the routed army, but Franklin was in chaos. After the battle on 30 November, the Confederates had made the town a major hospital area for Hood's army. On 16 December, Hood sent his wagon trains south, and they passed through the town for three days. Franklin was in a hectic state of abandonment. The sick and wounded who could not be moved were left for the Union army; thousands were sacrificed because there simply was no way to evacuate them all. Lee held off the Federals until Hood's last infantrymen crossed the pontoons across the Harpeth River on their way to Spring Hill.

Hood's army was so disorganized and reduced in size that it wasn't much of a fighting force; it was impossible to ascertain where anyone was, other than those fighting the rear guard. The army was strung out for miles — wagons, infantrymen, artillery, stragglers. Loring and other generals could not be pinpointed at one spot on this retreat as they were constantly in and out of the columns, moving the battle-fatigued troops on course

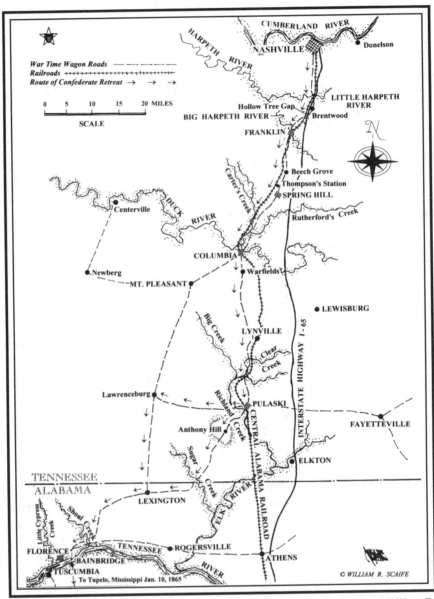

Hood's retreat from Nashville, December 16, 1864-January 1, 1865. (Courtesy, William R. Scaife)

toward Columbia and the Duck River. To add to the misery, the weather changed again: it rained heavily, which turned to sleet, which then turned to snow: "Wagon and gun carriage wheels sliced through the mud throughout the cold daylight hours while during the frozen nights the ruts thus created hardened into sharp-edged obstacles for the infantry to traverse. Large numbers of men were still barefoot and their bleeding feet left trails of blood" (Howell 402). The retreat was almost as disastrous as the battle of Nashville itself.

The torrential rains did bring a bit of luck. The rapid rise of the Harpeth River at Franklin and the increased swiftness of the current prohibited Thomas's infantry from crossing and continuing their dogged pursuit. Thomas had no pontoons and would have to wait for some to be delivered.

On the morning of the 17th, orders had been given to the tired Confederates to continue on toward Columbia. Hood had originally planned to make a stand there, but one look at his shattered army convinced him of the futility of that course. He therefore assigned command of the rear guard to General Forrest with instructions to hold Columbia as long as possible and then to follow him through Pulaski in the direction of Florence, Alabama. The next two days found the Army of Tennessee crossing the Duck River.

Hood's retreat in severe weather was likened to George Washington's stand some 88 years before. Colonel W. D. Gale went even further when he wrote, "I shall never forget the passage of Duck River — Washington crossing the Delaware was insignificant" (Gale 47).

The weather got worse. It rained for four more days and then grew severely cold. It is likely that in no other part of the war did the men suffer more than on Hood's march out of Tennessee.

On Christmas Eve, by some queer error, the pontoons that the Union infantry was waiting for in order to cross the Harpeth River were sent to Murfreesboro instead of Franklin. The gap between the retreating Confederate army and the pursuing bluecoats was becoming greater. The Federal infantry could never narrow it; only Union General J. H. Wilson's cavalry had the potential to make a strike.

Early on Christmas morning, the Union cavalry got across the Duck River above Columbia and began to pursue Forrest's rear guard. While Wilson and Forrest skirmished, the main body of the Confederate army arrived at the Sugar Creek crossing of the Tennessee River.

The Confederates were so short of horses that the ordnance train for the main army had been parked at Sugar Creek while the mules were used to help transport the pontoons to the river. If the army was to survive, it had to get across the Tennessee River. Pontoons were laid as rapidly as the arrival of the boats would allow. General Stewart's corps was put into position to protect both incoming roads. Loring confirmed, "Thus we toiled on till Christmas day, cold, drizzly and muddy. . . . We camped on the banks of Shoal Creek, and our corps formed a line of battle to protect the rear and let all cross" (Stockdale 169).

The last fighting of Hood's ill-fated Tennessee campaign occurred at Sugar Creek. In a dense fog, while waiting for Wilson's cavalry to attack, the gallant Confederates charged them, very successfully. The Yankee cavalry was driven back across the creek, and General Ross's cavalry brigade charged and chased them from the area.

It took two days for the army to cross the Tennessee River on the pontoon bridge. On the 28th, the march resumed to Florence. As the year came to a close, Hood thought that he was safe from Union pursuit. But the new year would not begin before another disaster would be added to his record.

On the 29th, a force of cavalry, numbering 600 men made up from detachments of the 15th Pennsylvania, 2nd Michigan, and 10th, 12th, and 13th Indiana Regiments under the command of Colonel William J. Palmer, started to move from Decatur, Alabama, westward in the direction of Hood's line of retreat into Mississippi. Avoiding Forrest's cavalry, Colonel Palmer overtook the five-mile-long Confederate pontoon train, consisting of 200 wagons and 83 pontoon boats, while ten miles out of Russellville, Alabama, on 31 December and burned it. Palmer also learned that a large supply train of Hood's, bound from Barton Station, was ahead: "I surprised it in camp. It consisted of 110 wagons and over 500 mules. We burned the wagons, shot or sabered all the mules we could not lead off or use to mount prisoners" (*OR*, vol. 45, pt. 1, p. 643). In nine days, Palmer had covered 265 miles, taken 150 prisoners, destroyed between 750 and 1,000 stand of arms, and burned two wagon trains. His successful raid merely added to the desecration of Hood's army as it crawled into its Mississippi resting place at Corinth, the northern terminus of the Mobile & Ohio Railroad. Here they would find critically needed supplies.

Post-battle rhetoric could hardly hide the fact that the artillery of the Army of Tennessee had been virtually destroyed. The Yankees had tallied 72 captured guns, 75 limbers, 20 caissons, and 6 wagons filled with artillery ammunition. The army was down to 67 pieces. More than half the companies were without guns and caissons, and nearly half of the ordnance had been lost. Many of the army's batteries were simply wiped out as fighting units. And even worse, some of the army's best artillery officers had been lost; only seven field officers remained. Seasoned officers who knew how to work with the infantry were needed, so Loring was sent to Columbus, Mississippi, and assigned to the artillery. This was a temporary assignment for Loring; no records indicate he was made chief of the artillery.

These were tumultuous days for the Army of Tennessee. It had hemorrhaged badly. The number of prisoners taken totaled 13,189, including eight generals. Deserters numbered in the thousands. Those killed and wounded during the battles of Franklin and Nashville were estimated at 8,600. During the campaign, Hood suffered perhaps 23,500 casualties from a total strength of about 38,000 men. Thomas's losses, in contrast, numbered less than 6,000 men.

As the word of the bloodletting at Franklin and Nashville got out, wailing was heard in homesteads across the Southland. Thousands of wives were widowed and children orphaned during the Yule season of 1864. With Sherman now in Savannah, it was the saddest, most dismal Christmas ever experienced in the South.

The Confederacy that had been so confidently launched in Montgomery nearly four years before was rapidly on the decline and unraveling. Every day added to the paralysis steadily creeping over the Southern cause.

In Richmond, Congress expressed increasing dissatisfaction with the Davis administration and talked of restoring Joseph E. Johnston to command and making Lee General in Chief. On 13 January, General Hood requested to be relieved from his command, which took effect ten days later.

While Hood's army was fighting in December, Sherman's army, after leaving Atlanta in flames on 12 November, moved across Georgia in his infamous march to the sea. While his bands played "Glory, Glory Hallelujah," his army of 62,000 teenaged adventurers marched across the state in 27 days, covering 222 miles, and pulled up in front of Savannah on 21 December 1864. Without Hood's army, Southern resistance was little more than a formality, as the Georgia militia was no match for the bluecoat juggernaut.

While Sherman spent about a month in Savannah clothing his men and filling the trains with ammunition and rations, his plans shifted toward South Carolina, the traitor state. He would move on Charleston and then on to the capital, Columbia. Unless the remaining Southern troops east of the Mississippi could combine against Sherman's march, the days of the Confederacy were numbered. The only answer to Sherman would be a concentration of scattered Confederate military units against him.

The call would go out for the help of the Army of Tennessee. Weathered veteran Loring and the last of the old guard officers would be compelled once again to be ready to move to a new theater of war for another year of fighting.

Chapter 15

Loring's Last Theater of the Civil War — Bentonville, North Carolina

*G*ENERAL P. G. T. BEAUREGARD *knew of the impending advance of Sherman's forces into South Carolina and ordered everything left of the Army of Tennessee to be moved east toward Augusta, Georgia. After a 400-mile trip on the broken-down Southern railroad system, pieces of the worn-out army began arriving at Augusta on 11 February but were too late to save Columbia, the capital of*

South Carolina. Sherman's advance was already heading north toward Fayetteville, North Carolina.

On 21 February, Loring received orders to proceed with part of the artillery to Augusta to join the force mobilizing there. He was then rushed east to join forces operating north of the Saluda River, near Newberry, South Carolina. From there, Loring's small command was directed to Pomaria, Unionville, and then Chester, where General Stewart and some of his units and General Cheatham's corps were located. With the Confederate abandonment of Columbia, the Southern counter-concentration strategy moved toward Smithfield, North Carolina, a small lumber and turpentine village west of Goldsboro on the North Carolina Railroad. It looked as though the town was on Sherman's route north. Trains could quickly carry the greater part of the Army of Tennessee directly to it, and General Bragg, facing the abandonment of Wilmington, North Carolina, could fall back to it.

Loring's command, with Stewart's corps, quickly left Chester by rail for their new destination, which changed to Goldsboro when it was found that the eastern part of the rail system was in chaos. But Loring's men had no sooner reached Goldsboro on 9 March than they were deployed to Kinston, 20 miles to the east.

On 18 March, General Joseph E. Johnston, who had been brought out of retirement at the request of Robert E. Lee and given the command of the Army of Tennessee on 22 February, learned that Goldsboro was Sherman's objective. He proposed that if the Confederates could concentrate promptly in the path of Union General Henry W. Slocum, the left wing of Sherman's Y-formation, they might destroy his exposed force before Sherman could come to the rescue. Johnston approved a spot two miles south of Bentonville, some 20 miles west of Goldsboro, as an ideal site to assemble the troops for a surprise confrontation.

By marching all that day, the troops of Generals Stewart and Bragg arrived soon after nightfall in Bentonville. General Hardee, coming from the vicinity of Averasboro, camped on the road six miles from the village. Slocum's column also halted late that day near Bentonville and went into camp.

Johnston's plan was simple. General Wade Hampton, with his horse artillery, would delay Slocum until Hardee had time to reach the field. This would bring Slocum to a halt; with Bragg's command he would smash him with a hammer blow between Hardee's and Stewart's forces.

The next morning, Union General H. C. Hobart was directed to deploy half of his 1st Brigade and move in line against the Confederates' line until something developed. General D. C. Buell's 2nd Brigade was sent to the left of the road to attack the Confederate right flank. With Buell in position on Hobart's left, General W. P. Carlin ordered his own command forward. He thought he was flanking the Confederates, who could be seen parked along the pike.

Unexpectedly, Carlin plowed into the hidden forces of "Old Blizzards" Loring and General D. H. Hill, who received him with a "sheet of fire" from a distance of about 50 feet. The Yankees reeled under the volley, while great gaps were made in their line.

However, right away, Johnston's plan began to unravel. General Hardee, the head of whose column was just appearing on the battlefield, was directed by Johnston to send his leading division to General Robert F. Hoke's assistance. But the division, having to pass through a dense thicket, did not reach the ground to which it was ordered until it was too late. Thus, Hardee's force had been split. There would be no anvil on which to bang Slocum.

General Johnston then ordered that Stewart and Hardee confer with each other about an advance. The hour for another attack — 2:45 p.m. — was agreed upon.

> There was never a battle line where so much of "rank" commanded so little of "file." Johnston, a full General, was in command, with Beauregard, of the same rank, as second in command. Bragg, another General, commanded one wing, and Lieutenant-Generals Hardee and Stewart, the others. Lieutenant-General D. H. Hill . . . commanded a corps; Lieutenant-General Hampton, the cavalry, with Major-General Wheeler, as his second in command. There were the Major-Generals, also: Hoke . . . ; Taliaferro and Stevenson . . . ; Cheatham, Bate and Brown . . . ; McLaws . . . ; "Old Blizzards" Loring, with one arm gone; Patton Anderson . . . ; Walthall . . . ; Butler . . . — and all of them together commanding but twenty thousand men, the faithful remnants of divisions and corps which had fought all over the South, for four years. (Henry 455)

Shrieking the Rebel yell, the Confederate right wing swept forward at the appointed hour. To observers elsewhere on the field, the scene was a reminder of past glories as the ragged, gray- and butternut-clad Confederates charged through the woods and across the fields in perfect order with colors flying. This would be the last grand charge for General Loring in the Civil War.

The Federals were driven nearly a mile and routed from their two lines of breastwork. Captured were 417 prisoners and eight pieces of artillery. For a brief moment on this Sunday afternoon, the old spirit of the Army of Tennessee was revived. Unfortunately, it was only the afterglow.

Again, advancing rapidly and firing as they charged, the Confederates chased the fugitives from the Union commands of Generals Buell, Hobart, and James S. Robinson westward through the fields and swamps until the bluecoats ended up safely behind the lines of the XX Corps. The critical moment for the Confederates had arrived. Flushed with success, they could move on General James D. Morgan's line and flank that lay exposed, opposite Bragg's position.

The other divisions of Hardee's wing, Loring, Colonel John G. Coltart, and Hoke, renewed the attack on Morgan's forces across the Goldsboro Road. Hardee led a column behind Morgan's line while Loring and Coltart attacked in front and Hoke moved up again on the enemy right. But because the Confederate assaults lacked coordination, Morgan's division survived these attacks. The Confederates made one last general effort about sunset, but their attacks on the left, center, and right of Morgan all failed. During the night, the two armies adjusted their lines and improved their fortifications.

Sherman's instructions for Slocum for the next day were to fight a defensive action until the remainder of the Union army could be rushed to his aid. Heavy skirmishing occurred on the field, but in comparison with the events of the 19th, the day passed quietly. General Loring went to the rear with sickness, and Walthall succeeded to his command.

On the morning of the 21st, Sherman's army was reunited and in position on three sides of the Confederate works. During that night, all of the Confederate wounded that could bear transportation were removed, and General Johnston, learning that Schofield had reached Goldsboro, ordered his army to cross Mill Creek by the bridge at Bentonville and retreat on Smithfield, North Carolina. Schofield's force alone was larger than Johnston's, and it was at most only a two-day march for him to join with Sherman.

While Johnston's army completed its withdrawal to Smithfield, Sherman moved on to Goldsboro where his men began arriving on the 23rd, joining with Schofield. The combined command equaled 90,000 men. In sad comparison, the returns of the Confederate infantry and artillery on 23 March showed a grand total of 13,363 effective present for duty. With these figures at hand, General Johnston sent a message to Robert E. Lee on the same day, which essentially dictated to Lee that he must move his force in front of Richmond.

> Sherman's course cannot be hindered by the small force I have. I can do no more than annoy him. I respectfully suggest that it is no longer a question whether you leave present position; you have only to decide where to meet Sherman. I will be near him (*OR*, vol. 47, pt. 2, pp. 1453-1454).

General Lee replied the same day, "Where, in your opinion, can we best meet Sherman?"

Could the two Confederate armies be joined to stop Sherman?

While both armies rested, Sherman journeyed by rail and boat from Goldsboro to City Point, Virginia, where he boarded the paddle wheeler *River Queen*. Here he discussed the coming end of the war with President Lincoln, General Grant, and Admiral Porter.

On 1 April, General Philip H. Sheridan attacked Five Points to the rear of Petersburg; the Union masses were behind General Robert E. Lee, and the South Side Railroad was at their mercy. Richmond would have to be abandoned, and it ceased permanently to be the capital of the Confederate States.

From Petersburg, Lee's Army of Northern Virginia groped westward in misery. Being boxed in by the Federal cavalry, it found itself at Appomattox Station on 8 April seeking its supply train from the south. But the Yankees captured this train destined for Lee; without his supplies and unable to open a route south to General Johnston, Lee realized that surrender was inevitable. The end had come. Lee asked for an armistice on 9 April 1865 and surrendered to General Grant the same day.

General John C. Breckinridge had been appointed Secretary of War on 4 February by President Davis. Shortly before the evacuation of Richmond, he had called together several congressmen to discuss the welfare of the soldiers: "What I propose is this: That the Confederacy should not be captured in fragments, that we should not disband like banditti, but that we should surrender as a government, and we will thus maintain the dignity of our cause and secure the respect of our enemies. This has been a magnificent epic. In God's name let it not terminate in a farce" (W. Davis 254). But the sudden collapse of Lee at Petersburg had left no time for surrender terms. The Confederate Congress knew the cause was lost and left Richmond quickly. Jefferson Davis and all of his cabinet — save Breckinridge — fled Richmond on a train to Danville, Virginia.

While parked at Smithfield during the first two weeks of April, Johnston reorganized the army for the last time, breaking up many regiments and divisions that numbered less than a hundred. The shrunken elements of the Army of Tennessee were a sad spectacle. For his corps commanders, Johnston appointed Hardee, Stephen D. Lee, and Stewart, who had Loring, Walthall, and Major General Patton Anderson for his division commanders.

On 10 April, Sherman's army headed out of Goldsboro in high spirits, moving "straight against Joe Johnston wherever he may be" (B. Davis 247). But at Smithfield, during a halt of Sherman's van, the momentous news was flashed from Virginia: Lee had surrendered the Army of Northern Virginia at Appomattox Court House on 9 April 1865.

Johnston heard of Lee's surrender as he retreated from Raleigh on 11 April and knew a similar fate awaited him. During the next few days, Johnston and his army moved toward the Greensboro area where they would join President Davis and his cabinet, the last remnants of the Confederate government still functioning while traveling on the railroad.

During the intervening period, Johnston's army was inactive. Numerous rumors concerning the coming surrender floated throughout the ranks, and discipline was lax to nonexistent. Loring and other officers began to discuss openly the likelihood of defeat and its possible consequences. Defeat was one thing for the volunteer soldier in the ranks, but for the Regular Army officers such as Johnston and Loring who had gone over to the Confederacy, it was something more dire, especially if Army regulations dealing with officers who deserted and took up arms for the enemy would be applied. There were indications that the old Army officers were being considered the ringleaders of the rebellion and would be brought to account when the war ended. Would they receive harsh treatment?

On 17 April, Johnston met Sherman under a flag of truce at the Bennett farmhouse near Durham Station, between the lines. The terms of the truce were simple and liberal, similar to those given Robert E. Lee. Sherman, ruthless and unfeeling in combat, was as considerate and magnanimous with Johnston's defeated army as Grant had been with Lee. Two days later, 20,640 men and officers were paroled. No charges would be preferred against the officers.

The Army of Tennessee, in one day, was dismantled and paroled. On foot, astride worn-out army horses and mules, or piled into patched-up, creaking army wagons and ambulances, the men started for their homes in the Southland. Somebody was needed to see that the ex-Confederates were returned back to their state capitals, and this was left up to the commanding officers. Loring and others would take their boys home.

General Loring and his van of Alabama and Mississippi veterans moved westward toward Georgia and Alabama; but it is unknown if he actually delivered his troops to Mississippi in May 1865. Perhaps he had designs of joining Lieutenant General E. Kirby Smith in the Trans-Mississippi Department, who was planning on continuing the war. St. Augustine-born Smith certainly would have welcomed his longtime friend. But with the surrender of Lee, Johnston, and Lieutenant General Richard Taylor on 4 May, Smith's army became disenchanted, and many of his men, sick of the war, abandoned their stations and went home. On 26 May, Smith surrendered the Trans-Mississippi Department. This locked Loring out of finding another command in the Confederate army.

Defeat had covered the South with a gray pallor of hopelessness. The Southern landscape was in shambles. Almost every family mourned the loss of at least one relative who had participated in the war. Railroads were torn up, churches and schools were closed, and every bank was insolvent. Homes, farms, and plantations had been destroyed by the thousands; entire towns and cities were reduced to rubble. The economy had collapsed with the Confederate currency and bonds. In general, those who returned home, unless they had great means of land or hidden assets, suffered greatly. The end of the war became a social as well as a military victory for the North.

Rather than stay behind and debate the meaning of "treason" or humbly await the return of their rights as citizens of the newly reunited United States, only to live as exiles in their native land, thousands of elite and wealthy Southerners, who could afford to, closed the gate behind them and headed to England, France, Mexico, Cuba, and Brazil.

But emigration was not for General Loring. With the termination of the war, Loring suddenly found himself unemployed for the first time in his life and without a profession. He had been a soldier for 30 years, a fighting man of experience and fame, but when he had volunteered for the Confederate army, he had given up all rights and claims to any U.S. Army pension or benefits; he could not return to the Federal ranks; he could not vote or hold office and had no clearly defined political or civil status. He was also without a home: Florida and St. Augustine had nothing to offer him since his family's property had been seized and the state was in Republican hands and undergoing Reconstruction.

After spending four years on the battlefield for Jefferson Davis and the "cause," he was an outcast and would be forced to enter some totally new endeavor. Gone were the days of the gold-gilded gray tunics and stars; gone were the orderlies who had held his mount and served him breakfast.

Despite a bleak future, it is documented that he visited his four nieces — Mrs. G. E. Spencer of Nevada; Mrs. Herbert Royston of Chicago; Mrs. M. E. Mauran of New Orleans; and Mrs. G. D. Knight of New York. Loring then settled in New York City — exactly when is unknown — where old Army and political friends apparently helped him find employment on Wall Street.

With the return of peace, the Federal government returned the seized railroads to their owners in 1865. As much as 90 percent of the rolling stock had been destroyed or damaged — locomotives, passenger cars, baggage cars, and express cars had to be replaced. Most railroad depots had disappeared and hundreds of bridges had been destroyed.

Capital for the purpose was obtained by promoters who convinced the public in this country as well those abroad, that railroad securities were among the safest as well as the most profitable investments. Loring became a consultant on matters of Southern investments, especially on "non-industrial" securities, such as those of the railroads, shipping companies, and banking concerns.

One piece of his correspondence that has survived is a business letter:

New York
31 March 1868

Cr. to John E. Wair,
61 Wall Street
N.Y.

I enclose you a letter received by me from Admiral Semmes, in Mobile. — I do not know the parties he refers to but shall please to do all I can to aid him.

My office is 36 New Street and shall [be] pleased to hear from you in case you can do any thing for him.

Respectfully
W. W. Loring
(St. Augustine Historical Society)

A Colonel Augustus M. Foute mentioned that he was engaged in the banking business for ten years with General Loring in New York. Loring was obviously taking a lengthy sabbatical from army life.

General Loring had asserted some time before Appomattox that it was apparent that the Chattanooga campaign spelled the end of the Confederacy. He stated in an interview after the war that "not a man in the Confederacy felt that the Union had really accomplished anything until Chattanooga fell." (Thomas, 338-339)

When asked, "You do not mean to say, General, that Vicksburg and Gettysburg were nothing?" he replied, "The loss of Vicksburg weakened our prestige, contracted our territory, and practically expelled us from the Mississippi River, but it left the body of our power unharmed. As to Gettysburg, that was an experiment; if we had won that battle the government at Washington would, perhaps, have tendered peace with a recognition of the Confederacy. Our loss of it, except that we could less easily spare the slaughter of veteran soldiers than you could, left us just where we were."

Continuing the conversation, General Loring was asked, "But in the latter part of 1863 some of your people lost hope?" He replied, "Not exactly that, but they experienced then for the first time a diminution of confidence as to the final result." Further, he stated that it was the fall of Chattanooga, in consequence of the Chickamauga campaign, and the total defeat of General Bragg's efforts to recover it, that caused the loss of confidence in Confederate success.

Regarding the reason Chattanooga was held to be so important, he replied,

As long as we held it, it was the closed doorway to the interior of our country. When it came into your [the Union's] hands the door stood open, and however rough your progress in the interior might be, it still left you free to march inside. I tell you that when your Dutch General Rosecrans commenced his forward movement for the capture of Chattanooga we laughed him to scorn; we believed that the black brow of Lookout Mountain would frown him out of existence; that he would dash himself to pieces against the many and vast natural barriers that rise all around Chattanooga; and that then the Northern people and the government at Washington would perceive how hopeless were their efforts when they came to attack the real South. (Thomas 338-339)

To another question, "But the capture of Chattanooga convinced you that even the real South was vulnerable, did it?" he commented, "Yes, it was only a question as to whether we could beat back your armies by sheer force of desperate fighting, and as you largely outnumbered us, and our resources were every day diminishing, the prospects to the thinking part of our people looked gloomy indeed." To a final remark, "But, general, there are people in the North who regard the Chickamauga campaign as a failure for the Union cause," he said, "Ah! We would gladly have exchanged a dozen of our previous victories for that one failure."

This judgement finds general support from competent military authorities. Chattanooga was undoubtedly the key to the unlocking of the Confederacy, of which Chickamauga was an extremely important first step. Richmond, on the other hand, was a holding action in effect, perhaps more accurately a stalemate, in proof of which the record of Union battles lost is cited. It was not until after Chickamauga, which prevented General Bragg's retaking Chattanooga, followed by the battles of Orchard Knob, Lookout Mountain, and Missionary Ridge, in November, 1863, and still later the clinching Battle of Nashville, in December, 1864, that the Confederacy was first cracked, then opened, and finally broken. (Thomas 338-339)

Chapter 16

In the Courts
of the Khedive

*W*HILE W. W. LORING, business-
man, labored in New York City
in the fall of 1869, an American
soldier of fortune named Thaddeus Mott was gracing the court of Ismail
Pacha, Khedive — ruler — of the Ottoman
province of Egypt during the ceremonial
opening of the Suez Canal on 16 November.
Mott's career, bearing, command of the
Turkish tongue, and excellent connections in
both Constantinople and New York had im-

pressed the Khedive. Prior to their meeting, Ismail's Egyptian army had been established by French military organizations who had trained Ismail's forces according to the French army manual. Then a sudden turn of events led to the young Khedive's decision to free himself of the French connection and the overlordship of Turkey. In the weeks following this breach, he methodically mustered out his French officers and laid his plans for acquiring other foreign advice and assistance in military affairs.

Within this year of turmoil, Thaddeus Mott, who had gained the confidence of Ismail, was made Féreek Pacha, equivalent to a major general. Mott began to persuade Ismail to add veterans of the American Civil War to his entourage of advisors. The Khedive was convinced.

As the guests at the opening of the Suez Canal in November of 1869 departed from Cairo, Mott left for the United States. He lost no time in consulting William Tecumseh Sherman, who had been made general of the armies after Ulysses S. Grant had been elected President. Perhaps no man in America knew more officers of the old Army than "Cump" Sherman. Soon Sherman guided Mott to Loring and other officers.

In late 1869, Loring heard the rumor that the Khedive of Egypt was seeking American officers for the Egyptian army. Hard upon the rumor came Thaddeus Mott, armed with authority to enlist Americans and with passage money to send them to Cairo. Loring met him, heard his plans, and accepted Mott's first offer. It was an opportunity to win on foreign soil the fame denied him in his native South. "Old Blizzards" agreed to go. (Hesseltine and Wolf 18) Sherman, of all people, had rescued him from his inertia on Wall Street. Under Sherman's guidance, Mott also selected Henry Hopkins Sibley, Loring's old compatriot from his service in New Mexico.

The word soon spread through the circles of the old Army that other Confederate generals — such as P. G. T. Beauregard, Braxton Bragg, and Joseph E. Johnston — were going to Egypt. These veterans had a high degree of technical skill, superior training, and a rich experience of four long years in the hardest fought, best equipped, and best directed war the world had seen. The Union and Confederate officers who would put on the Khedive's uniform were not on an "official mission" and never received anything approaching official status from the U.S. government, but they were recommended for the service by the head of the American Army, General William T. Sherman. They were experts in building forts, rail-

roads, and dams, in frontier explo-
ration, in surveying, and in the conduct of modern war. They were more
than romantic soldiers of fortune.
In early 1870, following the three-
week trip to Egypt, Mott delivered
Loring and Sibley to the Grand New
Hotel in Cairo. Prior to meeting the
Khedive, Loring was fitted for a new
uniform — a black, single-breasted
coat worn buttoned to the throat,
black trousers, glossy black patent
leather shoes, and a bright red fez
complete with a black silk tassel —
and received elementary instruction
in court etiquette, although the Khedive was no stickler for niceties with
his American friends.

William W. Loring. (Reprinted by permission of the University of Chicago Press.
From *The Blue and the Gray on the Nile*,
by William B. Hesseltine and Hazel C.
Wolf. Copyright © 1961 by The University
of Chicago.)

Ismail's first act was to assign
Loring as inspector general of the
Egyptian army. He was to outline
concisely the military needs of the
country. This situation was like noth-
ing Loring had ever known in his military career: he was in command of
the Egyptian army and navy. He was a Levan Pacha (brigadier general).

Loring began to send reports back to the Khedive that the army needed
complete reorganization and that the soldiers lacked drill, training in the
use of weapons, and discipline according to Western models. Furthermore,
what the army required immediately was more Americans, and at the head
it needed a chief of staff and a complete general staff to supervise the work
of reorganization.

Thaddeus Mott returned to New York to enlist more American recruits.
In the next five years, four dozen other Americans accepted commissions
in the Egyptian army. Mott returned to Egypt in the summer of 1870 with
Federal General Charles Pomeroy Stone. Loring and Stone would unite in
the joint venture to build the Egyptian army.

Under the direction of General Stone, the army would be reorganized
and made fit. Under Loring's direction, the defenses would be strength-

ened in order that, behind the rising fortifications, the development and expansion of Egypt might progress.

In 1871, General Loring was assigned to command Alexandria and placed in complete command of the army and navy. He was to report directly to the Khedive without the intervention of any Egyptian official. Loring was on his way. The palace of Moussaffa Khanah would be Loring's residence in Alexandria; later he was given use of Gabara Palace, the late residence of Säid Pacha. From these palaces, Loring directed the construction of coast defenses.

Loring and Sibley, who had come to Egypt together, devised the complete plans for the coast defense of the country. At the western end of the Bay of Alexandria, they built fortifications and mounted large-caliber guns that could, they believed, withstand any naval attack. From Alexandria eastward they planned a line of hidden forts, stretching 30 miles to Rosetta, each of which would mount a single high-powered gun. The forts would be so close together that they could effectively cover the entire coast.

The army had no General in Chief. Generals Loring and Stone were there to advise and make recommendations but never to issue any direct orders to the army. All orders emanated from the Minister of War's office and were sealed by him. The key to the organization of the Egyptian army lay not in the pachas themselves or in the direct chain of command that led from individual units straight to the Ministry of War; the key was the clerks — civilians, civil servants, and, incidentally, Coptic Christians, whose peculiar merit was their ability to read, write, and keep books. They swarmed in both the army and the civil establishment, scheming like petty members of a bureaucracy to hold their jobs and advance in favor. Illiterate officers were completely dependent on them, and lazy officers entrusted their duties to them. Having entrenched themselves with their pens, they resisted every reform that might threaten their position. With their ability to influence the pachas, they formed a solid phalanx against modernization. Both Stone and Loring battled the Coptic clerk system. "If only the non-commissioned officers and the privates could read and write, the civilian company clerks could be eliminated," remarked Stone (Hesseltine and Wolf 86).

The army over which Stone came to preside numbered perhaps 40,000 men in the ranks. Barely one-third of the officers were literate, and hardly any of the soldiers could read or write. Stone's first recommendation was for the education of the army. He established schools in each battalion where not only the officers but also the noncommissioned officers and soldiers could have instruction during at least an hour and a half each day. He ordered a staff school where students could be trained for higher studies. This school turned out very able officers, some of which went to Loring's command. He soon had 1,500 sergeants and corporals under instruction, teaching them reading, writing, arithmetic, and the keeping of regimental and company books. By 1873, more than 70 percent of the rank and file could read and write.

For transportation, General Loring used a carriage as well as the railroads. When in the field, he rode a dapple gray horse.

> The Khedive . . . presented [a bay horse, "Napoleon"] to General Loring, who was an old cavalry officer and a fine horseman, but General Loring had left an arm on the battle-field . . . when the City of Mexico was captured by the American troops. The horse was a plunger; he seemed to be on springs, and could bound into the air and keep up his bounds like a bouncing ball for a hundred yards or more without cessation, and at every leap take all four feet clear of the ground to a height of four or more feet. It is necessary to humor the mouth of a plunger, and General Loring could only shorten his reins by carrying them to his teeth, which Napoleon came near jerking out the only time the general ever mounted him. So Napoleon was passed on. (Morgan 277)

Loring also acted as a banker and loan officer for the Americans on his staff due to the Khedive's frequent delays in paying the men. Loring was very generous with his money when it came to his nieces in America. His ledger records numerous entries of drafts drawn on their behalf.

The general had a very active social life in Alexandria. His records indicate he purchased season tickets for the French Theatre, and he paid for his subscription to the opera, which he attended several evenings a week. He went to the circus, which was very popular in Alexandria, and at Christmas he sent General Mott bottles of green seal and treated him and his family to the opera. Loring also bought himself a ring with settings of diamonds and rubies, plus some fancy sleeve buttons, gloves, and new clothes. He was undoubtedly enjoying a richer life style than he would have had he stayed in the United States. As a pacha, it was reported he was being paid $10,000 a year in gold.

In his quest to learn the language of the country, Loring took both Arabic and French lessons. From the way he discharged his tutors, it is apparent he was not learning much from them. He finally did acquire enough French to converse with the Khedive, which satisfied Loring very much.

On 15 March 1872, Loring noted that he left in the company of General Sherman, then on a world tour, and General Stone for the Suez Canal. The trio went to breakfast at noon; formal dinner at seven; soirees at ten; supper at midnight. They ate from gold plates and drank from gold-rimmed crystal. Certainly Ismail's festivities were more elegant than those found in America. Could Loring have ever envisioned that seven years after the battles in Mississippi, Georgia, and North Carolina, he and Sherman would be enjoying each other's company in such grand style?

Chapter 17

The Battle of Gura

*I*N 1875, GENERAL STONE was ordered to prepare for an invasion of neighboring Abyssinia. As Egypt was the most enlightened commercial nation in northeast Africa, it was necessary for her to hold Abyssinia — being given to war, turmoil, and the slave trade — in check. The Khedive's object at this time was to punish King John for the slaughter of former Danish civilian Colonel Arrendrup's command, who, in the Khedive's service, had re-

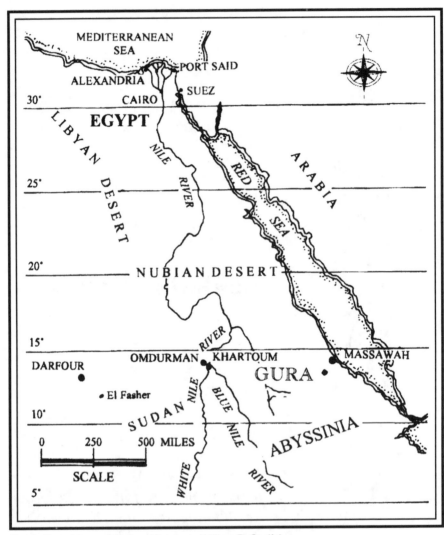

Egypt, Abyssinia, and Sudan. (Courtesy, William R. Scaife)

cently made an expedition into Abyssinia for the purpose of settling the boundary between the two countries. They would first make a demonstration and convince King John of their might and then, with an exchange of presents, negotiate peace on the frontier.

Stone insisted that the Egyptians be guided by American advisors. The Khedive yielded to this advice and Ratib Pacha, appointed to command the Egyptian expedition to Abyssinia, agreed, knowing full well that he had no intention of abiding by the counsel put forth by a "foreigner."

On Stone's summons in early December, Loring traveled to Cairo and sat in on the conference regarding the invasion. He was willing to accept the assignment as chief of staff and second in command to Ratib Pacha. Ten other Americans were also assigned to the expedition.

Aside from loyalty to the Khedive, Loring and Ratib had nothing in common and made an ill-sorted pair. Differences in personality — not to mention the wide differences in culture — doomed the partnership. Ratib had never even seen a battle and was not a fighting man.

The Khedive had impressed upon Ratib that he should have particular regard to Loring's counsel. To add emphasis to the injunction, Ismail, in the most solemn manner, put Loring's hand into Ratib's as evidence of fraternity and charged them that they should "be of one mind" (Loring, *Confederate Soldier*, 333). If Loring and Ratib were to be of one mind, it would have to be Loring's.

Loring and his staff of Americans and Ratib and his staff arrived at Massowah, on the Red Sea, on 14 December with 11,000 soldiers, 1,100 horses, and 1,200 mules. It was found that there were few camels there, and weeks passed until enough camels were available to start the vanguard.

In this crowded area — the seat of commerce for Abyssinia — and suffering from the hot climate, the officers and men grew irritable. All kinds of mistakes and minor annoyances beset them. Loring spent hours getting Ratib to order needed engineering instruments from Cairo. Part of the confusion sprang from conflicts with the Egyptian pacha system of running an army, a system by which each commanding pacha assumed responsibility for supplying his unit, maintaining its internal order and discipline. To the Americans, the pacha system seemed fraught with possibilities of corruption. In addition, it was necessary to translate orders into at least three languages. And Lutfi Effendi, the only translator and clerk, was constantly saying his prayers. "Tell him to cut them damned short," cried Loring (Hesseltine and Wolf 189).

Loring related that shortly after they arrived in Massowah, John Charles Kirkham, a Scot who had been for several years in the service of King John of Abyssinia and who had been part of the Arrendrup debacle, arrived in camp.

He was sent under the pretense of bringing back to the Egyptians a peace-offering of an officer and one hundred and five prisoners captured in the Arrendrup affair. Of these unfortunate people, twenty-seven were horribly mutilated.

King John had two objects in sending these victims back. One was the hope that Ratib Pacha, induced by apparent kindness, would let Kirkham pass through with a letter to Queen Victoria complaining of the Egyptians and their ambitious plot to invade Abyssinia. This cunning hint fell flat upon the ear of the Egyptian commander, who determined to let not one pass from under his authority.

The second idea . . . was that this savage reminder of these mutilated soldiers would impress the ignorant Egyptian soldiers with a dread of what they might expect from the cruelty and prowess of the Abyssinian. This well-timed embassy had the desired effect. Instead of lashing the Egyptians into a frenzy of righteous indignation and the desire to revenge their mutilated comrades, it filled them with dismay to see such evidence of the ferocity, the bravery, and the strength of the enemy. Furthermore, these unfortunate wretches, in telling their tale of sorrow and misery, did not fail to exaggerate the courage and power of the Abyssinians, the difficulties of advancing into the country, and the almost certain death that would follow the attempt.

The Egyptian officers talked with bated breath, and heard the conversation of these people with the soldiers in a quiver of suppressed fear. Altogether, it was a sad and horrible scene, and most damaging in its effects upon the morale of the expedition. (Loring, *Confederate Soldier,* 345-346)

The officers of the Egyptian army thus commenced bitterly deprecating the war, declaring it unnecessary and lamenting that they were all to be killed. They stated that Egypt had more land at home than they could cultivate and that it would have been more to the interest of the country to keep the army there to till the soil and take care of their suffering families. In discussing the invasion, officers and men saw an enemy behind every bush and rock.

Kirkham told Loring that in 40 or 50 days, King John would have a fighting force of over 60,000 men. The king had been scurrying about his country and appealing to his governors and chiefs to assemble their tribes to meet the invasion of the Egyptians and to defend their slave routes.

Prince Hassan, the third son of the Khedive, an active, stoutly built young man of 22, joined the invading army at Massowah in January. He presented a letter from Ismail asking Loring for kind attention to his son and another to Ratib requesting a place on his staff for him. The greatest possible care and solicitude were shown him.

> The Prince came to get a taste of campaigning and brought with him fifty retainers, a huge striped tent, innumerable animals, and baggage and equipment suitable for a princely establishment.
>
> Ratib was delighted. He was personally devoted to the royal family, and he welcomed the prince to his staff . . . and he too then received a permanent place at Hassan's rich and overflowing table. (Loring, *Confederate Soldier*, 340)

But Loring believed it best "to leave all this display of unnecessary luxury in the rear on account of the scarcity of transportation." Ratib, naturally, thought differently.

By January 1876, enough camels had been located for transportation and the necessary orders were issued to move the command out on the road to the Gura Valley, their destination. But the command had hardly left before the private Arab staff of Ratib commenced issuing orders in conflict to what Loring had given: "The opinion was forced upon me that Ratib was opposed to the campaign and took secret measures to delay it, thinking to deceive me in the field and the Khedive at home. After a barefaced wrong like that just mentioned, Ratib would proclaim his innocence and swear by the Prophet it should never occur again" (Loring, *Confederate Soldier,* 344).

This state of affairs did not bode well at the outset of the campaign, but Loring was determined to force it through with the aid of the American officers. "Having a fine army well armed, I knew that it was capable of winning success if properly handled."

Each day along the march found a bedlam of shrieking camels, yelling drivers, and cursing officers. Crates of crockery, boxes of wine, tables, and even stoves filled with hot coal were loaded upon the camels and mules. Along the trail, the animals kicked off their loads, scattering property and

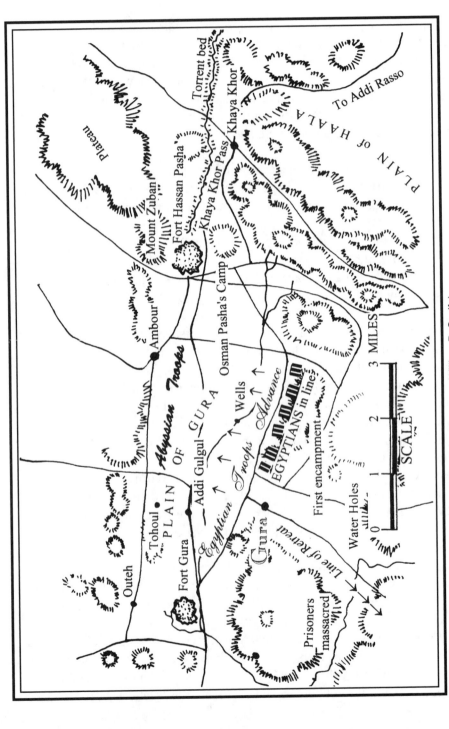

Plains of Gura and Halua, Battle of Gura, March 1876. (Courtesy, William R. Scaife)

creating minor stampedes. The Egyptian officers obeyed orders only when they came from Egyptians — an attitude certainly encouraged by the Coptic clerks and, so the Americans thought, by Ratib. In the opinion of the Egyptian soldiers, the Americans were merely ornaments to the commander. Moreover, in their minds, the prince was the true head of the expedition.

Loring was the first to confess to his shortcomings and would attempt to make amends for any offense he dealt out. He admitted that he could not punish subordinates consistently. He told the story of once striking a servant in Egypt and then giving him a silver dollar as recompense. "And ever after that," Loring recalled, "the rascal tried to make me strike him again" (Hesseltine and Wolf 186).

After marching six hours, the command reached Bahr Rezza, where Loring placed a depot. The next march led them to Addi Rasso, where a fortification was ordered for two companies and two guns. The march then commenced to the broad plains of Halua.

After camping in a pocket in the mountains of Khaya Khor, the next morning the army climbed the pass and made a gradual descent to the plateau of Abyssinia. From the pass, Loring got a glimpse of the plain of Halua and of the small somber valley of Gura, which was about eight miles long and two miles broad. After a great deal of scouting and shouting, Loring moved the army into the valley.

An insight into Loring's loyalties was revealed when, on the way to Gura, Colonel William McE. Dye, who accompanied him, urged Loring not to make a contemplated move. Loring roared, "By God, I will not put in unnecessary jeopardy the soldiers of the great and good man who has given me an asylum in my old age" (Hesseltine and Wolf 185).

Colonel Samuel H. Lockett had been sent forward to handle the building of Fort Gura. A blockhouse and breastworks were built for about 5,000 men. Soon word was brought that King John's army — perhaps as many as 50,000 warriors — was concentrated in the next valley.

> It was impossible for King John to keep the enormous cavalcade he had with him — men, women, and children (for they all go to war) — to remain many days in any one locality. Thus the King was forced to begin his movement. . . . It soon became known that he was south of us and making the first decided demonstration.

> Developing clearly his plan of operations, it was not long
> before his advance extended to the Mareb River, indicating his
> purpose to march to our rear. (Loring, *Confederate Soldier*,
> 393)

Loring and the bulk of the Egyptian troops were in the Gura Valley
behind good entrenchments. A second part was divided with one body in
the Khaya Khor Valley under Osman Bey and one, with most of the
artillery, in the fort of Khaya Khor Pass under Osman Pacha. Still a third
part, with supplies, was moving up from Bahr Rezza under General
Charles W. Field, Inspector General on Ratib's staff.

At a council of all the Egyptian officers, pachas, and beys, including
Prince Hassan, Loring presented his strategy for the coming campaign. He
argued that Fort Gura was impregnable and that something ought to be
done at once to meet and counteract King John. He urged that a force of
700 or 800 men should be left in Fort Gura, with a complement of artillery,
as this command could defy King John's army.

The rest of the command, over 6,000 strong, armed with Remington
rifles and a heavy park of artillery, should be moved to Khaya Khor, six
miles distant, and there be united with the command of Osman Pacha,
which was about 2,500 strong, who also had artillery. Loring further recommended that General Field should be brought from Bahr Rezza, about
35 or 40 miles distant, where he was engaged on duty with a command
about 1,500 strong.

By the time King John could concentrate in the valley, he would be met
with 10,000 effective men from Khaya Khor. Since King John was out of
supplies, and with his vast crowd of men, women, and children, he had to
go great distances to get water. From his present position, he would be
forced to take the Amhoor and Arato trails in order to obtain the supplies.
These two trails ran between Fort Gura and Khaya Khor.

> If we were concentrated at Khaya Khor, King John, on making
> an attempt to cross the valley, would be attacked in flank with
> the whole army and with no hesitation. With our strength, dis-
> cipline, and splendid armies, such a sudden blow at his hordes,
> unprepared for an attack, would certainly be crowned with suc-
> cess. Under no circumstances should we divide our forces; that
> would be fatal. . . . Nor should we place our forces outside of

the fortifications or beyond their protection. (Loring, *Confederate Soldier*, 398)

Later in the evening, Prince Hassan came to Loring's tent and said he approved what he had outlined but advised letting Ratib have his own way. No plan of operations was agreed upon, and as usual, everything was left to chance and Allah.

On 6 March, Ratib invited Loring to go with him to Khaya Khor. Believing something was wrong with the fortifications, Loring took Colonels Dye and Henry C. Derrick along so they might express their opinions. He quickly discovered that Osman Pacha and Osman Bey were present for this strategy meeting.

Colonel Derrick then said in substance that a sufficient command should be left at Fort Gura and the rest of the command brought to Khaya Khor. Colonel Dye was of the same mind.

Agreeing with them in this, Ratib turned to Osman Pacha and Osman Bey, the other two present, who did not understand a word of what had been said, and conversed a few minutes in Turkish, not long enough to tell them what had been said, to which they smiled in response. Ratib, apparently amused, turned toward us and said we were all agreed. His whole manner was marked by insincerity and cunning. (Loring, *Confederate Soldier*, 403)

The conference ended and Loring returned to Fort Gura. On 6 March, Loring again argued with Ratib about not delaying the movement to Khaya Khor. "Ratib stared incredulously, as though he had not thought about it, and finally said that he did not intend to give any orders for a movement" (Loring, *Confederate Soldier*, 403). By this time, the Americans had concluded that the Egyptians were errant cowards. The army was drifting along toward a rapidly approaching catastrophe.

In the meantime, King John was concentrating all his strength in the immediate direction of Khaya Khor, undoubtedly with the intention of entering the valley near there. On the morning of 7 March, Osman Pacha, commanding Khaya Khor, finally informed Ratib that the enemy was near him.

Without further notice, Ratib verbally ordered about 2,500 men, with a

number of Krupp guns, to be left at Fort Gura and about 5,000 men to be
moved out of the fort. After the troops had been marched out for a few
minutes, the command halted within a few yards of the fort instead of
marching directly to Khaya Khor.

Just then, a dispatch came indicating that the dust of the enemy was
seen on the Arato and Amhoor Roads leading into the valley between the
two forts, near Khaya Khor. Upon this news, Ratib moved diagonally
across the valley to the right and a little in advance of the fort and halted
again. At this point, Loring wrote, "I now felt that he had determined not
to join his forces, and that the best thing to be done was to secure him in
the position he had taken and save his army" (Loring, *Confederate Soldier*,
404).

Ratib stood on a prominent elevation where, with his field glass, he
could scan the valley. He soon saw the great clouds of dust moving, which
denoted the rapid approach of King John's army. The enemy then
appeared in great numbers on a ridge diagonally across the valley, about
two miles away.

Loring determined that Ratib did not intend to move out of his position.
Finding that his right-most flank was probably one mile distant from
Khaya Khor, Loring inquired of Ratib whether he was in communication
with that fort and informed him that in a short time the enemy would fill
the valley and get between him and his forces there. Unless he effected a
junction with the troops at Khaya Khor, he would jeopardize his army. But
Ratib had no plan of action.

King John, who had been hesitating, finally threw a strong line of
sharpshooters along the entire front, opening a brisk fire, to which the
Egyptians replied, sending at the same time cannon shot at his force on the
ridge and those toward the right. This forced the King to circle around
nearer Khaya Khor, evidently trying to make his way into the glen on the
right. The enemy was silenced in the front from the sustained fire but was
evidently approaching the battery on the right, which had been left without protection. The enemy was thickening in the valley and was bolder in
its movements.

A mile and a half of our position, and in its immediate front,
marshalled in barbarian splendor upon an elevated ridge, were
the serried hosts of the foe, full 50,000 strong, their banners and
shields glittering in the declining sun, waiting for orders of their

king, the ablest and most renowned African warrior of modern times, to move en masse across the valley. Around to our right and rear, there were also lurking in great numbers their bravest and most venturesome warriors. (Loring, *Confederate Soldier*, 410)

Shortly, Colonel Derrick approached Loring and explained that the enemy was taking over the right. Derrick accompanied Loring to Ratib and made the same statement. At this time, the Egyptian cavalry on the right had taken flight and was coming to the rear, mixed with infantry. Loring recalled:

Ratib, who is of swarthy complexion, upon hearing [Derrick's news] became ashy pale, whereas before this he had concealed emotion. Without giving us time to say a word he rode rapidly to the left, possibly, it was thought by us, to do something toward saving his army. But he took no steps to that end. Frightened out of the last vestige of manhood, he had deliberately run away [toward Fort Gura], and he did not stop until he was out of all danger. Looking at him for a moment to see what his intentions were, I turned my horse and gathering a number of staff rode rapidly to the right. (Loring, *Confederate Soldier,* 412)

Loring was now in charge of the army.

Heard over the cannon fire, the wailing of the Egyptians, and the clamor of the Abyssinians was Loring in wild excitement, issuing orders in torrents of words that the Egyptians never understood. Loring rushed troops from one point to another, and on his reddened face the sweat of exhilaration glistened.

We were soon near the battery of the right, and were soon met by the retreating infantry and cavalry mixed in chaotic confusion. . . . It was then that we saw regiment after regiment turn deliberately in their tracks and walk away, Egyptian officers setting the example. Making no haste, they laughed while firing their guns in the air as though it were fine sport. Soon the fugitives became an unwieldy mass, and resisted all effort to stem their retreat. The American and foreign staff threw themselves in their front, but after extraordinary efforts were forced along with the retiring column . . . it had become a rout . . . men and officers, artillery, camels, horses, and mules were out of all control and in the greatest disorder. (Loring, *Confederate Soldier,* 412-413)

When King John realized that the Egyptians were retreated in a confused mass, he instantly assembled his clans and rushed into the valley, gathering plunder.

With Ratib completely paralyzed with fear, there was not an Arab officer to assist in organizing a force to protect the rear, and only an Arab officer could control the men and keep them from their impending fate. At this crisis, Loring, noticing the head of the column bearing away from Fort Gura, then a mile in the distance, sent Captain Henry Irgins to turn the force in the right direction toward the fort. For some unaccountable reason, the column did not change its direction.

Had Ratib gone in person to the head of the column [the army] would have followed him beyond a doubt. Instead, he rode deliberately away from his command and when his party was immediately opposite the fort, entered it for safety. . . . Ratib was safely in the fort, and from the parapet he could see his army step by step, marching into the power of the enemy. At least he could have made a diversion but he did not. (Loring, *Confederate Soldier*, 417)

Loring arrived at the fort, and he and a few others retraced their steps for the purpose of guiding the retreating command. "We tried every means to attract the attention of the Egyptians and to get them to turn upon the small body of enemy cavalry on their right flank," but this effort failed (Loring, *Confederate Soldier,* 419). The Egyptians slowly continued to turn away from the fort and marched into the enemy's clutches, which beyond a doubt would result in their general massacre.

Loring then sent Osman Bey Nageeb, the last Egyptian to leave the troops, to Ratib to report the facts and to inform him that he could march several thousand of the fresh troops inside the fort safely out to open the way for the rescue of his people and that he would find no difficulty in driving back the small body of cavalry on their right flank.

Here I stood, physically and mentally fatigued, and witnessed
this sickening spectacle, after one of the most anxious and labo-
rious days in my long life, and as the column of Egyptians was
winding its slow length along, we knew that it was creeping into
the entangling web of a remorseless and cruel foe. Still no effort
was made from the fort, no message was sent, no aid, no troops;
the silence of death reigned there; it was the shadow of the
doom that awaited the remnant of the army which had so gaily
marched out of Fort Gura in the morning. (Loring, *Confederate
Soldier*, 420)

The enemy forced Loring and his party to return to the fort as the last
of the Egyptians entered the hills and disappeared from sight. The
Abyssinians closed in upon their rear with a ringing shout of triumph. This
was hardly a battle but a bloodbath. During the night, the Abyssinians, just
a short distance away in the hills, made hideous, prolonged yells and
howls, rejoicing over the scenes of bloody tragedy. This struck additional
terror into the heart of Ratib and his remaining men.

During the night and early the next morning, 8 March, a number of
Egyptian wounded came into the fort and reported a great many still in the
valley and on the hills, one or two miles away. Loring prepared to take
command of the cavalry and ride forth to save these men, but Ratib would
not let a soldier go out of the fort.

King John began forming upon the hills and slopes at sunrise. From his
movement, it was expected that his many thousands would be at once
pushed upon the fort in an attempt to end the matter in a single assault. He
reasoned that the demoralized Egyptian force would undoubtedly fall as
easy prey upon his strong demonstration. But the king had not counted on
the Egyptians' accurate and deadly return fire from within the fort. Loring
related:

The Krupp guns playing into the dense masses on the slope of
the hills and tearing through their ranks caused them to sway
and surge, and very soon a shot dismounted the only gun the
Abyssinians had, which was doing us considerable harm. . . .
After several futile attacks, those of the enemy in our immediate front gave way. When they had fled a considerable distance,
running as though they had abandoned the fight, a sortie was

made from the fort, the Krupp guns still continuing to pour well-directed shots into the enemy on the slopes of the hills, and these too showed signs of weakening. The scattered throngs in the valley around us, seeing the discomfiture of their assaulting party, fled precipitately; those on the hills catching the excitement, music and shouting ceased, and King John and his army took to their heels. (Loring, *Confederate Soldier,* 426-427)

The Abyssinians left a number of killed and wounded on the field near the fort. As soon as they had disappeared from the hills, the Egyptian officers and men rushed out of the fort and at once began killing the wounded Abyssinians and mutilating the dead, cutting off their hands and feet and scattering them about. They threw the dead bodies upon dry brush and set fire to them; others placed straw upon the victims' faces and torched them.

Upon learning of this heinous activity, Loring hastened to Ratib and urged him to stop such devilish work.

I reminded him that King John had nearly one thousand Egyptian prisoners, naked and bound hand and foot, in his camp not two miles off; that as the great outrage had already been committed of killing the wounded, the only thing to do now was to bury the dead so deep that the Abyssinians could not find one of them when they came to seek their wounded in the coming night. If finding their dead so horribly mutilated, just as certain as the sun rose the next day every Egyptian they had in their camp would be murdered. (Loring, *Confederate Soldier,* 428)

The Egyptians did not succeed in burying the dead, and the next morning, a ghastly spectacle was left for the Abyssinians to look upon. The hills then resounded with the discharge of firearms and the cry of over 600 unfortunate officers and men, the Abyssinians' prisoners, shot down and lanced in cold blood.

Ratib, trying to figure out how to conceal his losses, sent a letter and telegram to the Khedive announcing that he had gained a great victory on 7 March, sending an exaggerated account of the force he had combatted and the miraculous numbers of the enemy killed. It was not surprising that in response to these messages, an order came to demand of King John all arms, cannon, and prisoners he might have. Cairo was tired of the expensive war. The Khedive therefore ordered Ratib to make peace at once with King John upon almost any terms. It was at this point that Loring broke off his relationship with Ratib: "His correspondence, begun in secret, was becoming complicated, and he desired me to aid him. I declined, from that time thereafter, unless he undeceived the Khedive and gave me all the despatches that had passed between him and Cairo. As he did not do so, I ended my intercourse with him, as far as possible" (Loring, *Confederate Soldier,* 433-434).

Ratib sent an emissary to King John proposing peace. The Abyssinian monarch listened, for he was satiated with blood and plunder and had also lost severely in the battle of 9 March. But peace would have to be on the terms of the Abyssinians. Profuse promises to do all that was demanded were immediately made by Ratib. There then followed liberal presents and gifts to King John. Hostilities were thus suspended by mutual consent.

The badly defeated Egyptians wanted to return to Egypt. They had sustained 2,000 officers and soldiers killed, 1,500 wounded, and 800 more taken prisoner and massacred. The American-trained army had performed poorly and was a great disappointment to the American officers.

After an absence of five months, Loring returned to Alexandria. He was raised to Féreek Pacha — major general — the highest military grade in Egypt and Turkey. He was decorated with Egyptian orders, a neck badge and breast star of the Order of Medjidieh. He was also awarded the Order of Osmanieh.

But rumors soon surfaced that the Khedive intended to dismiss the American officers from his service rather than send them out on another expedition. The blame for the defeat was laid on the Americans. Ratib, who had control of the telegraph, censored — even stopped — official and personal mail so that American countercharges got no hearing. And Prince Hassan, who had supported Loring against Ratib, hid his own less-than-courageous conduct at Gura by attesting to the blunders of the Americans. They were still considered foreigners.

The declining prestige of the Americans seemed to go hand-in-hand with the declining finances of the Khedive. By the middle of 1876, his treasury was almost depleted. The Abyssinian War had disrupted his profitable trade, and thus revenues had declined substantially. Suddenly, he could not pay the Americans. Loring, Stone, and all officers of the Amer-

Loring (front, center) and Ulysses S. Grant (seated, front, hat in hand) at the Great Pyramids, 1878. (Courtesy, St. Augustine Historical Society, FL)

ican staff went unpaid for several months. Some, in disgust, took long vacations to Europe with the money they had saved. There was no work in Cairo and Alexandria for the rest of 1876.

The year 1877 was also relatively uneventful for Loring, and as he neared the age of 60, he knew his days in Egypt were numbered. He began to think ahead about retirement and maybe a pension, after all, from the U.S. government. In a letter dated 26 May 1877, Loring wrote to Senator S. W. Williams, a former Confederate general, in reference to his pension: "Now that the 'lion and the lamb' have laid down together, I think it likely Congress will pardon all the Rebels and thus finish the whole thing! Don't you think so?" (St. Augustine Historical Society).

Early in 1878, the Americans in Cairo hoped for a restoration of some part of their prestige with the visit of former President Ulysses S. Grant. In January, General Grant, with his wife, son, and a retinue of lucky reporters, arrived during a trip around the world. From the train, amidst great fanfare, Grant cried out, "Why, there's Loring, whom I have not seen for thirty years" (Wessels 80).

The Americans led Grant and his party to a banquet. There was much excitement in the receiving line where the American generals vied with Arab chiefs and pachas to make the affair imposing. Loring said: "When I came up, among the crowd, wearing my Egyptian uniform, General Grant turned his eye on me, and without a moment's hesitation, extended his hand and called me by name. It was thirty-one years since he had last seen me. That was at the taking of the City of Mexico at Garita de Belen, where I lost this arm. Grant and I were in the charge together" (Wessels 81).

In the end, General Grant's visit was of no help in restoring the dimming glory of the Americans in Egypt. Those of the general staff in Cairo and Alexandria had outlived their usefulness to Egypt. Rumors persisted that the Khedive was going to send them home.

In the spring of 1878, a commission of inquiry, forced by Ismail's European bondholders, came out with a demand that the size of the Egyptian army be reduced from 60,000 to 9,000 men and the American officers be dismissed. On his return to America, General Loring spoke bitterly of the English and how they grabbed Egypt.

The discharge date was set for 30 June 1878. Each officer received full pay, an additional six months' pay as indemnity for the termination of the contract, and an extra 75 pounds for expenses on the return to the United

States. General Loring did not leave Cairo immediately. Settling payment accounts took time to be resolved, and Loring returned to the U.S. a "leisurely year after the dismissal day" (Hesseltine and Wolf 239). It was now 1879.

Loring and the other Americans

> chalked up some remarkable accomplishments. They made contributions to Egyptian education, brought engineering skill to the aid of a progressive khedive who was trying to modernize his country, made significant geographical discoveries, and conducted extensive physical and sociological surveys on distant frontiers. Paradoxically, it was only in the area of military affairs that they had but limited success. (Hesseltine and Wolf 2-3)

They were the advance guard of a newly invigorated America whose representatives — technicians, soldiers, salesmen, cultural agents, missionaries, and administrators — would soon go forth to every part of the world over the next 75 years.

Chapter 18

The Return Home

ONG AFTER THE guns fell silent and after the Compromise of 1877 ended Reconstruction in the South, Sherman, the commanding general of the U.S. Army, set out on a tour of reconciliation, following the path of his march from Chattanooga to Atlanta and on to the sea. From Savannah he continued on to St. Augustine, where he had been stationed, and then on to New Orleans.

After his European tour, General Ulysses

S. Grant also made a tour of America. General Frederick T. Dent, commander of the troops at the St. Francis Barracks in St. Augustine and also brother of Grant's wife, invited the general to St. Augustine. Grant agreed to stop by a few weeks later on his return trip from south Florida.

During his stay in the Ancient City, Grant was feted and displayed and shown the best the town had to offer. But the cheers for Grant had hardly died when word went out that General Loring was coming home. Loring, who had arrived in New York and had spent some time visiting his four nieces, was returning to St. Augustine.

The train whistle seemed a little brighter than when Grant had graced the depot. Loring was met by a committee appointed by Mayor H. F. Oliveros and Bartolo Genovar, president of the St. John's County Commissioners, and the St. Augustine Brass Band, who headed the parade from the railroad station to the plaza. Here, a platform had been built in front of the Confederate Monument. This platform had been erected through the efforts of Anna Maria Dummett, a childhood friend of Loring. Around it a vast multitude assembled to greet their native hero. Mayor Oliveros addressed Loring:

> Today St. Augustine welcomes home one of her noblest sons.
>
> The compliment of welcoming you has been extended to me as a native born citizen, grown to manhood since your absence. We greet you with open arms and happy hearts. General, this is no welcome to a hero, nor a statesman, nor one aspiring to public honors, but sir, we welcome you as a humble citizen of St. Augustine, after a separation of thirty years.
>
> Welcome, thrice welcome, to the home of your childhood. Look around, General, and see the happy hearts of the old, and the merry smiles of the young — all have come today to welcome you home again. (Wessels 85)

The Plaza had an elaborately decorated arch with inscriptions that read "Welcome Home" and "Mexico, Egypt for Valor." General Loring remained in St. Augustine for several days, and the visit climaxed with a grand ball given in his honor.

Loring then faced being at "liberty" at age 60. His army days were over, and finding employment during the postwar depression was out of the

Loring Pacha. Féreek and General. (Courtesy, Museum of Florida History, Tallahassee)

The iniquity of oblivion scattereth her poppy and deals with the memory of men without distinction to merit and perpetuity . . . who knows whether the best of men be known, or whether there be not more remarkable men forgot, than any that stand remembered in the known account of time.

— Sir Thomas Browne, 1686. From W. W. Loring,
A Confederate Soldier in Egypt (New York: Dodd, Mead & Co, 1884).

question. The general was a cosmopolite at heart, and thus he turned to the
lecture circuit and the political arena for his means. He made his headquarters at the St. Denis Hotel in New York, and from there he toured the
country and made many trips in and out of Florida for a six-year period.

The general was considered an authority on Egypt, and reporters liked
to quote him and sought him out regularly for his opinions. Perhaps they
liked his genial manner and his willingness to talk emphatically. He was
still a fine-looking man, tall and impressive, with an iron-gray mustache
and imperial beard. His bearing was military. He wore his left sleeve
pinned to his breast with a rosette of red and green ribbons, an emblem of
his Egyptian honors, in his buttonhole. He spoke didactically, and
newspapers and magazines wrote his stories, which gained for Loring a
good deal of recognition in military, political, and business circles.

Loring's Florida activities were consumed with politics and business.
He campaigned for the Democratic party in Tallahassee and was himself a
candidate for a seat in the U.S. senate, but was not elected. The general,
however, was very resourceful, and if he did not wildly succeed in politics,
he did make money in business. Loring became active in the promotion
of the Jacksonville, St. Augustine & Indian River Railroad with two other
gentlemen. These men were visionaries before Henry M. Flagler the railroad entrepreneur — one of the many who developed Florida in the late
1800s.

Loring had begun to write the story of his time in Egypt while still in
Cairo, but after Colonel William Dye's book on the same subject hit the
market in 1880, Loring hurried to complete his work. He finished *A Confederate Soldier in Egypt* in April 1884. With the publication of the book
came personal appearances and lectures. The huge number of veterans'
groups kept his presence in demand.

In 1886, his longtime friend from Egypt, General Stone, got a symbol-
ic offer of employment in New York City. He was asked to design and construct the base for a huge statue to be executed by a Frenchman and presented to the United States by the schoolchildren of France: the Statue of
Liberty. He called on Samuel H. Lockett to aid him in drafting the plans.
Loring was in on all of this activity, as he lived in New York City at the
time.

On 11 May 1886, General Loring wrote to his friend George A. Porter-
field, from the Romney expedition: "I am so very young that I look to the
future with the same bright anticipation I did at sixteen" (*Southern His-*

torical Society Papers, 16:89). But though these Confederates were young at heart, the ending of their lives and careers were upon them. Lee, Grant, and many others had passed over.

General Loring, who had spent the summer and fall visiting relatives in Chicago, came back to New York to continue work on his autobiography, *Fifty Years a Soldier*. But before he could take up his pen again, death came.

The *New York Times* reported on 31 December 1886:

> General Loring felt slightly indisposed Wednesday afternoon, and it was believed to be an attack of indigestion; in fact it was treated as such. At four o'clock yesterday morning he had an acute attack so alarming that Dr. Norris, of New York Hotel, was summoned. The physician found the patient stricken with pneumonia and during the afternoon called Dr. Phelps in consultation. Notwithstanding their combined medical skill, Gen. Loring failed rapidly and sank into unconsciousness, from which he never rallied.

After an illness of only eight hours, the general died at the St. Denis Hotel on 30 December 1886. Charles Chaille-Long, a member of Loring's staff in Egypt, was at his bedside. General Loring had never married. He left his four nieces and two nephews, Charles and William A. Loring of Savannah.

Loring was not a West Point graduate, so the military honors of that institution would not be bestowed upon him. Instead, he was cremated, and on 2 January 1887, Dr. William Reed Huntington at Grace Episcopal Church in New York City officiated at the burial. The headlines were seen across the nation.

General Stone survived his comrade less than a month. He never recovered from the chill he had taken at the dedication of the Statue of Liberty on 28 October. In mid-January 1887, he caught cold, and on 24 January passed away.

Although Loring had died in New York City and his ashes had been buried at Grace Episcopal Church, there were those who felt St. Augustine should be his final resting place. In March 1887, a committee was formed to handle the ceremonies for his return to his home.

It was decided that the old Spanish Market on the eastern front of the Plaza would be utilized as the place of rest for the remains of General Loring while lying in state. Friday, 18 March 1887, would become a red-letter day in the annals of the State of Florida and in St. Augustine's long and distinguished history.

The *Florida Times Union* in Jacksonville reported on 19 March 1887 that

> one of the most striking features of the parade was the fraternizing of the veterans of both armies. The Jacksonville Post of the Grand Army of the Republic went over to St. Augustine as the guests of the Jacksonville Camp of Confederate Veterans. After arriving there they were joined by a number of other veterans, and at an impromptu meeting . . . it was decided that instead of maintaining separate organizations, they should march in the procession with the Confederates and Federals, two and two, arm in arm. . . . It was a genuine union of the Blue and the Gray, and was accepted as the symbol of a reunited people. It was felt, too, to be peculiarly appropriate that such a fraternization should occur at the grave of General Loring, who had worn both uniforms — who had been a soldier of the Republic as well as of the Confederacy.

Loring's longtime friend from the battles of West Virginia in 1861 and 1862, Dr. and Reverend Charles Todd Quintard, now bishop of Tennessee, read the impressive burial service of the Episcopal Church. As he recited slowly and deliberately, an officer stepped forward with one of Loring's swords, which he unsheathed and broke in two, casting the sheath, broken blade, and hilt into the grave. The final military salute was fired by the artillery and the cadets.

After the return from Woodland Cemetery, the veterans held a reunion at Bartolo Genovar's Opera House on St. George Street. The old battle cries were made to resound again, and the exchange of friendly sentiments was followed by cheers. Speeches and handshaking closed the jubilee. It was later said that this was the largest body of troops that had been assembled under arms in Florida since the close of the Civil War.

For more than three decades, Loring's ashes rested at the cemetery.

Loring Memorial in downtown St. Augustine.

However, many in St. Augustine, including Loring's nieces, thought that the general should have a more fitting memorial than a lonely hillside grave. In 1920, the Anna Dummett Chapter of the Daughters of the Confederacy and the General Loring Chapter of the Children of the Confederacy, both of St. Augustine, under the leadership of Sister Esther Carlotta and others, began a campaign to have a memorial erected in downtown

St. Augustine. A plot, 15 feet square, at the corner of Cordova and King Streets (once called Post Office Square) was obtained from the federal government. A money-raising event was conducted by the concerned organizations, and on 6 July 1920 Loring's ashes were removed from the cemetery and placed beneath the site, which is now designated as the garden of the Government House. A tall, marble obelisk was erected on 13 July 1920 and a dedication made on 30 December of the same year.

The preservation of liberty and freedom was the motivating factor in the South's decision to engage in what they called the second American Revolution. The tenacity with which Confederate soldiers and officers fought underscored their belief in the rights guaranteed by the Constitution. As the century closed, in order to preserve their memory and reputation, the Sons of the Confederate Veterans was organized in Richmond, Virginia, in 1896.

Over the years, hundreds of camps were formed in the Southland perpetuating the names and glory of various Confederate veterans. On 10 August 1973, General W. W. Loring was so honored when the General William Wing Loring Camp No. 1316 was chartered in St. Augustine.

Select Bibliography

Books and Articles

Ambler, C. H. "Romney in the Civil War." *West Virginia Quarterly* 5, no. 3 (1944).

Ambrose, Stephen E. *Struggle for Vicksburg.* Harrisburg, PA: Eastern Acorn Press, 1967.

Anderson, Colonel Keller. *Confederate Veteran* 16, no. 11 (1908).

Andrews, Colonel Garnet. "A Battle Planned, but Not Fought." *Confederate Veteran* 5, no. 6 (1897).

Barr, Alwyn. *Charles Porter's Account of the Confederate Attempt to Seize Arizona and New Mexico.* Austin: Pemberton Press, 1964.

Bearss, Edwin C. *The Battle of Jackson/The Siege of Jackson/ Three Other Post-Vicksburg Actions*. Baltimore: Gateway Press, 1981.

_____. *Decision in Mississippi*. Jackson, MS: Mississippi Commission on the War Between the States, 1962.

_____. *The Vicksburg Campaign*. 3 vols. Dayton, OH: Morningside House, 1985.

Bearss, Margie Riddle. *Sherman's Forgotten Campaign: The Meridian Expedition*. Jackson, MS: Gateway Press, 1987.

Boatner, Mark M. *The Civil War Dictionary*. New York: David McKay Co., 1957.

Bond, Captain J. L. *Confederate Veteran* 5, no. 9 (1897).

Bradley, Mark L. *The Battle of Bentonville*. Campbell, CA: Savas Woodbury Publishers, 1996.

Brown, Norman D. "The Approach to Atlanta." Presented at a symposium at the University of Texas, Austin (undated).

Clark, Louise M. *The Regiment of Mounted Rifles*. Vancouver, WA: Ft. Vancouver Historical Society of Clark County, 1964-1966.

Cox, Jacob D. *Campaigns of the Civil War IX: Atlanta*. Dayton, OH: Morningside House, 1987.

_____. *The Battle of Franklin, Tennessee*. Dayton, OH: Morningside Bookshop, 1983.

_____. *The March to the Sea: Franklin and Nashville*. Wilmington, NC: Broadfoot Publishing Co., 1989.

Crownover, Sims. "The Battle of Franklin." *Tennessee Historical Quarterly* 14, no. 4 (1955).

Davis, Burke. *Sherman's March*. New York: Vintage, 1988.

Davis, William C. *The Orphan Brigade*. New York: D. Appleton and Co., 1893.

Dewhurst, William W. *The History of Saint Augustine, Florida*. New York: G. P. Putnam's Sons, 1885; Bowie, MD: Heritage Books, Inc., 1990.

Eisenschiml, Otto, and Ralph Newman. *The American Iliad*. New York: Bobbs-Merrill Co., 1947.

Faust, Patricia L. *The Historical Times Illustrated Encyclopedia of the Civil War*. New York: Harper and Row, 1986.

French, Samuel G. *Two Wars*. Nashville: Confederate Veterans, 1901.

F.W.M. "Career and Fate of General Lloyd Tilghman." *Confederate Veteran* 1, no. 9 (1893).

Gale, Colonel W. D. "Confederate Disaster at Nashville." *Confederate Vet-*

eran 2, no. 2 (1894).

Greene, F. V. *Campaigns of the Civil War*. New York: Charles Scribner's Sons, 1882.

Greenwell, Dale. *The Third Mississippi Regiment-C.S.A.*. Pascagoula, MS: Lewis Printing Services, 1972.

Greif, J. V. "Baker's Creek and Champion Hill. What Abe Buford's Brigade and Others Did There." *Confederate Veteran* 4, no. 10 (1896).

Hart, Herbert. *Old Forts of the Southwest*. The Old West Series. Alexandria, VA: Editors of Time-Life Books, 1964.

Hay, Thomas Robson. *Hood's Tennessee Campaign*. New York: Walter Neale Publisher, 1929.

Henry, Ralph Selph. *The Story of the Confederacy*. NY: Broadfoot Publishing Co., 1989.

Hesseltine, William B., and Hazel C. Wolf. *The Blue and the Gray on the Nile*. Chicago: University of Chicago, 1961.

Hogane, Major J. T. "Reminiscences of the Siege of Vicksburg." *Southern Historical Society Papers* 11 (1883): 227.

Hood, J. B. *Advance and Retreat*. New Orleans: Hood Orphan Memorial Fund, 1880.

Horn, Stanley F. *The Army of Tennessee*. Wilmington, NC: Broadfoot Publishing Co., 1987.

_____. *The Decisive Battle of Nashville*. Knoxville: University of Tennessee Press, 1956.

Howell, Grady, Jr. *To Live and Die in Dixie: A History of the Third Mississippi Infantry*. Jackson, MS: Chickasaw Bayou Press, 1991.

Hughes, Robert M. *General Johnston*. New York: C. Appleton & Co., 1893.

Johnston, General Joseph E. *Narrative of Military Operations During the Civil War*. NY: D. Appleton, 1874.

Keleher, William A. *Turmoil in New Mexico, 1846-1868*. Albuquerque: University of New Mexico Press, 1952.

Loring, W. W. *A Confederate Soldier in Egypt*. New York: Dodd, Mead & Co., 1884.

Losson, Christopher. *Tennessee's Forgotten Warriors: Frank Cheatham and His Confederate Division*. Knoxville: University of Tennessee Press, 1954.

Manahan, T. A. "Letters from Veterans." *Confederate Veteran* 2, no. 8 (1894).

Maury, Dabney M. *Recollections of a Virginian.* 2nd ed. New York: Charles Scribner's Sons, 1894.

McDonough, James Lee. *Five Tragic Hours: The Battle of Franklin.* Knoxville: University of Tennessee Press, 1934.

McKinney, Tim. *The Civil War in Fayette County, West Virginia.* Charleston: Pictorial Histories Publishing Co., 1988.

_____. *Robert E. Lee and the 35th Star.* Charleston: Pictorial Histories Publishing Co., 1993.

_____. *Robert E. Lee at Sewell Mountain.* Charleston: Pictorial Histories Publishing Co., 1990.

Morgan, James Morris. *Recollections of a Rebel Reefer.* New York: Houghton Mifflin Co., 1917.

National Cyclopedia of American Biography. Clifton, NJ: James T. White & Co., 1893.

Nevin, David, and the Editors of Time-Life Books. *The Mexican War.* The Old West Series. Alexandria, VA: Editors of Time-Life Books, 1978.

Noll, Arthur Howard. *Doctor Quintard, Chaplain C.S.A. and Second Bishop of Tennessee.* Sewanee: The University Press of Sewanee, Tennessee, 1905.

Packwood, William H. "Reminiscences." *Oregon Historical Society Quarterly* 16.

Patterson, Gerard A. *Rebels from West Point.* New York: Doubleday, 1987.

Pemberton, John C. *Pemberton, Defender of Vicksburg.* Chapel Hill: University of North Carolina Press, 1942.

Phillips, G. C. "Witness to the Battle of Franklin." *Confederate Veteran* 14, no. 6 (1906): 261.

Scaife, William R. *Allatoona Pass: A Needless Effusion of Blood.* Atlanta, GA: Etowah Valley Historical Society, 1995.

_____. *The Campaign for Atlanta.* Saline, MI: McNaughton & Gunn, 1993.

_____. *The Chattahoochee River Line: An American Maginot.* Atlanta, GA, 1992.

_____. *The March to the Sea.* 2nd ed. Saline, MI: McNaughton & Gunn, Inc., 1993.

_____. *Hood's Campaign for Tennessee.* Atlanta, GA, 1986.

Settle, Raymond W. *The March of the Mounted Riflemen.* Lincoln: University of Nebraska Press, 1940.

Sherman, William T. *The Memoirs of General William T. Sherman.* Civil

War Centennial Series. Bloomington: Indiana University Press, 1957.

Simpson, Harold B. *Simpson Speaks on History*. Hillsboro, TX: Hill College Press, 1986.

Southern Historical Society Papers 16:89.

Stevens, Tillman H. "Other Side in the Battle of Franklin." *Confederate Veteran* 2, no. 4 (1903).

Stockdale, Paul H. *The Death of an Army: The Battle of Nashville and Hood's Retreat*. Murfreesboro, TN: Southern Heritage Press, 1992.

Sword, Wiley. *Embrace an Angry Wind (The Confederacy's Last Hurrah)*. Lawrence: University Press of Kansas, 1992.

Tanner, Robert G. *Stonewall in the Valley*. New York: Doubleday and Co., 1976.

Tower, Lockwood. *A Carolinian Goes to War: The Civil War Narrative of Arthur Middleton Manigault, Brigadier General*. Columbia: University of South Carolina Press, 1983.

Thomas, Wilburn. *General George H. Thomas, the Indomitable Warrior*. NY: Exposition Press, 1964.

Utley, Robert M. *Frontiersmen in Blue: The United States Army and the Indian, 1848-1865*. Lincoln: University of Nebraska, 1967.

Van Arsdol, Ted. "Vancouver Barracks." *Columbian* (1966). Courtesy of Clark County Historical Society.

Waterbury, Jean Parker. "The Treasurer's House." *St. Augustine Journal of History* 31 (1994).

Wessels, William L. *Born to Be a Soldier*. Fort Worth: Texas Christian University Press, 1971.

Wilson, D. J. *Confederate Veteran* 2, no. 9 (1894): 281.

Wingfield, Marshall. *General A. P. Stewart: His Life and Letters*. Memphis: West Tennessee Historical Society, 1954.

Woodworth, Steven E. *Jefferson Davis and His Generals*. Lawrence: University Press of Kansas, 1990.

Archives and Universities

Arizona Historical Society, Northern Arizona Division, N. Fort Valley Road, Route 4, Box 705, Flagstaff, AZ 86001.

Atlanta History Center, 3101 Andrews Drive, NW, Atlanta, GA 30305.

The Carter House Chapter of the Association for the Preservation of Tenneesee Antiquities, 1140 Columbia Ave., Franklin, TN 37064.

Commissioner of Internal Revenue Service. U.S. Government. Deed, St.

John's County, FL.

Florida Department of Military Affairs, St. Francis Barracks, P.O. Box 1008, St. Augustine, FL 32085. Robert Hawk, Historian.

Florida Department of State — Museum of Florida History, Bruce Graetz, Historian/Curator. R. A. Gray Building, 500 South Bronough St., Tallahassee, FL 32399.

The Hill College History Complex, The Harold B. Simpson Confederate Research Center, P.O. Box 619, Hillsboro, TX 76645.

The Huntington — Department of Manuscripts, 1151 Oxford Road, San Marino, CA 91108.

William Hicks Jackson Papers. Association for the Preservation of Tennessee Antiquities (APTA)-Nashville Chapter, Belle Meade Plantation, Nashville, TN.

Letter book and papers of Major General W. W. Loring from April 3, 1862, to May 11, 1862. Virginia State Library, Archives Division. Richmond, VA.

Loring report. To Colonel William G. Freeman, adjutant-general, Headquarters, U.S. Army, NY (no date).

Loring to Army Headquarters, Camp Scott, Utah Territory, 11 June 1858. Gen Ex. Docs. No. 1, 35 Cong., 2nd sess. 182-187.

Mississippi Department of Archives and History. Jackson, MS.

National Archives and Records Service. Reference Service Branch. Washington, DC.

The Official Records of the Union and Confederate Armies, 128 Vols., Washington, DC, 1880-1901 (noted as *OR*).

Oregon Historical Society, Sieglinde Smith, Reference Librarian, 1230 S.W. Park Ave., Portland, OR 97205.

The St. Augustine Historical Society, 271 Charlotte Street, St. Augustine, FL 32084.

Tennessee State Library and Archives, 403 Seventh Ave. North, Nashville, TN 37219.

William R. Perkins Library. Special Collections Department. Duke University, Durham, NC.

Joseph F. Siano private collection. Quincy, MA.

University of Toledo Libraries. Toledo, OH.

U.S. Army Fort Bliss Museums Division — 3rd Cavalry Museum, Dick Fritz, Curator, Fort Bliss, TX.

U.S. Army Military History Institute. Carlisle Barracks, PA.

P. F. Whitehead Letters, Feb.-Dec. 1864. McCain Library and Archives, University Libraries, University of Southern Mississippi, Hattiesburg.
C. T. Quintard Papers. William R. Perkins Library. Special Collections Department. Duke University, Durham, NC.

Index

by Lori L. Daniel